Lanzarote

Travel with **Insider Tips**

How this Guide Works

Our guide introduces you to the sights of Lanzarote (and briefly to Fuerteventura) in four chapters. The map below presents an overview of how the chapters are arranged. Each one has been allocated a special colour. In order to help you plan your trip, we have subdivided all the main points of interest in each chapter into three sections: the must-see sights are listed under the *TOP 10* and also highlighted in the book with two stars. You'll find other important sites that didn't quite make our *TOP 10* list in the *Don't Miss* section. A selection of other places worth seeing appears in the *At Your Leisure* section.

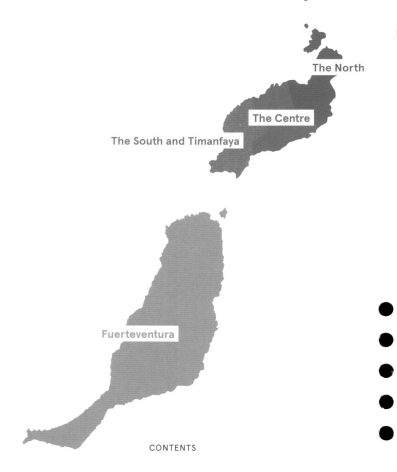

The North

The Centre

The South and Timanfaya

Fuerteventura

CONTENTS

★★ TOP 10 6
That Lanzarote Feeling 8

The Magazine

Fields of Fire 14
César Manrique 18
Guanches & Conquistadors 21
The Water Problem 24
Canarian Cuisine –
Simple but Original 28
Viticulture with a Difference 32
Beetle Juice 35
Rio-like Carnival 38
Canarian Wrestling 41

The North

Getting Your Bearings 44
My Day on the Trail of
César Manrique 46
★★ Teguise 52
★★ Jameos del Agua 55
★★ Fundación César Manrique/
Taro de Tahíche 58
★★ Cueva de los Verdes 61
Jardín de Cactus 63
Haría 65
At Your Leisure 68
Where to ... Stay 71
Where to ... Eat and Drink 72
Where to ... Shop 74
Where to ... Go Out 75

The Centre

Getting Your Bearings 78
My Day on Foot to Arrecife 80
★★ Arrecife 86
★★ Puerto Calero 90
Puerto del Carmen 92
At Your Leisure 94
Where to ... Stay 96
Where to ... Eat and Drink 98
Where to ... Shop 101
Where to ... Go Out 102

The South and Timanfaya

Getting Your Bearings 106
My Day Visiting Volcanoes 108
Parque Nacional de
★★ Timanfaya 112
★★ La Geria 116
★★ Playas de Papagayo 118
Yaiza 119
At Your Leisure 122
Where to ... Stay 124
Where to ... Eat and Drink 125
Where to ... Shop, Go Out 127

Fuerteventura

Getting Your Bearings 130
My Day on the Neighbouring
Island 132
★★ Betancuria 138
Corralejo 140
At Your Leisure 143
Where to ... Eat and Drink 146

Walks & Tours

Teguise 150
North 156
South 161

Practicalities

Before You Go 168
Getting There 169
Getting Around 170
Accommodation 171

Food and Drink 171
Shopping 172
Entertainment 173
Calendar of Events 173
Useful Words and Phrases 198

Appendix

Road Atlas 177
Index 187
Picture Credits 189
Credits 190

Magical Moments

Be in the right place at the right time and experience
magical moments you will never forget.

Wildly Romantic 67
Thought-Provoking Art 89
Sundowner in El Golfo 121
Just Like the Sahara 142

Wonderful prospects: Enjoy the sea view as you hike along the Papagayo coast

Even dromedaries need a break – here seen resting in the "Fire Mountains" of Timanfaya

TOP 10

★★ TOP 10

Not to be missed! Our top hits – from the absolute No. 1 to No. 10 – help you plan your tour of the most important sights.

❶ ★★ Parque Nacional de Timanfaya
Head to the "Fire Mountains" and you'll feel you've landed on the moon – the region was shaped by a volcanic eruption in the 1700s (p. 112).

❷ ★★ Teguise
A jewel from the Colonial Era. The island's former capital with its well-preserved centre is a wonderful place for a stroll (p. 52).

❸ ★★ Jameos del Agua
This "eighth wonder of the world", a complex created by César Manrique in a collapsed volcanic tunnel, is one of the best-visited attractions on the island (p. 55).

❹ ★★ La Geria
Lanzarote's most significant wine growing region. The grapes ripen on vines in black lava fields, protected from the wind by thousands of low stone walls (p. 116).

❺ ★★ Fundación César Manrique
You can see work by César Manrique and other artists displayed in his former home. The house itself, now the headquarters of the César Manrique Foundation, is an architectural masterpiece in its own right (p. 58).

❻ ★★ Playas de Papagayo
Named after a parrot, these beaches in the south are the most beautiful on Lanzarote. They boast several swimming bays, light-brown sand and crystal-clear water (p. 118).

❼ ★★ Arrecife
Head to the island's capital to experience a taste of urban living. Visit the small museums, enjoy some drinks, go shopping and take a walk through the streets and alleyways (p. 86).

❽ ★★ Cueva de los Verdes
This network of lava tunnels was created by volcanic activity many thousands of years ago – it's a fantastic subterranean world (p. 61).

❾ ★★ Puerto Calero
Welcome to this watery wonderland! You can spend time admiring yachts in the marina, take a day trip aboard a catamaran, or dive right down to the bottom of the sea in a submarine (p. 90).

❿ ★★ Betancuria
The most beautiful town on Fuerteventura. Once the island's capital, it's home to some handsomely restored colonial houses that hark back to a bygone golden age (p. 138).

That Lanzarote Feeling

Find out what makes the
Canary Islands tick and experience their
unique flair – just like
the Lanzaroteños themselves.

Magnificent Markets

Lanzarote's *mercados* ("markets")
are a part of daily life on the island.
They sell fresh produce (including
fruit and vegetables, cheese, meat
and sausages) and often clothes,
household goods and crafts. The
stallholders enjoy having a bit of
a chat with their customers. There
are some beautiful markets in
Teguise (the famous Sunday
market, which attracts streams of
visitors to the small town), Arrecife,
Haría, Playa Blanca, Tinajo and
Mancha Blanca, among others.

Volcanic Wine

Sit in a fish restaurant, somewhere
overlooking the sea, perhaps during
the blue hour, eat grilled Atlantic
fish with the traditional *papas arrugadas* (literally "wrinkly potatoes") and
a spicy red *mojo* sauce, and accompany
the meal preferably with a dry white
wine from grapes ripened in the volcanic La Geria wine region (p. 116); it
is a very civilised way to end the day.

Everyday Arrecife

Tourism has hardly made a mark
in Arrecife, the island's largest
town, with the exception of the few
hours the cruise ships set their
guests ashore. In the evening, the
capital's inhabitants have the city
to themselves. They meet up for
a beer in one of the restaurants on
Charco de San Gines or along the
elegant food mile by the new
marina. In the water, fishing boats
and yachts bob up and down against
the backdrop of a medieval castle
once used to ward off pirates.

Canary Island Nightlife

If you'd like to experience Lanzarote's
local nightlife, head to Arrecife when
darkness falls – the bars and pubs
here don't start to fill up before 10pm.
The main party strip is the Calle José
Antonio, where several cafés, pubs,
music bars and clubs stand side by
side. You'll find a much more chilled,
authentic local atmosphere here
than in the tourist hotspots.

A rough volcanic island with fertile soils: Lanzarote manages to produce some good wine in unusual surroundings!

Caravans of camels heading back to Uga
after a hard day's work

Reminiscent of Rio de Janeiro – the street parade
on Carnival Monday in Arrecife has a lot to offer.

Let Sleeping Camels Lie

Every morning, you'll see camels heading out from the small village of Uga (east of Yaiza) to do a day's work in the Timanfaya National Park. Uga is where the camels sleep. Setting out from the edge of the National Park, the animals ferry holidaymakers on fascinating tours of the region's unusual landscape. When evening comes, the creatures head back home in long, swaying rows, with one small caravan following on from the next.

Into the Volcano

You can peer down into a volcano crater in Caldera de los Cuervos. The symmetrical crater basin of the picture-book volcano reveals a narrow passage into the "heart of the volcano" and a view of volcanic slag and bizarre lava formations devoid of any trees or bushes. It was hellishly hot down here just 300 years ago.

It's Party Time!

Once a year, people all over the island (and particularly in Arrecife and Teguise) let their hair down to celebrate a lavish carnival that's reminiscent of the famous parties in Rio. Smaller festivities are also held throughout the year. Almost every community holds an annual mass or procession to honour their local saints, followed by a village festival complete with good food, dancing and fireworks.

Manrique's Legacy

Despite the many years since his fatal accident, César Manrique's presence is still very much felt on Lanzarote. There is no one else that has left such a distinctive mark on his home island. Not all the Lanzaroteños appreciated his extravagant lifestyle, or even his abstract painting for that matter – but he was one of them; there's no doubt about that. His superb landscape designs, such as the skilful transformation of lava grottoes into tourist attractions or his clifftop lookout point Mirador del Rio, helped to make Lanzarote known around the world.

Ray of Hope Aloe Vera

Inland, one's eye is drawn to the black fields – laboriously wrested from the volcanic landscape and proof of the difficult time farmers have on this arid island. Cereal cultivation has been given up almost altogether; onions, pumpkins and other green vegetables are only grown for personal use. A new ray of hope for the few remaining people in agriculture is aloe vera. This medicinal plant needs very little water and can cope with the dry conditions on the island. The gel produced from the thick, fleshy leaves is used in care products and as a home remedy for sunburn.

The perfect Lanzarote idyll:
Haría in the "Valley of the Thousand Palms"

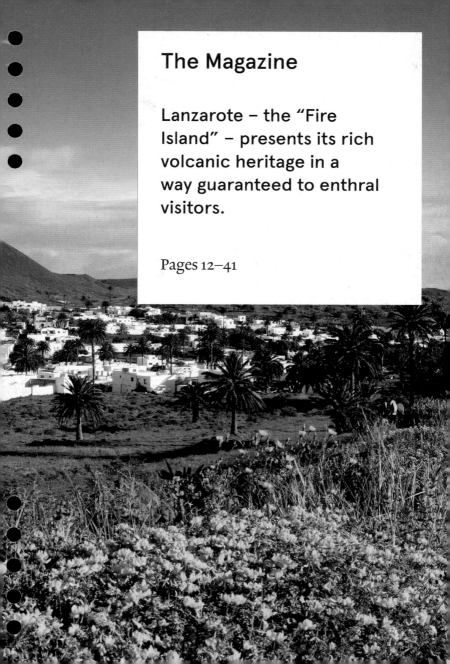

The Magazine

Lanzarote – the "Fire Island" – presents its rich volcanic heritage in a way guaranteed to enthral visitors.

Pages 12–41

Fields of Fire

"Suddenly the earth opened up near Timanfaya... the lava flowed towards the north as rapidly as water but it soon thickened and slowed down, flowing as if it were honey... In an instant, the mass of glowing lava reached out and destroyed the villages of Maretas and Santa Catalina in the valley. The darkness caused by the mass of ashes and smoke covering the sky and shutting out the sun caused the inhabitants of Yaiza to flee..."

Diary of the Yaiza parish priest, Don Andrés Lorenzo Curbelo, 1 September, 1730.

The Timanfaya eruptions lasted for another six years, the longest and largest recorded historical eruptions in the Canary Islands, with 26 volcanoes blowing their tops, or sides, at one time or another. It is said that the sounds of the explosions were so loud that

Spectacular views in the Fire Mountains, here at Pico Partido

The lava coast of Lanzarote between El Golfo and the Salinas de Janubio is called Los Hervideros (Hot Springs), and the waves surge particularly wildly here.

they were heard in Tenerife, 250km (155mi) away!

When the ground stopped shaking, about 200km² (78mi²) – one-third of the island, including many villages and hamlets plus the most fertile valleys and estates – was buried under the lava. It is estimated that the average depth of lava in the area of today's national park is an incredible 4m (13ft) – over twice the height of the average man. Ironically, the huge lava field, which was spewed from the volcanoes, also increased the island size by one-third.

Fortunately, Canarian volcanoes are what are known as the Hawaiian type, which are relatively slow to burn and give plenty of notice before erupting. The area was therefore evacuated and remarkably no one was killed or even injured. With

their most fertile fields laid waste, many of the islanders were reduced to destitution and sought to flee Lanzarote. Some did, but the Spanish authorities, fearing that an empty island would be seized as a strategic maritime base by rival powers (including the English), prohibited further evacuation under pain of death.

In 1824 three more volcanoes exploded just outside the boundary of the current national park. It is said that the heat was suffocating and sailors could hardly see the island because of the dense mist generated. Once again, there were no casualties and the damage, compared to the previous eruptions, was minimal, but it was still a terrifying experience: "On 29 September the volcano burst through the lava deposit of 1730, and flaming torrents flowed down to the sea. A noise like loud thunder had continued unceasingly, and prevented the inhabitants from sleeping, even many miles away. It is now 18 October and there is no doubt a furnace under our feet... Yesterday the volcano burst through a bed of lava in the centre of a great plain, sending up into the air a column of boiling water 150ft high." (From letters written by Don Augustin Cabrera, a local inhabitant). Since then there have been no more explosions. Yet even now, almost 200 years later, it is possible to observe geothermic activities in some areas of the island; they are one of the attractions at the Timanfaya National Park (p. 114).

The Volcanic Landscape

More than 300 volcanic cones undulate on the horizon. There are three main types of volcanic debris on Lanzarote. The biggest type is known as a bomb, which can range from the size of a grapefruit to a large boulder. Next in size comes pumice, *escoria* or slag – smaller, lightweight rock, honeycombed by hot gases. The smallest is called *picón* or *lapilli*, the tiny light cinder particles put to good effect by Canarian farmers and wine growers. This porous black gravel absorbs moisture on the surface at night which drips down to the plant roots during the day – thus enabling dry field cultivation.

Not all lava is alike. When thick, slow-flowing lava cools and breaks up, the rocks are rough and jagged. This lava is called *aa* (pronounced "ah-ah") based on the Hawaiian terminology and forms the classic Canarian *malpaís* (badlands) landscape. Thinner, faster-flowing lava, which cools quickly and is consequently smoother in texture, is known as *pahoehoe* or *pahoe-pahoe* from Hawaiian *pa howe howe*, which translates as "smooth unbroken surface". This kind of lava often looks like sculpted rope.

Another important feature is the volcanic tube, which is created by rivers of lava. The tube forms when the outer layer of the lava flow cools and solidifies, but the lava beneath the surface remains fluid and continues to flow. When the roof of a volcanic tube collapses it is known as a *jameo* ("ha-may-oh").

Learning More about Volcanoes

The best exhibition on the island's volcanic activity is the Casa de los Volcanes in the Jameos del Agua (p. 55). The Interpretation Centre at Mancha Blanca (p. 115) has a similar but less interesting exhibition, but a fascinating walk is led from here into the Montaña Termesana during which national park rangers expertly elucidate the volcanic phenomena of the region (see p. 111).

By far the best way of learning about the island's vulcanology is to take the Canary Trekking tour. It is led by a former park ranger who will happily answer your questions. Taking part in one of these walks may well prove to be a highlight of your holiday (tel: 609 537 684; www.canarytrekking.com). The tour ends at the site of the 1824 eruptions – you'll get the chance to look right down into the volcanic "chimneys" caused by the enormous boiling waterspouts.

Top: On foot through the Timanfaya Region
Centre: 300 years after the eruption: Hardly any plants grow on Lanzarote's volcanoes
Bottom: It's 100–120°C (212–248°F) just below the surface of the ground. Dry brushwood catches fire when placed in a shallow hole.

César Manrique

Even almost 30 years after his death, you will still come across the name César Manrique wherever you go on Lanzarote. The artist's works count among the most popular tourist attractions, drawing in millions of people from all over Europe to admire and enthuse about them. More than almost anyone else, he was responsible for highlighting the special features of the island.

Manrique was a painter, sculptor, architect and landscape designer rolled into one, an all-round talent dipping into what seemed to be an endless pool of ideas – and a constant source of amazement even to his fellow islanders. It is universally agreed that the set-piece attractions and artworks that Manrique has bequeathed to the island are extraordinary in themselves, but the measure of his greatness is also in what is not on the island and the values that he has embedded into future generations of Lanzaroteños. César Manrique was born in Arrecife in 1919. He studied at art college in Madrid and at the age of 23 staged his first exhibition in Arrecife with the aid of Pepin Ramírez, a family friend who would later become a vital ally.

Manrique's early artworks were

conventional in style and subjects, with many works featuring the island and its islanders, but when Surrealism burst on the scene in the mid-1950s he became a torch

Artist and Genius: César Manrique

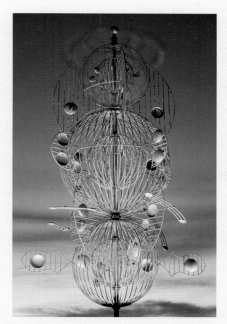

César Manrique's oeuvre includes many kinaesthetic objects – large mobiles standing at exposed (and often widely visible) locations all over the island.

carrier for the movement and opened Spain's first non-figurative art gallery. He rapidly made a name for himself, and in 1964 Nelson Rockefeller, who had bought some of his works, invited him to exhibit in the USA. Manrique flourished there and lived in New York for two years before the call of his beloved island beckoned him home.

By now Pepin Ramírez was president of the Cabildo island council and enthusiastically supported the ideas that his old friend had in store for Lanzarote. Noting the effect that mass tourism and increasing commercialisation was exerting on developing holiday destinations (such as Gran Canaria and Tenerife), Manrique and Ramírez drew up a series of guidelines that are still implemented to this day. The most apparent were a ban on advertising hoardings, electricity pylons and high-rise buildings, and all new buildings had to conform to the native island style – whitewashed with doors and windows painted green. Manrique was of the firm opinion that it was necessary to blend in with nature, and he endeavoured to find a balance between man and his environment.

Manrique had begun to conceive his magnificent seven visitor attractions (now known as the Centros de Arte, Cultura y Turismo) even while he was in New York, mailing his ideas for the first of these, the Jameos del Agua, to Ramírez. His works were to be "dreams that capture the sublime natural beauty of Lanzarote". Over the next decade he was to add the International Museum of Contemporary Art at the Castillo de San José (p. 88); the Cueva de los Verdes (p. 61); the Mirador del Río (p. 69); the El Diablo restaurant, Timanfaya (p. 113); the Casa Monumento al Campesino (p. 94); and the Jardín de Cactus (p. 62). He was also busy working on major projects elsewhere; the Lago Martiánez lido at Puerto de la Cruz in Tenerife; two *miradores* (belvederes) on the Canary Islands of El Hierro and La Gomera; and La Vaguada, a Madrid shopping centre.

For Manrique, the transitions between art, architecture and nature were smooth, and in many of his works these three major areas are seen in a successful synthesis. Lava is seen in harmony with a filigree wind chime or a modern sculpture, a traditional building with a cactus placed next to it. The volcanic element of the artist's home island always played a role in his work; he felt such a strong tie to it that he even set up his home in an arid lava field. His eye for detail is particularly visible in his architectural intervention in the lava tubes of Jameos del Agua: plants sprout from volcanic niches and white steps blaze against the anthracite-coloured lava flow.

By 1988 Manrique's celebrity status meant that he could no longer work undisturbed by fans and well-wishers at his famous house at Taro de Tahíche (p. 58) and he moved to Haría. His house continued to function as the Fundación César Manrique. He continued working full time into his 70s, but in 1992 he was tragically knocked over by a car and killed, just 50m away from Taro de Tahíche. He is buried in a simple grave at Haría.

Manrique's former home in Tahíche

Guanches & Conquistadors

When the Genoan sea captain Lancelotto Malocello arrived on Lanzarote in 1312, a curious sight awaited him. Here were people only slightly removed from the Stone Age, people who knew neither about the wheel nor about how to work metal.

Lancelotto Malocello – whose first name provided the inspiration for "Lanzarote", the island's modern moniker – seems to have built the first small fort here. A century later, the Norman nobleman Jean de Béthencourt (image p. 22) journeyed to the Canary Islands on the hunt for the much sought-after orchella lichen which was used in the production of purple dye for textiles. He was supported in his mission by Castile and Pope Clement VI, who was interested in converting the island's inhabitants to Christianity. For that reason, Béthencourt's party included a number of priests.

When they arrived on Lanzarote, Béthencourt and the priests encountered a peaceful people with high moral standards: "Go throughout the world and nowhere will you find a finer and better formed people...with great minds were they to receive instructions." Other researchers added that their hair was long, the men wore plaited beards and that their clothes and shoes were made of goatskins.

Alexander von Humboldt, the famous German naturalist, geographer and expert on the Canaries, concurred with these positive sentiments in an account of the islanders written in 1799: "On the arrival of the Spaniards, its [Lanzarote's] inhabitants were

The Early Islanders

The Canary Islands were probably settled by Berbers from the north-west of Africa around 500BC. These native inhabitants are often known as "Guanches". *Guanche* is actually the name for the inhabitants of Tenerife, however, and roughly translates as "Son of Tenerife". The native people of Lanzarote called themselves "Majos".

In 1402, Jean de Béthencourt conquered four Canary Islands and declared himself king.

the Spanish mainland. Rubicón was declared the first bishopric on the Canary Islands in 1404, and was relocated to Las Palmas/Gran Canaria in 1485.

Jean de Béthencourt was able to occupy Fuerteventura with support from the Castilian throne in 1405. El Hierro and La Gomera were also captured, but Gran Canaria and La Palma did not fall. Lanzarote, Fuerteventura, El Hierro and La Gomera were given the status of *Islas de Señorio* ("Islands under a Lordship") as if they had been taken by a nobleman. The land belonged to the conqueror, but the new settlers from the Iberian Peninsula were allowed to use it for agriculture in return for a tax (30% of their harvests). Béthencourt later handed the responsibility of running the islands over to his nephew, Maciot de Béthencourt.

distinguished from the other Canarians by marks of greater civilisation. Their homes were built with free stone [without cement, lime or mortar] while the Guanche inhabitants of Tenerife dwelt... in caverns."

Conflicting Interests

Béthencourt landed on the south coast of Lanzarote (east of today's Playa Blanca) and built a fort and a church in a place then known as Rubicón. Some of the island's 1,000 or so native inhabitants – whom the Priests hoped to convert to Christianity – allowed themselves to be baptised and chose to cooperate with the conquistadors. They were given land in return for helping to conquer the other islands. Anyone who refused baptism ran the risk of being taken into slavery in the Canaries or shipped off and sold on

Not long after, in 1418, Maciot de Béthencourt gave the Canary Islands to the Andalusian Counts of Niebla as a gift. To complicate matters, the Portuguese Prince known as Henry the Navigator then received the right to the Canary Islands via a Papal Bull in 1433. Three years later, both Portugal and Castile laid claim to the archipelago. It was not until 1479 that their conflict was resolved by the Treaty of Alcáçovas: Castile obtained the Canary Islands, while Portugal got West Africa and the other islands off its coast.

Jean de Béthencourt's ship on its way to the Canaries in 1402

The Water Problem

Even as the plane approaches the runway, you get
an impression of what is later confirmed as you
tour the island: Lanzarote is extremely arid, almost
desert-like, and has practically no natural forest.
In short: there is just not enough water.
Why the island is so different from its evergreen
neighbours is very simple.

The Canarian archipelago lies under the influence of the north-easterly trade winds, which pick up moisture from the sea and carry it to the islands. On the northern side of the mountains, these air masses are forced to rise and clouds are formed, which produce rain or at least moisture in the form of dew and mist. However, this only occurs where the hills and mountains are high enough to stop the flow of air. This means that this "natural moisture

Tourism and especially the many hotel complexes have played an important part
in increasing water consumption on the dry island of Lanzarote.

Enormous wind turbines soar high across Lanzarote's countryside. They play an important role in the island's power production.

transfer" in fact only takes place on the neighbouring islands of Lanzarote, which have significantly higher ground. La Palma and La Gomera, but also Tenerife receive a relatively good amount of rain. Subtropical rain forests with rich vegetation have even been able to develop on the north faces of these islands.

Lanzarote and its neighbour Fuerteventura are just too low. The Fire Island's highest point does not even reach 700m (2,296ft), and the moist air thus just blows over the island without giving up much of its valuable freight. This does not mean that it never rains on Lanzarote, but it is a lot less than for example on La Palma, the wettest Canary Island.

The problem is not new and not a result of the climate change, but actually as old as Lanzarote itself.

Traditional Water Management
In earlier times water was obtained with relatively simple methods.

Almost every house had a cistern, in which at least the little that fell from the heavens was collected from the roof using a sophisticated system. In some places, for example Teguise and Tahíche, there were larger cisterns, which supplied

The energy-hungry desalination plant (above) is powered among other things by the wind energy (top) produced on the island. Water consumption on the island has increased and can no longer be met by the island's rainfall.

THE MAGAZINE

water to the whole town. In addition, of course, each town had one or more wells. To supplement these methods so-called *galerías* (water tunnels), were laboriously drilled into the mountains to tap the groundwater resources there. With the water obtained in this way, it is at least possible to get by in the years bringing relatively little rain. However, as a result of recurring periods of drought, the island has experienced many years of acute water shortage.

With the arrival of tourism in the 1960s, and the enormous increase in the population that occurred as a result, there was a dramatic rise in water consumption. The ground-water level sank, so that the water in many wells became salinated. At times, the island became dependent on water supplies from external sources; attempts were made to get the situation under control by bringing water over by tanker from Gran Canaria.

Water from the Sea

1964 saw a turning point with the construction of the first desalination plant in Arrecife. At the time, Lanzarote was one of the first regions to make use of this technology. Today, more than 90% of the island's service water is taken from the sea – without desalinated seawater, Lanzarote's present situation would not be viable. Whilst in 1960 the island's population was 60,000, now

Everyday life in the countryside: Undaunted, a farmer waters his field.

it has more than 140,000 inhabit-ants – and more than 2.5 million tourists visit Lanzarote every year.

The water harvested from the sea has its price though: desalination plants use a tremendous amount of energy. Although some of the energy needed comes from the Los Valles wind farm, the majority of the electricity is produced by the island's fossil-fuelled power station. What is more, although the desalinated water that comes out of the tap is perfectly hygienic, it does not taste particularly nice. Good mineral water is thus brought in from Gran Canaria and Tenerife.

Canarian Cuisine – Simple but Original

There is no point in beating about the bush: real gourmets will struggle with the Canarian cuisine, which is probably why the hotels tend to opt for a more international menu. However, rural Canarian cooking naturally offers some original specials that you really need to try.

Anyone visiting the Canaries has definitely got to try *gofio*.

For all intents and purposes, the quintessential ingredient of the Canarian cuisine is the potato, which is served as a sort of jacket potato side dish with fish and meat but which can also be ordered separately in many restaurants. It is cooked in a small amount of salted water until a white salt crust appears on the rather wrinkly skin.

That is why Canarian potatoes are often called *papas arrugadas* or "wrinkly potatoes". Relatively small potatoes are used for this purpose; they are harvested on the Canaries about three times a year. Some of them are actually the product of dryland farming done on Lanzarote, but most of them come from the neighbouring islands or from the Spanish mainland.

Unlike jacket potatoes, it is usual to eat *papas arrugadas* with the skin, but only after dipping them in a spicy *mojo* sauce. This comprises of oil, vinegar, local herbs and plenty of garlic. One of the main sorts is *mojo rojo* with red pepper and a bit of chilli; the green version *mojo verde* is made with lots of fresh coriander. Green *mojo* is usually served with fish dishes and red *mojo* with meat. Every restaurant worth its salt always makes its own *mojo*.

The Canarian National Dish

You either like *gofio* or you don't. If you like polenta, then you should try it. This staple food, once eaten by the original inhabitants of the Canaries, is traditionally made from the flour of roasted barley but is now also made from wheat and corn. It is regarded as being extremely good for you. As the bran and germ are ground with the endosperm, it is a healthy, full-grain product corresponding to our

---

Tasty Tapas and Starters

Albóndigas meatballs
Calamares fried battered squid
Chorizos al vino tinto paprika sausage in red wine
Gambas prawns
Jamón serrano mountain cured ham; pata negra is the best variety, and very expensive.
Mejillones mussels
Pimientos peppers. These may be stuffed with a variety of fillings.
Pimientos de padrón are the hot spicy variety. They are sometimes served smothered in melted cheese.
Pulpo octopus
Tortilla potato omelette

---

modern understanding of wholefood nutrition. Full of fibre, vitamins from the B-complex and minerals, it contains a lot of the things the body needs. People used to just mix the flour into a sort of porridge consistency with water or goat's milk, which was then eaten as a side dish. In the meantime, there are dozens of different dishes with it. Restaurants, for example, serve *gofio escaldado* with fish, but *gofio* can also just be stirred into a casserole to thicken the sauce. Not only main courses contain this nutritious flour, it is also an ingredient in sweets and desserts, such as *mousse de gofio*,

Freshly caught and prepared straightaway – that is how fish tastes best.

gofio pancakes or *gofio* ice-cream. You can also eat it in the morning instead of muesli: put *gofio* in a dish with banana, the juice of an orange and some honey and add a pinch of cinnamon or vanilla. You won't often find *gofio* on a hotel buffet though, unless they happen to be doing a "Canarian evening".

Island Classics: Fish, Shrimps & Co.

Naturally, as on every island, fish and shellfish play a prominent role, and it is no different on Lanzarote. One of the most popular edible fish is freshly caught *vieja* (parrotfish), which is mainly served boiled. In fish restaurants, fish is generally *a la plancha*, as they call it on the Canaries, which means it is grilled. Atlantic fish is available every-where, and *cherne* (bass grouper), *sama* (pink dentex) and *atún* (tuna) are often on the menu.

One of the best local fish, popular owing to its firm white flesh is the *alfonsiño* (red bream). Mostly from coastal waters (bred in aquaculture) are the *dorada* (gilt-head sea bream) and *lubina* (sea bass), which fish lovers also known as *loup de mer*.

A more elaborate dish is fish baked in the oven in a salt mantle or the Canarian fish stew *cazuela de pescado*, in which the fish, potatoes and onions are seasoned with herbs such as coriander, safran and plenty of garlic.

Another typically Canarian dish is *sancocho canario*, a salted fish (generally grouper) usually eaten on public holidays, which is eaten with *gofio* and green *mojo* sauce. Although smoked salmon is not typically Canarian, it has become popular since it was introduced to Lanzarote by the smokehouse in Uga (p. 127) and is now served as a first course by many upmarket restaurants.

Practically every tapas bar sells *gambas al ajillo*, prawns in a sizzling olive oil and garlic sauce; they are served, as they are on the mainland, in a small ceramic dish.

Meat also features on the menu of course. Typical dishes include marinated rabbit and goat ragout, but you will naturally also find poultry, steak and chops. Since there is practically no livestock farming on the island, almost all the meat is imported.

Shellfish, appetisingly prepared fish and aromatic *mojo* – typical "Fire Island" food. Ideally, these delicacies should be eaten at a table overlooking the sea to savour the full island atmosphere.

Viticulture with a Difference

On Lanzarote, the right wine to accompany your fish dish does not necessarily have to come from the mainland. Local vintners have been making up for lost ground over the last few years, and what is even more eye-opening than some of the good wines they produce is their unique method of growing the vines.

The people on Lanzarote are very innovative – and they have to be if they want to survive on an arid volcanic island. A lot is demanded of the farmers and wine makers in the area of agriculture and viticulture. Owing to the lack of rain, they have to organise

In the biosphere reserve La Geria on Lanzarote, the vines benefit from the fertile volcanic soil.

Without the necessary expertise, the grapes would not thrive on this arid island: vines grow protected from the wind, their roots girded by lapilli.

themselves in a completely different way.

Wine, like onions and other vegetables, is cultivated using the dry farming method, in other words without artificial irrigation. This method is extremely ingenious: vines are planted in soil covered with lapilli, volcanic ejecta available in abundance on

Lanzarote. These almost black, barely pea-sized granules have hygroscopic (water-attracting) properties; they absorb the dew from the air at night, and this moisture drips down to the roots during the day. The approximately 20 to 30 cm thick lapilli layer stops the ground from drying out.

In order to protect the vines from the wind, they are planted in funnel-shaped pits, called *zocos*, and surrounded by a low semicircular stone wall. On both sides of the road through La Geria, the largest wine-growing area on Lanzarote, thousands of vines merge together to create a unique landscape picture – the New York Metropolitan Museum of Art rather appropriately even referred to the region as a total work of art.

Especially in the afternoon when the sun is going down, the interplay of the light and shade in the vineyard conjures up an enchanting picture.

Malvasía, Moscatel & Co.

The Malvasia is the traditional grape variety grown on Lanzarote. Originating from Crete, the first vines were brought to Lanzarote at the beginning of the 16th century.

One of the oldest wineries is the Bodega El Grifo in La Geria. Founded in 1775, just a few decades after the devastating eruption of Timanfaya, the family business has remained the market leader on Lanzarote to this day; around 500,000 bottles leave the modern filling plant each year, a small percentage of which are exported to Germany and Switzerland. Adorning the label on the bottle is a bird of prey designed by the artist César Manrique. El Grifo cultivates predominantly Malvasia on more than 60 ha (148 acres) of land. Practically all of the work in the vineyard, including the grape picking, is done by hand, which is naturally reflected in the price. Unlike the vines on the European mainland, the grapes reach full maturity in the summer, which is the reason why the grape harvest begins at the beginning of August on Lanzarote.

Instead of the heavy red Malvasia wine that used to be pressed here, mainly dry and semi-dry white wines are now produced with the help of state-of-the-art cellar techniques. They are a straw-yellow colour and their fine acidity leave a pleasant aftertaste on the tongue. Appealing red and rosé wines are pressed from the Listán negro grape, and some Moscatel is also cultivated. El Grifo also has a fine sparkling wine produced using the traditional Champagne method with second in-bottle fermentation. Wines from Lanzarote are covered by a protected designation of origin (D. O. = *Denominación de Origen*).

Beetle Juice

Lipsticks using the carmine red obtained from bugs? That's right: For years breeding the cochineal beetle was a mainstay of Lanzarote's economy. A cactus, brought in from Mexico served as the host plant. These days the farming areas lie fallow, but on the drive through the north of Lanzarote, especially Guatziza, overgrown cactus fields provide a reminder of the "golden age" of the little beetle.

The cochineal beetle lives in small colonies on the cladodes (pads) of the prickly pear (Opuntia). The undemanding plant arrived on the Canary Islands in the 16th century, mainly as an ornamental plant and to fence off fields but also for its edible cactus fruits. From about 1830, Opuntia was grown specifically to breed the cochineal

A field of cacti – the favourite food of the cochineal beetle

Those lucky enough to find someone who knows about the cochineal beetle will hear fascinating stories about its history.

beetle. At that time there was enormous demand for red dye in the growing European textile industry. The market was mainly covered with imports from Mexico, whose inhabitants already knew in pre-Columbian time how to produce red dye from the insect. After Mexico gained its independence, its former colonial power, Spain, began producing the cochineal red itself. The climate on the Canary Islands proved to be optimal for cultivating Opuntia. What was more, on arid Lanzarote, there was plenty of fallow land that could be cultivated for the undemanding cactus.

From Export Hit to Niche Product
In the mid 19th-century, at the height of the cochineal boom, there were thousands of workers involved in the business. Even the children had to help collect the little insects. A spatula was used to scrape them from the cactus pad; then they were dried and the "blood-red" colour they contained extracted using a solvent. From a kilo of cochineal insects, it was possible to get 50 grams of red dye. Thousands of tons were exported each year and for Lanzarote the work-intensive cochineal breeding formed the basis of the island's economy for decades. That is until synthetic aniline dyes were discovered – the Badische Anilin- & Sodafabrik, founded in Germany in 1865, played a decisive role in the demise of cochineal breeding, by providing the global market with cheaper and more colour-stable dyes.

Nowadays, cochineal red is only found in a smaller group of products, natural textiles, carpets and natural cosmetics, where it is used i. a. for lipsticks. As a food dye (E 120), it adds a deep red colour to jams, sweets, drinks and Easter eggs. For a long time, the most well-known drink to be coloured with cochineal was Campari until, in 2006, the company also decided to change to artificial colours.

Whole families once earned their living breeding the cochineal beetle; these days it is more of a recreational pastime.

Rio-like Carnival

Celebrations on Lanzarote tend to be loud, lively and long. The highlight on the festival calendar is always the carnival for which the whole island starts to prepare months in advance. Springlike temperatures mean most of the events take place outdoors.

The *Carnaval*, as it is called on Lanzarote, has its stronghold in the capital of Arrecife, but Teguise, Puerto del Carmen and even the smaller towns and villages have their own celebrations. To ensure that you don't miss anything, none of the events in the various locations ever take place at the same time, and as a result the

Colourful and cheerful: the festivities in Arrecife are reminiscent of carnival in Rio.

Gruesomely good-looking: In Arrecife you need to watch out for the mischievous musicians.

partying carries on over several weeks. It generally kicks off mid February in Arrecife and San Bartolomé; and In Yaiza and Playa Blanca towards the end of March. The show begins with the *Verbena de la Sábana*, for which only sheets are allowed to be used for the costumes. Afterwards, the carnival queen is chosen; her costume is lavishly adorned with feathers and lots of sequins. One of the highlights of the colourful activities is in Arrecife the Sunday before the actual Carnival weekend when the drag queen is crowned. For this, men slip into the female role and pose on the stage, decked out in bright make-up and with wigs and high heels. On Carnival Monday, the procession of carnival groups and different floats makes its way along the streets, loudly accompanied by South American rhythms.

The Little Devils of Teguise

In Teguise the scary-looking *diabletes* (little devils) populate the streets of the old town. They wear black bull masks, complete with red tongue and horns, as well as a white cotton costume with red and black stripes and circles, which is covered in bells. Vigorously brandishing their sand-filled leather pouches attached to a stick, they give everyone a fright, particularly the children. Their counterpart in Arrecife is the *Parranda de los Buches*, in which a group of musicians dressed in historical costumes sing old shanty songs at the top of their lungs and

Devils and damsels: *Carnaval* on Lanzarote displays many different facets

taunt spectators with an inflated *buche* (fish stomach). During the parade, they are usually at the front. Local colour is guaranteed.

Crowning Finale

On Ash Wednesday, performed with great fanfare, *El Entierro de la Sardina* (the Burial of the Sardine) sees the

Carnaval laid to rest. This ritual that has taken place on the Canaries for centuries also marks the beginning of Lent. Here again, the capital of Arrecife is the main centre of attention. A huge papier-mâché sardine is carried through the streets in a procession accompanied by weeping women (who are actually men) dressed in mourning. When it arrives in its appointed place in front of Castillo de San Gabriel, a firework is lit inside the sardine and it is literally blown to pieces. This ends the colourful activities in Arrecife. However, in line with "The carnival is dead, long live the carnival," just a few days later, activities take off again in Puerto del Carmen, only a couple of miles down the road.

Glittering headdresses and magnificent costumes – the island can be extremely colourful.

Canarian Wrestling

The Lucha Canaria – a form of traditional Canarian wrestling – is popular throughout the Canary Islands. Lanzarote boasts a number of wrestling arenas where competitions are regularly held.

In the 15th century, the Spanish chronicler Alvar García de Santa María wrote that wrestling was particularly popular among the native population. He described it as a gallant martial art in which participants were less concerned with beating their opponents than uniting with them in a peaceful embrace after the fight.

The rules for tournaments have been written down since 1872. Two teams, each consisting of 12 male – or female – wrestlers, enter into competition against one another. The barefoot athletes wear trousers rolled up to their upper thighs. Two *pollos* (fighting cocks) take their starting positions on a circular, sand covered surface *terrero* and bend their upper bodies forwards in a bow before grabbing the other fighter's rolled up trouser leg with their left hand. They must then try to wrestle the opposing *luchador* (wrestler) to the ground in the space of two minutes with a series of pushes, pulls, jerks, lifts and throws; only punches, kicks and uppercuts, are not allowed. After a maximum of three rounds have been played, the wrestler who has brought their opponent down twice is the victor. He or she must then take on the winner of another fight (facing a maximum of four opponents in total). The team that reaches 12 points first during the competition (which lasts around 2 hours) is victorious. Tao (over 1,000 seats) and Tinajo (over 1,500 seats) have their own dedicated Lucha Canaria arenas.

Ready to Go: Two *Pollos* in the Starting Position

The stamp César Manrique has left on the north of the island is second to none – the Jameos del Agua complex is one of his finest works

The North

An attractive holiday region
with unspoilt countryside,
a colonial legacy and lots
of beautiful landscape art
by César Manrique

Pages 42–75

Getting Your Bearings

The north of Lanzarote is home to the island's most spectacular man-made sights – the man in question who made them all was César Manrique. Devotees can trace much of his life story at sites within the loop that makes up the main roads of the north: his boyhood holidays in Famara; his extraordinary home at Tahíche; his great subterranean garden; his belvedere visitors' attractions; and even his last resting place in Haría.

The north is not just about one man, however – travel around and you'll discover some impressively stark natural contrasts contained in a very small area. These phenomena include the desert-like *jable* around Famara, the lush oasis of the Haría valley, the stark lichen-covered *malpaís*, the cultivated lava fields around the Monte Corona, and the cactus fields surrounding Guatiza. The north also has the best views on the island, courtesy of its many *miradores* (lookout points).

Rich in contrasts, nature here demands to be explored. One attractive option is a boat trip to the little neighbouring island of La Graciosa, for instance, where in some parts you may end up feeling like Robinson Crusoe. On the coast, the Costa Teguise holiday resort welcomes tourists with a good infrastructure and wonderful beaches, while inland, quiet, dignified and lovingly restored, the former capital Teguise is possibly the island's most beautiful town. If the conquistadors were to march back into Teguise tomorrow, they would probably still recognise large parts of it. At the weekly Sunday market, Teguise's charm is particularly irresistible.

TOP 10
2 ★★ Teguise
3 ★★ Jameos del Agua
5 ★★ Fundación César Manrique
     (Taro de Tahíche)
8 ★★ Cueva de los Verdes

At Your Leisure
13 Costa Teguise
14 La Caleta
15 Mirador del Río
16 Órzola
17 La Graciosa

Don't Miss
11 Jardín de Cactus
12 Haría

Pedro Barba

La Graciosa 17

Caleta
del Sebo

Mirador 15
del Río

16 Órzola

. Las Tabaibitas

Las Rositas . · Yé
                  · Casas   LZ-1
                  La Breña

LZ-201

**Cueva de
los Verdes**

Máguez ·   **8** ★★
                     3 ★★
                          Jameos
Haría 12   Los Picachos ·   **del Agua**
                 LZ-10

                 · Arrieta
            Tabayesco ·

La Caleta 14
            LZ-10   LZ-1

            Los Valles ·   · Mala

       Las Laderas ·   Charco del Palo
      LZ-402   El Mojón ·   Guatiza
                              11 Jardín de Cactus
Teguise 2 ★★

       Teseguite ·   LZ-1

   Nazaret ·
LZ-30   LZ-10 Las Cabreras ·

                    Urbanización
                    · Ciudad Jardín
Fundación César · Tahiche
Manrique 5 ★ LZ-34
                              13 Costa Teguise
            LZ-1

                 Las Caletas

                    5 km
                    ⊢────────⊣
                    3 mi

My Day
on the Trail of
César Manrique

What ingenious ideas the man had! On Lanzarote you encounter the artistic creations of César Manrique around almost every corner. In the north of the island, there is so much of his work that it would be difficult to visit it all in one day. It's better to just pick what interests you most.

10am: Village Square, Cactus Garden or Lava Grotto?

As soon as you leave the capital **7 ★★ Arrecife**, you are already spoilt for choice. In the holiday resort of Costa Teguise, for example, Manrique designed the Pueblo Marinero complex; however, it is a bit early in the day to stop at one of the restaurants surrounding the pretty village square.

The **11 Jardín de Cactus** in Guatiza, a few miles further north, is (not just) a must for fans of the prickly plant. Decide for yourself.

An alternative, which is at least equally attractive is a visit to the **3 ★★ Jameos del Agua**. Manrique's skilful restaging of these volcanic tubes that formed after the eruption of the volcano 3000 years ago and collapsed in several places is regarded by many people as the artist's ultimate creation – making it highly unlikely that you will ever find yourself alone here.

Noon: Off to See the Eagle

After all the hustle and bustle of your fellow tourists in Jameos del

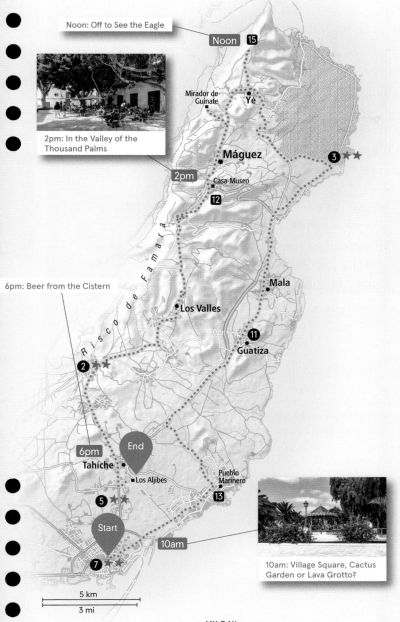

Noon: Off to See the Eagle

Noon 15

Mirador de Guinate ● Yé

2pm: In the Valley of the Thousand Palms

● **Máguez**

3 ★★

2pm

Casa-Museo ■
12

6pm: Beer from the Cistern

Mala

Risco de Famara

Los Valles

11

Guatiza

2 ★★

6pm

End

Tahíche ●

■ Los Aljibes

Pueblo Marinero

13

5 ★★

Start

7 ★★

10am

10am: Village Square, Cactus Garden or Lava Grotto?

5 km
3 mi

At the Mirador del Río created by Manrique, you can gaze out from a height of around 480m (1,574ft) across the salt pans of the Salinas del Rio to the neighbouring island of La Graciosa – don't forget to take a picture!

Agua, drive up to the Risco de Famara. There are lots of fantastic *miradores* (lookout points) waiting to be discovered along the clifftops. The most famous one is the one designed by Manrique, **15** Mirador del Río, from which there is a spectacular view across the water to the little sister island of La Graciosa. There is an alternative to this too though: from Mirador de Guinate on the LZ 201 south of the little hamlet of Yé, you can have almost the same view all to yourself – and, what's more, there is no entrance fee. To do this, follow the road through

Guinate until it ends at the edge of the scarp. Take a deep breath and just enjoy the experience!

2pm: In the Valley of the Thousand Palms

In **12** Haría the church square offers a good place for a break. Here, in the shade of the laurel trees you can enjoy a small snack or just lap up the serene atmosphere sitting on a bench. Manrique spent the last years of his life in Haría, in a house located on the outskirts of the town in the middle of a palm grove. After his fatal accident, the house and the adjacent studio

10am

2pm

At the top: Guatiza is where Manrique completed his last major project, the Jardín de Cactus

Above: The Casa-Museo in Haría enables visitors to see Manrique's former home and his studio

2pm

Haría, the place in which Manrique lived, after he had left Tahiche, exudes a quiet and peaceful atmosphere.

were opened up to the public: Casa-Museo (p. 66). Everything exhibited there gives the impression of being exactly the way Manrique left it – in the bar a Campari bottle that has been opened, in the studio an un-finished painting on the easel, surrounded by dozens of paint-brushes and paint pots. Make time in the garden next to the pool to watch a video about Manrique's life – the historical recordings and

Noon

5pm

At the Mirador de Guinate you can savour a wonderful view across the Atlantic – and also of Lanzarote itself: to the south-west you can discern the volcanoes.

interviews provide an intimate picture of the multi-talent.

5pm: Manrique's Final Resting Place

The artist is buried in the <u>Haria Cemetery</u>, which is located on the edge of town on the road to Arrieta. Very few tourists come here. The gravestone is easy to find, just a few steps away from the cemetery chapel. Fresh flowers generally adorn the grave; the only extravagance is a, in the meantime, 5m (16ft) columnar cactus soaring over the resting place – Manrique had a soft spot for prickly plants.

6pm: Beer from the Cistern

César Manrique was an epicurean, which is made clear by the fact that on Lanzarote alone, he designed more than half a dozen restaurants – he even designed the logo on their menus. In <u>Tahíche</u> (p. 58), his former home town, he initially set up an art gallery in a disused cistern, now also

10am

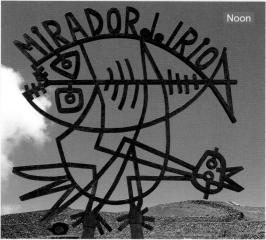

Noon

Left: Manrique's grave at the Haría cemetery
Top: A lava cavern in Jameos del Aqua
Above: "Signpost" at the entrance to the Mirador del Río

a restaurant, Los Aljibes. There, you should accompany the grilled dishes with a glass of freshly tapped craft beer from the house brewery. The restaurant is slightly tucked away on the road leading to Costa Teguise (LZ 34) just behind a large roundabout. Close by is the artist's first house, now home to the ❺ ★★ Fundación César Manrique the location of which you should keep in mind for the following day.

Los Aljibes
✠ 181 E3
✉ Calle Bravo Murillo 6
☎ 610 454 294
🕐 Mon 1–8, Tue–Sat 1–10:30, Sun 1–9:30

❷ ★★ Teguise

Don't Miss	A wonderful little town that was once the capital of the island
Why	Colonial atmosphere in the purest of forms
When	The mornings, during the week for a stroll through the town, and on Sunday for the market
Time	At least half a day
What Else	The Castillo de Santa Bárbara offers the best view of the city
In Short	A town of contrasts: easy-going browsing to shoulder-to-shoulder shopping

For six days of the week the town shows its serene side, then on Sunday thousands of visitors flock here to its tourist market, which takes over the centre. Folklore dancers and musicians perform in the Plaza Miguel beside the handsome Iglesia de Nuestra Señora de Guadalupe.

View from Castillo de Santa Bárbara over Teguise, one of the oldest towns on the Canary Islands

On the square, guarded by two stone lions, is the Palacio Spínola, built between 1730 and 1780, complete with a chapel, a patio and an attractive well. A visit will give you a good idea of how the wealthy citizens of the capital enjoyed life in the 18th century. The Museo del Timple in the Palacio Spínola tells you all about the history, development and

The church of
Nuestra Señora
de Guadalupe

creation of this small, typically Canarian guitar. Also on the
square is the rustic stone Caja de Canarias bank, built in
1680. It was originally called La Cilla, a place used for storing
"tithes" (a kind of tax given to the clergy).

Just off the main square, the adjoining squares of Plaza
18 de Julio and Plaza Clavijo y Fajardo are lined with beautiful
historic buildings, now home to shops and restaurants. Just
off here is a very picturesque snowy white-topped building
with a characteristic outside Canarian balcony. This is the

See how the wealthy lived inside the Palacio Spínola.

17th-century Casa Cuartel, formerly an army barracks.

The town has two attractive former convents. The Centro de Arte, which displays a selection of temporary art exhibitions, is now housed in the Convento de Santo Domingo. Don't miss the Palacio del Marqués between the 16th-century Convento de San Francisco and the Iglesia de Nuestra Señora de Guadalupe on Calle Herrera y Rojas. Built in 1455, it is the oldest building in town and plays host to the beautiful Patio del Vino garden bar and café (p. 73).

Overlooking the town is the 16th-century Castillo de Santa Bárbara (also known as Castillo de Guanapay). It sits right on the lip of the Volcán de Guanapay and enjoys 360-degree views. The castle was a refuge for the townsfolk who fled here to avoid frequent pirate raids. Those left in the town were often slaughtered, most savagely in 1586. You can learn more about the history of pirate attacks in the fort's Museo de la Piratería.

INSIDER TIP There are lots of **restaurants**, **cafés** and **bistros** in Teguise – you'll be spoilt for choice (p. 72).

🛈 📍181 D4

Convento de San Francisco (Museo de Arte Sacro)
✉ Plaza de San Francisco
🌐 www.turismoteguise.com
🕐 Tue–Sat 9.30–4.30, Sun 10–2 💶 €2

Convento de Santo Domingo
✉ Calle de Santo Domingo ☎ 928 845 001 🌐 www.turismoteguise.com
🕐 Mon–Fri 10–3, Sun 10–2 💶 Free

Palacio Spínola
✉ Plaza de la Constitución
☎ 928 845 181
🌐 www.casadeltimple.org
🕐 Mon–Sat 9–4 (in summer until 3), Sun 9–3 💶 €3

Castillo de Santa Bárbara
✉ 1km (0.6mi) east of Teguise
☎ 928 845 001
🌐 www.museodelapirateria
🕐 Daily 10–4 💶 €3

❸★★ Jameos del Agua

Don't Miss	Collapsed volcanic tunnels transformed into a perfect tourist attraction
Why	Nature and art in harmony
When	Ideally late afternoon when most of the tour buses have gone
Time	Two to three hours
In Short	A perfect example of Manrique's ingenuity

Regarded by many as César Manrique's most spectacular creation, the Jameos del Agua was also his first tourist centre on the island. His design took a volcanic tunnel that had fallen in here and there and transformed it into a fantasy grotto. When the Hollywood legend Rita Hayworth visited the site in 1966, she declared it "the Eighth Wonder of the World".

You descend stairs into the first *jameo* (p. 16) to find a cool crepuscular café-bar area, luxuriant with tropical plants. Huge lobster pots serve as hanging baskets for giant ferns whose bright green foliage contrasts with the dark volcanic

The "beach" and palm trees of this artificial landscape in a collapsed volcanic tunnel

In the tunnel between the first and second *jameo* is an enchanting cave lake inhabited by tiny albino crabs.

rock. Bird song and New Age or classical music completes the mood. As your eyes adjust you can see little niches and alcoves that really come into their own in the evenings when this becomes a night-spot (Manrique called it "the most beautiful night-club in the world"). In the adjoining cave tunnel is a perfectly transparent lake – the still water is populated by hundreds of tiny, almost fluorescent spider-like albino crabs. They once lived deep in the ocean, up to 2,000m (6,500ft) beneath the waves, but were stranded here long ago. They're a biological rarity today and are threatened with extinction.

As you emerge up the meandering steps from the dusky tunnel, there is a shock in store. The second *jameo* is a South Seas-style swimming pool, bright blue with a blinding white "beach" (painted stone), picturesque black and grey volcanic rocks and a tall palm tree set at a picture-postcard angle over the pool. Don't bring your swimming costume, as swimming is not permitted. At the far end of the pool the final part of the cave system is home to an auditorium that seats 600 spectators. It has near-perfect acoustics and is used for folk-lore shows and concerts.

Ascend the steps for a great photo opportunity over the pool and you will find a series of rooms housing the Casa de los Volcanes exhibition area and research centre. This is an excellent hands-on introduction to the world of volcanoes and will answer just about any question on vulcanology in Lanzarote, the Canary Islands or indeed worldwide. For instance, one exhibit demonstrates what happens as magma

The auditorium is a large concert hall integrated into the lava grotto.

rises to the surface: its gas explodes in bubbles erupting through the Earth's crust. Fascinating film recordings show lava flowing into the sea.

INSIDER TIP There are two **bars** at either end of your visit. The first may be a little too dark for some people. If so, go to the one up the steps above the swimming pool. Both sell snacks, although they are rather expensive. The classy **restaurant** (tel: 928 848 024; daily 12–4, Tue, Sat 7pm–0.30am), renowned for its first-class local cuisine, is also open during the evening on Tuesdays and Saturdays. Smarter clothing is required at these times (no shorts). There's often music playing while you dine.

✝ 179 F2 ☎ 928 848 024
◐ Daily 10–6:30 ✦ €9.50

❺ ★★ Fundación César Manrique (Taro de Tahíche)

Don't Miss	César Manrique's house: Taro de Tahíche
Why	This extravagant property was the centre of César Manrique's life for over 20 years
When	There is always a lot going on here, or at least whenever you want to get involved
Time	At least two hours
What Else	There is a filigree "wind toy" at the entrance
In Short	Luxury living in the middle of an inhospitable lava field

Nature and architecture: A subterranean living space built in a collapsed lava tunnel. The walls are made of volcanic rock.

Just after Manrique had returned from America, he was driving past Tahíche when he noticed the branch of a fig tree protruding from a lava field. He discovered it had taken root in a *jameo* (p. 60) around 5m (16ft) in diameter. Manrique noticed there were a further four *jameos* of similar size, and with characteristic resolve determined that this would be the site for his house, to be known as Taro de Tahíche.

When Manrique approached the landowner and offered to buy the land he was told it was worthless and he could take as much as he required. This was in fact the perfect challenge and opportunity for him. Here, in the most barren landscape of Lanzarote, he would use its natural features to create a masterpiece, which would show the outside world, and particularly the students who had taunted him at college in Madrid, that the island was much more than just a cinder heap.

Manrique's former home, wonderfully embedded in nature, remains fascinating to this day.

Wandering through Casa del Volcán!

The approach is heralded by one of Manrique's most imaginative and colourful *juguetes del vientos*; these "wind toys", of which quite a few can be found on the island, are kinetic objects that look like enormous mobiles. As you step into the first room of the house and look through the large picture window onto the lunar-like waste ground created by the lava field, you begin to appreciate the extraordinary vision of Manrique: across a naked lava field, the eye is drawn to an evenly shaped volcanic cone.

The ground floor is a gallery devoted mostly to works by Manrique and plans and drawings of his projects. <u>Pieces from his private collection</u>, including works by Picasso and Miró, are also on display. It is interesting to note the broad range of Manrique's styles, from his early conventional naturalistic works to his later abstract oeuvre.

Downstairs is where the real fun is. Curved whitewashed narrow passageways lead from one *jameo* to the next. Furnishings are minimalist, original 1960s chic, and, as at Jameos del Agua (p. 55), there is a bright blue-and-white painted swimming pool and luxuriant flora.

Manrique lived here until 1988. A victim of his own fame, he moved out to Haría so that he would be less disturbed by casual visitors. Since then, the house has been a visitor attraction administered by the Fundación César Manrique, a body created by Manrique in 1982 in order to promote artistic, environmental and cultural activities.

No Smoking Policy

King Hussein of Jordan was an admirer of Manrique, visited Lanzarote regularly, and bought a holiday home here (now the property of the King of Spain). While Manrique was showing him around his house the king took out a cigarette. Although he was indulgent of other people's habits, Manrique never allowed anyone to smoke in his home and, with a smile, asked his distinguished guest to refrain, adding "In this house, I am king!"

INSIDER TIP The cafeteria in the Fundación does not offer anything particularly special. It is better to go to **Panadería Artesanal Levain** (Av. Néstor de la Torre 20, Tahíche; Tue–Sun 8–8), in which you can find delicious fruit and cheese cakes. It is in Tahíche near the large roundabout on the road towards Órzola.

---

i ✛ 181 D2
✉ Taro de Tahíche (just off the roundabout with the giant silver wind mobile)
☎ 928 843 138
🌐 www.fcmanrique.org
🕐 Daily 10–6 ✦ €8

❽ ★★ Cueva de los Verdes

Don't Miss	A volcanic cave of enormous proportions
Why	It provides fascinating insight into the island's volcanism
When	Given its popularity, no time is better than another
Time	About an hour
What Else	During the tour, a real surprise awaits you
In Short	Here one seems to come a bit closer to the Earth's core

You may have visited caves before but probably never one created by molten lava. The Cueva de los Verdes belongs to an enormous tunnel system, which was not explored along its whole length until the 1980s.

Follow the guide on the exciting tour through the lava tunnel labyrinth.

The Cueva de los Verdes (The Green's Cave) and Jameos del Agua (p. 55) are part of a 7km (4.3mi)-long volcanic system that was created around 5,000 years ago by the eruption of the Volcán de la Corona (Monte Corona) around 5km (3.1mi) away. The event also connected the volcano with the Atlantic. The cave takes its name from a family who once lived here. It was regularly used by the islanders as a refuge from pirates and slave traders in the 16th and 17th centuries.

Access to the cave is by a guided tour, taking you on a 2km (1-mile) journey (around 50 mins) through this spectacular labyrinth. It is artfully lit and stairs lead from one gallery to another. The tour ends with a memorable optical illusion.

From the geological perspective, the different-coloured minerals are interesting. In some places on the roof, one can see lava drops, which were produced when the lava was cooling down. Steps connect each level with the next; in total the visitor goes down about 50m (164ft) below the Earth's surface; at the end of the tour, the guide creates an unforgettable optical illusion. The concert room inside the cave is also known for its amazing acoustics. You can find out what's on when from the tourist offices.

The Cueva de los Verdes has a refined system of indirect lighting – there are some great colour games.

INSIDER TIP The nearest refreshments are at the Jameos del Agua (around 400m away), but you have to pay admission. The nearest recommended alternatives are the fish restaurants at **Órzola** or **Arrieta** (p. 73).

i ✝ 179 E2 ☎ 928 848 484
🕐 Daily 10–6, until 7pm in mid-summer 🐟 €9.50

⑪ Jardín de Cactus

Don't Miss	Prickly plants from all over the world
Why	The largest cactus collection on the island
When	Whenever you want needles
Time	A good two hours
What Else	Around Guatiza there are fields full of abandoned opuntias
In Short	Manrique's last big project is just as fascinating as the rest of his work

Even the least horticulturally inclined visitor will find this an amazing landscape. Putting aside any preconceptions about cacti and even about gardens, this is where nature meets modern art.

Spiky and fascinating: The Jardín de Cactus

On the drive to Guatiza, visitors can't help but notice the vast stretch of fields full of opuntias. The cochineal beetle from which it is possible to obtain a coveted red dye was bred here

Manrique's Jardín de Cactus with its landmark *gofio* mill resembles an arena – a gathering place for thousands of cacti.

until just a few decades ago (p. 35). Manrique's idea to set up a cactus garden right next to the now fallow fields was thus not inopportune.

As the location for the garden, the artist used a former gravel pit, in which he had tiers integrated, very much like an amphitheatre. In the Jardín de Cactus, you can admire more than 4,500 cacti, from the magnificent gold barrel cactus ("mother-in-law's cushion") to the soaring Mexican columnar cacti. In-between them Manrique placed bizarrely shaped stone columns made in part of red volcanic stone. The garden's landmark is a restored *gofio* mill, which is visible for miles around. The garden was opened in 1990 and was actually César Manrique's last major project; as he loved cacti, he invested even more energy than usual into this venture.

INSIDER TIP You have a lovely view of the cactus garden from the **café** in the garden complex.

ⓘ ✢ 181 F5 ☎ 928 529 397 ◕ Daily. 10–5.45 ✦ €5.80

⑫ Haría

Don't Miss	White houses, dark lava fields, a green palm valley
Why	One of the island's most beautiful villages
When	Whenever you feel like an excursion
Time	Half a day
What Else	The "Valley of the Thousand Palms" offers beautiful long walks
In Short	The green oasis of the volcanic island

Haría is a pretty place with white cubic cottages and a nice plaza. It is no wonder that the large village in the "Valley of the Thousand Palms" is often compared with a North African oasis. For Lanzarote, Haría is surprisingly green; in the summer, onions and some wine are cultivated in the volcanic fields.

Haría's smart houses and leafy, shaded streets make it a real jewel in the north of the island.

The valley itself, unique in Lanzarote for its plentiful supply of water, is best viewed from one of the *miradores* to the south (p. 158). Haría, which sits at a relatively lofty altitude, used to be a popular summer retreat for well to-do islanders who fled to the mountains to escape the heat.

The centre of the village is the pretty avenue-cum-square of Plaza León y Castillo, lined with trees, several restored old houses and the church of Nuestra Señora de la Encarnación. Adjacent is a small Museo de Arte Sacro (Sacred Art Museum). Haría is a magnet for the art and crafts community and has some good shops. Artisans from all over the island come here on Saturday to participate in Lanzarote's biggest and best craft market (p. 75) The village was a favourite of César Manrique (p. 18) who lived here from 1988 to 1992. His former house and atelier on the edge of the village is now open to the public: Casa-Museo. He is buried in a simple grave in the Haría cemetery.

Strolling beneath the blossom in Plaza de La Constitucion

INSIDERTIP You'll find good Canarian tapas (p. 29) and wines (p. 32) at **Bar del Centro Cultural** (Plaza León y Castillo 14).

 ✛179 D2

Museo de Arte Sacro
✉ Plaza León y Castillo
🕐 Tue, Thu, Sat 10–2
❦ Free (donation)

Casa-Museo César Manrique
✉ Calle César Manrique s/n
☎ 928 843 138 ⊕ www.fcmanrique.org
🕐 Daily. 10.30–6 ❦ 10 €

Wildly Romantic

On the rugged north-west coast, a light sandy beach snuggles around the semi-circular bay of Famara like a crescent moon and creates a very inviting walk. Almost all year round, waves roll in here with great force; only surfers are out on the water, and the sea is far too dangerous for inexperienced swimmers. Presenting an awe-inspiring backdrop to the beautiful beach and the churning sea are the around 500m (1640ft) high cliffs, their naked walls falling almost vertically into the water below. Nature demonstrates its full strength here and man looks small and insignificant in comparison.

At Your Leisure

13 Costa Teguise

In the early 70s, there was not a single hotel here; today Costa Teguise is Lanzarote's third biggest tourist centre after Puerto del Carmen and Playa Blanca. César Manrique was a consultant, most notably designing the gardens and pool at the Gran Meliá Salinas hotel (p. 71) and the Pueblo Marinero, a district reflecting the style of a typical Canarian village and with a square surrounded by restaurants and with a small stage.

Initially it was patronised by the rich and famous, including King Hussein of Jordan and wealthy Spanish residents. Manrique's influence and many of the resort's wealthier clients were lost as subsequent development meant the resort was no longer an exclusive place to stay.

Costa Teguise was originally conceived as a holiday resort for the well-to-do; early guests included King Hussein of Jordan, and members of the Spanish royal family also stayed in Meliá Salinas on a number of occasions. In the meantime, however, normal tourism has arrived here as well. Inland, accommodation of the more or less run-of-the-mill style found everywhere have been built. Of the three beaches, the Playa de las Cucharas is the largest, part of which is reserved for the windsurfers, for which there are several surf schools

The café of Mirador del Río affords a dream view of the sea and across to La Graciosa.

where equipment can be rented on site. Golf players can enjoy the wonderful 18-hole course (p. 173).

✛ 181 F2

🔟 La Caleta

The approach to La Caleta de Famara is called El Morro del Jable, a barren plain made up of compacted sand blown across from the Sahara. La Caleta is the little white fishing port where Manrique spent his holidays as a child. The Risco de Famara sea cliffs, which rise up to a height of 450m (1,500ft), provide a magnificent backdrop to Famara, a 3km (2mi)-long stretch of beach to the east. The golden sand here can be a great sight in summer, but it turns a dull brown in winter and you may not be able to see the cliffs for mist. Conditions are excellent for surfing and it's the best beach on the island to learn how to (p. 173). Nevertheless, rubbish sometimes washes up here and swimming can be dangerous – none of which seems to deter the holidaymakers who stay in the Urbanización Famara bungalows behind the beach.

✛ 178 C1

🔟 Mirador del Río

Originally the site of a gun battery built in 1898 – during the Spanish-American war – this is probably the most spectacular *mirador* (lookout point) in the whole archipelago (photo p. 68, 148). It was carefully designed, by César Manrique (of course!), so that neither the entrance nor the curvy white stone corridor gives you any hint of what is coming next – which is a super-wide angle, almost aerial view, through full-length windows, right across the bright blue straits of El Río to La Graciosa (p. below) and the islands beyond.

The two uninhabited rock islands behind Graciosa are Alegranza and Montaña. The precipitous cliff of Risco de Famara plunges down 480m (1,575ft) to the Playa del Risco, next to which the red salt pans of the old Salinas del Río glitter in the sun.

✛ 179 E3 ☎ 928 526 551 🕐 Daily 10–5:45, until 6:45pm in mid-summer 🏷 €4.75

🔟 Órzola

Set almost at the northern tip of the island, this little white fishing village, known for its restaurants and bars, is the end of the road for most vehicles. A dirt track carries on 2km (1mi) north to a beautiful golden surfing beach, the Playa de la Cantería. Don't swim here – the currents are dangerous.

Shortly before Órzola is the wonderful white beach of Caletón Blanco. An unsurfaced path leads to a bay with clear and warm water. Ferries to the island of La Graciosa dock in Órzola. The family-friendly Las Pardelas Park (p. 38) with its animals and adventure playground etc., lies to the south of Órzola on the narrow road to Yé.

✛ 179 F3

17 La Graciosa

If you want to get away from it all, this is the place. Around 500 people live on the island and it gets a couple of hundred day-visitors in summer, but with 27km² (10.5mi²) to choose from, you can usually find solitude.

The boat docks at the main settlement of Caleta del Sebo, which has a couple of reasonable bar-restaurants and a few basic *pensiones* if you want to stay overnight. There is a campsite just south of Caleta del Sebo (ask at the Oficina Municipal in Caleta del Sebo for permission to camp) and the smaller settlement of

A romantic walk on the lonely Playa de las Conchas on La Graciosa

Pedro Barba has some upmarket accommodation.

There are several golden beaches around the island, and the gorgeous Playa de las Conchas (6km/4mi from Caleta del Sebo) is one of the most beautiful in the archipelago; alas, strong currents make it too dangerous to swim here. The Bahía del Salado, found not far from the harbour, is the favourite beach among islanders. The Playa de la Cocina is a preferred spot for naturists. To get around you can either walk, or hire a mountainbike at one of the shops in Caleta del Sebo. There are no tarmac streets, cars (generally jeeps) are few and far between – so it is an ideal terrain for nature lovers and hikers.

Island conqueror Jean de Béthencourt (p. 21) gave the island its gracious name in thanks for reaching dry land after the long voyage from La Rochelle. He also christened the other islands in the Chinijo Archipelago: Montaña Clara (clear mountain), Alegranza (joy) and the small islet, Roque del Infierno (Hell's Rock). These are all uninhabited and protected as nature reserves.

Getting here: Take the Líneas Marítimas Romero or the Líneas Biosfera Express (p. 170) from Órzola (approximately every hour/half hour). Last trip back is at 5:30; 6 in summer; 7 in high summer. Journey time: 15 minutes.

✛ 179 D4 ⊕ www.graciosaonline.com. (in Spanish only)

Where to...Stay

Expect to pay per double room, per night:

€	under €60
€€	€60–€100
€€€	€100–€150
€€€€	over €150

COSTA TEGUISE

Beatriz Costa & Spa €€€€
You can't miss this huge four-star plus hotel at the far end of the resort. If you like your hotels big and brassy, then this is the place to come. All 346 rooms have either a balcony or terrace with a view of the pool.
+ 181 E3
✉ Calle Atalaya 3
☎ 928 590 828
🌐 www.beatrizhoteles.com

Grand Teguise Playa €€€
Overlooking the small beach of Playa del Jablillo, this popular, recently renovated four-star hotel has 314 rooms, all with terraces, ocean views and most mod cons. It has a lush interior atrium of hanging plants and palms, and the grounds hold two large swimming pools. There is an Italian and a Spanish-Canarian restaurant.
+ 181 F3
✉ Avenida del Jablillo ☎ 928 590 654

Mansión Nazaret €€
This charming three-storey apartment hotel offers the most characterful accommodation in the resort. The exterior features wrought-iron and dark-wooden typical Canarian balconies. You then enter into an Art Nouveau hall, and bedrooms and lounges are furnished in rustic late 19th- and early 20th-century style.
There is a lovely swimming pool (heated in winter) bordered by palm trees and plants, and the nearest beach is just 200m away.
+ 181 E3
✉ Avda. Islas Canarias 1 ☎ 928 590 868
🌐 www.nazarethotels.com

Meliá Salinas €€€
One of the resort's original hotels, Las Salinas was built in the late 1970s and

Garden landscape in the inner courtyard of Meliá Salinas

despite recent refurbishment is beginning to look a little dated. This luxury five-star hotel is still one of the best addresses on the island and a member of The Leading Hotels of the World Association. César Manrique designed the murals in the foyer and landscaped the beautiful pool and garden area. All 300-plus rooms look out over the resort's best beach, Playa de las Cucharas. Facilities include mini golf, three tennis courts and a Beauty and Wellness Centre. If you really want to push the boat out, stay in one of the hotel's ten gorgeous romantic garden villas, each with a private swimming pool.
+ 181 E3
✉ Avenida Islas Canarias 16
☎ 928 590 040
🌐 www.melia.com

LOS VALLES

Casa El Aljibe €€€€
Set in the quiet rural surroundings of Los Valles, this gorgeous rustic holiday accommodation for two people, built into a large high-vaulted subterranean antique water tank (aljibe), is possibly the nicest conversion on the island. Years of mineral deposits have resulted in beautifully coloured stonework. The living room (equipped with satellite TV and hi-fi) is in the bottom of the aljibe, while the bedroom is on a mezzanine level, set on antique timber rafters. A large, well-appointed kitchen sits above ground and looks onto a lovely

courtyard and garden shaded by a large fig tree. There is an outdoor jacuzzi and a swimming pool.

✛ 179 D1
✉ Calle San Isidro 72
☎ 917 907 907 🌐 www.casasrurales.net

HARÍA

Casa Rural Villa Lola y Juan €
This large farm estate, located in the very centre of the village, nestles among abundant fruit orchards and grapevines and acts as a rural apartment hotel offering guests a swimming pool, a solarium with great views of Haría, a tea room and other hotel services.
There are various types of apartment to choose from: Two doubles, two suites, one master suite (with a jacuzzi) and one single-room apartment. All come with a large terrace and are individually decorated with 1930s original and repro furniture. Breakfast is included.

✛ 179 D2
✉ Calle Fajardo 16 ☎ 639 208 384
☎ 917 907 907
🌐 www.casasrurales.net

YÉ

Finca La Corona €€€
In the very north of the island under the shadow of the mighty Monte Corona, this is a conversion of an old farming estate into six upmarket holiday homes (five accommodating four people, one accommodating two).
It enjoys spectacular views and is a haven of peace and tranquillity.
The (one- or two-floor) fincas are large and well-equipped: they have marble bathrooms decorated with natural wood, satellite TV and CD players and their own terrace areas. All of the guests have access to a heated pool with an area suitable for children as well as a barbecue spot; in addition, you can rent mountain bikes. The beautiful surrounding countryside demands to be explored on foot.

✛ 179 E3
✉ Las Rositas 8 ☎ 619 231 904
🌐 www.rural-villas.com

Where to...Eat and Drink

Expect to pay for a three-course meal for one, excluding drinks:

€	under €15
€€	€15–€25
€€€	over €25

NAZARET

LagOmar €€–€€€
Designed by César Manrique as a private home for Omar Sharif, LagOmar is built into the face of a cliff, with curving whitewashed corridors linking natural caves and niches. Add plants, unusual artefacts, soft lighting, great tunes and you have an enchanting location, which is now open to the public as a museum.

Its little restaurant which is open in the evenings awaits guests with meticulously laid tables; specialising in Mediterranean cuisine, the magret de canard is well worth consideration.

✛ 181 D4 ✉ Nazaret, Calle Los Loros
☎ 928 845 665 🌐 www.lag-o-mar.com
🕐 Tue–Sun 6pm–11pm

TEGUISE

Acatife €–€€
Acative is actually the original name of Teguise, once used by the indigenous population. The namesake restaurant opposite the parish church is one of the oldest on the island. The lofty dining area is subdivided into five intimate dining rooms. The menu is full of traditional Canarian dishes such as kid or rabbit in red wine sauce. It is always packed on Sundays when the market stalls go up along the streets around the restaurant.

✝ 181 D4 ✉ Calle San Miguel 4 ☎ 928 845 037
🕐 Tue–Sat 12–11, 7–1am, Sun 9–4

Bodega Santa Bárbara €–€€

Tucked away behind the church, this pleasant little café-cum-tapas bar shares a modern but traditional-style building with two smart shops and an art gallery. It has a courtyard terrace on two levels and plays jazz and chill-out music.

✝ 181 D4 ✉ Calle La Cruz ☎ 928 845 200
🕐 Sun–Fri 11–5

La Bodeguita del Medio €–€€

This atmospheric little hole-in-the-wall bar is usually spilling out onto the pavement, where its tapas menu is cleverly carved onto wooden tables. It also doubles as a shop selling local delicacies.

✝ 181 D4
✉ Plaza Clavijo y Fajardo 5 ☎ 928 845 680
🕐 Mon–Fri noon–9, Sat–Sun noon–4

La Cantina €€

This long-established Teguise restaurant serves its guests tasty Canarian dishes at moderate prices. There's a fantastic wine list, a wide selection of tapas, and even the burgers with fries are worth recommending. The service is very friendly and efficient. Now and again you'll get to enjoy some live music with your food. The area surrounding the eatery is also worth a look.

✝ 181 D4
✉ Calle León y Castillo 8 ☎ 928 845 536
🌐 www.cantinateguise.com 🕐 Daily 11–11

La Tahona €–€€

Locals and tourists rub shoulders in this rustic restaurant-bar almost next to the Convento de Santo Domingo. Go for a good old-fashioned peasant's dish such as pork ribs with corn cobs or grandmother's beef stew, or typical Canarian favourites such as goat, *ropa vieja* a casserole chickpeas.

✝ 181 D4 ✉ Calle Santo Domingo 3
☎ 928 845 892 🕐 Thur–Tue 10am–11pm

Patio del Vino, Palacio del Marqués €€€

This garden courtyard, set in the oldest house in town (p. 155), is one of the prettiest refreshment spots on the whole island. Here they serve a variety of tapas with a good island wine.

✝ 181 D4 ✉ Calle Herrera y Rojas 9
☎ 928 845 773
🕐 Mon–Fri noon–8, Sun 9:30–4

Restaurante Hespérides €€–€€€

This small restaurant, which uses organic produce in its kitchen, is located in an old townhouse. There's a simple menu with a variety of very tasty, interesting dishes. They serve a mix of traditional and innovative cuisine – you'll get the chance to try such creations as salads made with smoked salmon and dark chocolate.

✝ 181 D4
✉ Calle León y Castillo 3 ☎ 928 593 159
🕐 Daily noon–11

HARÍA

El Cortijo de Haría €–€€

This 200-year-old whitewashed farmhouse has been beautifully restored and numerous palms have been planted, which add a sculptural feel. Sit inside the dark traditional cosy rooms or outside on the large sunny terrace under huge shady umbrellas. Suckling pig, roast lamb, rabbit with rosemary and grilled meats are just some of the house specials.

✝ 179 D2
✉ El Palmeral ☎ 928 835 686
🌐 http://elcortijodeharia.blogspot.de
🕐 Daily noon–6 (Jul, Aug, Sep until 8)

La Puerta Verde €€

Here you will find international cuisine under German management. If you only want to drop in, sit in the inner courtyard for a coffee and cake break. The restaurant is located at the top end of town: follow the path going up behind the church.

✝ 179 D2
✉ Calle Fajardo 24 ☎ 928 835 350
🌐 www.facebook.com/PuertaVerdeHaria

ÓRZOLA

Charco Viejo €€

Popular with locals and visitors, this friendly harbourside fish and shellfish restaurant has an open kitchen where you can see the cooks at work. Try the sole, tuna and fish of the day or go for the mixed fish grill.

⌖ 179 E3 ✉ Calle La Quemadita
☎ 928 842 591 ◐ Daily 8am–10pm

ARRIETA

El Amanecer €€

Fish in Arrieta is a must – there is one restaurant after the other along the main road. El Amanecer is very popular and generally bursting at the seams; the tables at the back looking out across the water soon fill up. What is good here are the lavish seafood dishes and the grilled tuna fish.

⌖ 179 E2 ✉ Calle La Garita 46 ☎ 928 848 390
◐ Fri–Wed noon–6

COSTA TEGUISE

El Pescador €€

El Pescador has an unusual interior of elaborately hand-carved wooden panels depicting traditional island scenes, which tend to either intrigue or disconcert diners. This is one of the best fish and seafood restaurants in Costa Teguise. There is outside seating too, looking onto the lively Plaza Pueblo Marinero. Specialities include *zarzuela*, paella, *cherne* (bass grouper), in green sauce and king prawns in garlic.

⌖ 181 F3 ✉ Plaza Pueblo Marinero
☎ 928 590 874 ◐ Mon–Sat 3–11

Patio Canario €–€€

Set just off the main part of the Plaza Pueblo Marinero, this restaurant serves good rice and fish dishes in addition to the tapas, pizza and pasta. The dining area is in an attractive courtyard.

⌖ 181 F3
✉ Plaza Pueblo Marinero ☎ 928 346 234
⊕ www.patiocanariolanzarote.com
◐ Wed–Mon noon–midnight

Villa Toledo €€€

The restaurant's trump card is its location immediately above the Playa Bastián. Delicious veal dishes are served on the spacious terrace. Those who like neither meat nor fish should go for the mushroom risotto.

Next to the restaurant area there is also a wonderful terrace on which to chill.

⌖ 181 F3 ✉ Avenida Los Cocederos s/n
☎ 928 590 626 ◐ Daily 1–11

Where to...Shop

TEGUISE

With its quiet, traffic-free streets and relaxed historic setting, Teguise makes browsing an enjoyable pastime for even the most reluctant shoppers. Good-quality arts and crafts, jewellery and clothing are the main items. There are few bargains, but many items will be handmade and unique. Indigo (Galería La Villa, Plaza Clavijo y Fajardo 4) has a wide selection for women of all ages. Artesanía Lanzaroteña (Plaza de la Constitución 12) has a good range of gifts, including guitars, hats, wine and jams. Emporium, located in an old cinema in the Calle Notas, specialises in products from Asia (China, Mongolia, Tibet, India, etc.). You'll find furniture, porcelain, jewellery, paintings, home accessories and textiles on offer. They're also happy to arrange good-value shipping. It's worth paying a visit to Emporium just to see the building in which it's located. Almost right next door, Galeria Oe (Calle Notas 11) makes pieces of sand-and-lava encrusted pottery and large rock-and-sand pictures. For food and drink try the Bodeguita del Medio (p. 73). Many shops in Teguise close on Saturday, but all are open on Sunday.

COSTA TEGUISE

Most of the shops in Costa Teguise are found on the Playa de las Cucharas (you'll spot sportswear, electronics and jewellery in the Centro Comercial Las Cucharas), in the Avenida del Jablillo and near the Hotel Meliá Salinas.

HARÍA

Several artisans who receive financial support from the town hall work in the Taller de Artesanía de Haría (Calle

Barranco de Tenesía, next to the Mercado de Abastos de Haría). You can watch them as they ply their trades, creating ceramics, jewellery, dolls, embroidery, paintings, etc. (Mon–Sat 10–1, 4–7; closed Monday afternoon).

MARKETS

Costa Teguise Every Wednesday night from 6pm till late, there is a craft market in the Pueblo Marinero where you can find a selection of handmade items and novelties.
Haría is the venue for the island's largest arts and craft market every Saturday (10am–2:30pm). You can buy basketware, sand-and-volcanic-rock ware, cacti, island wines and foods, lava stone and olivine jewellery. The quality and prices are high.
Teguise The Sunday (9am–2pm) market here is by far the biggest on the island. There is an enormous choice of handicrafts, textiles and bric-a-brac. Just remember to examine things closely, because a lot of the "genuine" products are nothing of the sort.

Where to...Go Out

NIGHTLIFE

Two of the island's most beautiful and un-usual nightspots are in the north the Jameos del Agua (p. 55) and LagOmar (p. 72), both designed by César Manrique. Dress to im-press – no shorts. The Jameos del Agua and the Cueva de los Verdes (p. 61) also have auditoria where occasional classical concerts are staged. The much vaunted acoustics make them well worth checking out. Costa Teguise's nightlife starts in the Pueblo Marinero square, where you'll find live music and lots of bars. A couple of the most pop-ular locations are the cocktail bars Number One and Hook (soul, pop, rock). Number One in the Centro Comercial Las Cucharas wins a lot of points with its sea view terrace.

WATER SPORTS

The island's best windsurfing conditions are at Costa Teguise, which has been hosting Windsurf World Cup competitions for over a decade.
Good operators are Windsurf Paradise (tel: 657 641 107; www.windsurflanzarote. com) and Windsurfing Club Las Cucharas (CNS) (tel: 928 590 731; www.lanzarote windsurf.com) which also offer surfing, boogie board rental, kayak rental, trekking and mountain biking.
The beach at Famara is the place for surfers and kiteboarders. Famara Surf School caters for beginners and experts. Children can start on boogie boards from the age of nine (tel: 616 107 621; www.famarasurf.com). Lanzasurf offers surfing for both experts and beginners (Calle Chiromoya 15, tel: 697 238 115; www.lanzasurf.com).
If you want to learn the exciting sport of kitesurfing (p. 173), contact Costa Noroeste to enrol at their Surf Camp and Kiteboarding Academy (tel: 928 528 597; www.costanoroeste.com).

DIVING

Reserva Marina del Archipélago Chinij, Órzola and La Graciosa are excellent locations for diving and deep-sea fishing. Go with Punta Fariones, based at the Punta Fariones fish restaurant in Órzola.
Diving is very popular at Costa Teguise and dedicated diving schools include: North Diving Lanzarote (Calle La Garita 33, Arrieta; tel: 928 848 285, www.northdiving-lanzarote. com); Aquatis Diving Center, on the promenade of Playa de las Cucharas (tel: 928 590 407; www.diving-lanzarote.net); Calipso Diving, Avenida de las Islas Canarias (tel: 928 590 879; www.calipso-diving.com). Native Diving offers diving and surfing, and is based at Be Live Grand Teguise Playa Avenida del Mar (tel: 928 346 096; www. nativediving.com).

CYCLING

Try Tommy's Bike (tel: 628 102 177; www. tommys-bike.com) if you want to rent bicycles while you're in Costa Teguise. Bikes are also available in Caleta del Sebo on La Graciosa.

On the beach promenade in Arrecife you can always find a quiet place to relax.

The Centre

Two disparate neighbours rub shoulders here – the sedate capital of Arrecife and the pulsating holiday resort of Puerto del Carmen.

Pages 76–103

Getting Your Bearings

For many years Arrecife was derided as the "ugly duckling", and most holidaymakers gave it a wide berth. These days visitors to the island metropolis marvel at the two resplendent, medieval-looking castles and the modern marina just a few steps away from the town centre. To the west of the capital, Puerto del Carmen is Lanzarote's largest holiday resort.

Puerto del Carmen wears its heart on its sleeve. Its long sandy beaches and profusion of restaurants, bars, clubs and shops on the promenade tell you that fun in the sun is what goes down here.

If you want culture, history and sightseeing you have to head out of town to the rural heart of the island. At San Bartolomé and Tiagua, the Museo Etnográfico Tanit and Museo Agrícola El Patio, respectively, tell you all about the old island ways over the last two centuries. A growing number of people are also choosing to make their holiday base here, in the island's stylish *casas rurales* and *hoteles rurales* (country houses and rural hotels).

For a feel of contemporary Lanzarote, hop on the bus to Arrecife, or perhaps take the water taxi from Puerto del Carmen to Puerto Calero, from which even underwater excursions are on offer – for all those who also want to see the island from a completely different perspective.

TOP 10
7 ★★ Arrecife
9 ★★ Puerto Calero

Don't Miss
18 Puerto del Carmen

At Your Leisure
19 San Bartolomé
20 Monumento al Campesino
21 Bodegas El Grifo
22 Museo Agrícola El Patio

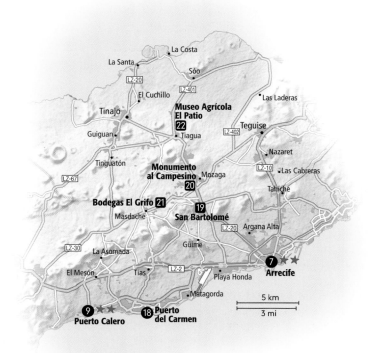

My Day
on Foot
to Arrecife

The beautiful trail from Lanzarote's largest holiday resort Puerto del Carmen to the capital of Arrecife winds along parallel to the water. Don't be put off by the airport directly next to the promenade – for quite a few of the people walking here it is actually the highlight of the day. Remember to take your swimming things with you and perhaps a clean t-shirt to change into later!

 **10am: Start in Puerto del Carmen**

The best starting point for the coastal walk is the Playa de los Pocillos on the eastern outskirts of ⑱ Puerto del Carmen (bus stop at the Costa Mar shopping centre). From the broad sand beach, follow part of the dismantled and now car-free esplanade. You first pass Hotel Jameos Playa in front of the slightly narrower Playa Matagorda. Shortly afterwards, the former esplanade turns into a promenade and cycle path, which goes all the way into the town centre of the island capital. In the distance, you can already see the end destination, the hotel tower of Arrecife's Gran Hotel.

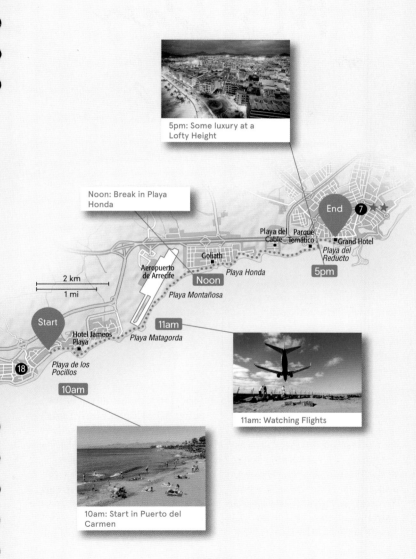

5pm: Some luxury at a Lofty Height

Noon: Break in Playa Honda

Playa del Cable

Parque Temático

End

7

Grand Hotel

Playa del Reducto

Goliath

Playa Honda

Noon

5pm

Aeropuerto de Arrecife

2 km

1 mi

Playa Montañosa

11am

Playa Matagorda

Start

Hotel Jameos Playa

Playa de los Pocillos

18

10am

11am: Watching Flights

10am: Start in Puerto del Carmen

The walk initially takes you along the promenade of Playa Matagorda (above), around lunchtime it is interrupted for a short stop at Playa Honda (upper right) and then reaches the Parque Temático with its artworks (lower right) in the afternoon.

11am: Watching Flights

After about an hour, you will reach Punta Montañosa the site of the international airport. Right behind the barbed wire fence is the runway, on which you probably arrived a few days previously. There is always a lot going on here, not just in the air but on the ground as well. This spot is a popular meeting place for plane spotters who can watch the holiday flights landing here. Every few minutes large Boeings and Airbuses from Condor, Ryan Air & Co. roar just over them – not much more than 100m (328ft) above their heads! Unlike at many other airports, people are allowed to take as many photographs as they like and to record videos. Don't stay too long though – multilingual signs warn about the emission of hot aviation fuel.

Noon: Break in Playa Honda

From the airport, it is not far to Playa Honda, an area predominantly still in local hand. There the flight noise is no longer audible; you can find a seat on the surprisingly quiet terrace of the beach restaurant Goliath and, with a bit of luck perhaps even at the front overlooking the ocean. While the food may not come into

The highlight for plane spotters: the airport's approach path

the category of haute cuisine, the burgers served here are really good and the drinks always cooled to the right temperature.

🕑 2pm: Small Theme Park
The Gran Hotel Arrecife is a lot closer in the meantime. At El Cable, another bungalow park, you have already reached the outskirts of Arrecife. Recently opened at the edge of the town, on a spit of land that had been discounted by developers for many years is the Parque Temático. The makeover is very pretty; palms have been planted on the once desolate wasteland, palms, and a whole array of art objects, including a shipwreck, give the park a distinctive flair. Right behind it is the 500m (1,640ft) long town beach of Arrecife.

5pm

Above: The shipwreck in Parque Temático is a sculpture by artist Luis Ibánez
Left: The Gran Hotel is the only "real" skyscraper on the island.

3pm: Bathing Fun on the Capital's Beach

Few holidaymakers it would seem have caught up with the fact that Arrecife also boasts a first-class beach. As long as you not there on a summer weekend, when the locals stake out their Playa del Reducto, you won't have to share the sandy beach with many other bathers. Swim a round in the sickle-shaped bay protected by a natural reef and treat yourself to an hour or two lazing in the shade of a coconut tree afterwards.

5pm: Some Luxury at a Lofty Height

Now it's time to spruce up as much as you can after a long walk for the big finale. Awaiting your visit on the 17th floor of the noble Gran Hotel (p. 96) is the Star City Coffee & Gastro

The palm-lined beach Playa del Reducto at the foot of the Gran Hotel is (with the exception of weekends) often fairly deserted.

Bar. A glass lift behind the reception zooms you up the 75m (246ft). Accompany the spectacular view with a delicious snack, which is not as expensive as you might expect for a five-star establishment. After Puerto del Carmen, you can return either with one of the taxis waiting in front of the Gran Hotel or catch the No. 2 bus (which departs from the bus station by Parque Temático).

Length of the walk: approx. 10km/6mi

Goliath
✉ Calle Ctra. de las Playas, Playa Honda
☎ 928 839 429
🕐 Sun–Thu 10–midnight,
Fri, Sat 10am–1am

Star City Coffee & Gastro Bar
✉ Parque Islas Canarias, Arrecife
☎ 928 800 000
🕐 Sun–Thu 9:30–midnight,
Fri & Sat 9:30am–1am

❼ ★★ Arrecife

Don't Miss	Capital with two museum castles on the waterfront
Why	Urbane Canarian savoir-vivre holds sway here
When	Whenever it fits in the itinerary
Time	At least half a day
What Else	It is well worth going off the beaten track to explore the area around the harbour basin Charco de San Ginés
In Short	Arrecife is starting to spruce itself up

The evening envelops Charco de San Ginés: natural harbour basin and peaceful urban oasis.

A few years ago, Arrecife was not one of the places on Lanzarote that you really had to see. That has changed in the meantime. Many tourists come here to shop and, in the meantime, the promenade by the harbour is a lovely place to go for a stroll. Apart from the Calle León y Castillo, a popular boulevard to browse during the week, the island capital also has its fair share of quiet areas away from the maddening crowds. What is more, with the museum for contemporary art housed in its old fort, the seaport town is now a renowned address for modern art.

Arrecife began life around 1403 as the nearest port to the old capital of Teguise (p. 52). Arrecife means reef and is a natural harbour protected by a barrier of islets and reefs. This, together with its proximity to the rich fishing grounds of North Africa, enabled it to build up the largest fishing fleet in the archipelago. In 1852 it became the capital of Lanzarote. Today it has a population of around 60,000, representing more than 40 per cent of the total island. For a long time, the harbour town was just a transhipment point and administration centre. The booming tourism brought in a lot of money to the public purse, but until recently relatively few tourists actually came to the town. However, the town has recently spruced itself up both for the people who live there and those who come to visit. In the meantime, Arrecife is even a popular stop for cruise ships.

Two attractions: The Iglesia de San Ginés (above) and the Castillo de San José (below), now home to a contemporary art gallery

The new centrepiece of the small island metropolis is the promenade Avenida La Marina (formerly Avenida General Franco), lined with palm trees and subtropical plants – and the tourist office can be found in the pretty pavilion. Houses spanning several styles and centuries form the backdrop on the town side of the street, while a causeway leads over a drawbridge to Arrecife's oldest surviving building, the Castillo de San Gabriel, which was built in 1590 to fend off pirates. The castle now houses an exhibition about the town's history (Mon–Fri 10–5, Sat 10–2). From the roof of the fortress, there is a beautiful view of the town and of a volcano cone in the distance.

Beyond the car-free shopping street of the Calle León y Castillo, you'll find the Iglesia de San Ginés (1665) in a peaceful square. Its beautifully restored interior features late

baroque statues of the city's patron saint, San Ginés, and the Virgen del Rosario. Behind it is a large, peaceful lagoon, the Charco de San Ginés. This is a lovely spot for a stroll with its old fishermen's houses, boats at anchor and a good choice of bars and restaurants.

From Charco, it is only a few steps to the Marina Lanzarote, in which a modern shopping centre and an elegant row of restaurants awaits you; usually you will find a lot going on here when a cruise ship has come into the port just to the east of the marina.

A little further out, at the end of the port, is the capital's main visitor attraction, the Castillo de San José. It was built in the late 18th century and restored by César Manrique 200 years later to hold the internationally acclaimed Museo Internacional de Arte Contemporáneo (MIAC), which exhibits contemporary art over two storeys – including works by Manrique himself. The contrast between the ancient dark stones and the vibrant modern artworks is striking. The castle is also home to a restaurant that is well worth seeing (p. 100), as it was also designed by César Manrique.

Arrecife has plenty of good places to eat and drink

INSIDER TIP Arrecife is full of good places to eat and drink. Slightly off the main tourist routes you can sit in **Tasca la Raspa** (Avenida César Manrique 20; tel; 928 808 405; Mon–Sat 11–2, Sun 12.30–0) and enjoy a bit of peace and quiet by the old harbour basin Charco de San Ginés. Try one of the small fish dishes with a glass of house wine.

 ✛ 181 E2

Museo Internacional de Arte Contemporáneo (MIAC)
✉ Castillo de San José,

Avenida de Puerto Naos
☎ 928 812 321 ⊕ www.cactlanzarote.com
🕐 Daily 10–8 ✦ €4

Thought-Provoking Art

You don't have to go up onto the roof of Castillo de San José. The panoramic window in the castle restaurant also offers a great view of the cruise ship dock opposite and of the harbour basin in which Jason deCaires Taylor installed a group of sculptures in the water. At low tide, you see the horses standing knee-deep in the water; at high tide it is more or less only the heads of their heavy concrete riders that protrude from the water. The sight is as fascinating as it is thought-provoking: if climate warming continues, then this art is also doomed.

❾ ★★ Puerto Calero

Don't Miss	Wander along the smart little jetty and admire the boats
Why	An exclusive marina, not just for skippers, and well worth a visit
When	There's almost always something to see here
Time	One to two hours
What Else	Dive down to the bottom of the ocean in a submarine
In Short	Here you can take in some chic harbour atmosphere

The island's top marina, Puerto Calero provides berths for over 400 boats. Most visitors simply use it as a boarding point for a catamaran or submarine trip (p. 102). You can also just stroll at leisure along the promenade or enjoy the harbour atmosphere from one of the restaurants.

Life passes by peacefully in the Puerto Calero marina

The marina was built following plans by Lanzarotean architect Luís Ibáñez Magalef, and took inspiration from the Spanish Colonial style. The maritime colours of blue and white have been used to replace the green and white hues that are typical to the island.

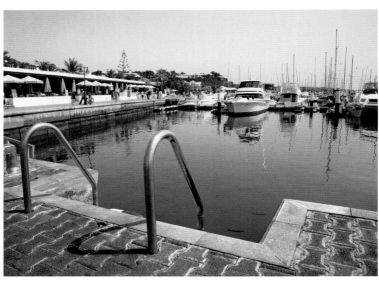

A dozen or so restaurants and bars (p. 99) line the flower-decked quayside and offer a relaxed, elegant waterside setting, which won't suit the party crowd. If you wish, you can arrange to sail along the east coast on a catamaran to the Papagayo beaches or take a trip on a bright yellow submarine and find out what Lanzarote looks like under the water.

This submarine leaves from Puerto Calero a number of times every day (Mon–Sat) on its underwater tours.

Apart from the harbour itself, there is not much to see here, with the possible exception of the sundial on the gable wall opposite the gourmet restaurant Amura. A small selection of places to stay can be found to the north of the harbour basin. Apart from a small bathing area near Hotel Hesperia Lanzarote, however, there is no beach here.

Getting Here

Five times a day a fairly reasonably priced water taxi does the trip between Puerto del Carmen and Puerto Calero (tel: 928 842 055, www.lineasromero.com). The journey takes 15 minutes. A bus trip costs less of course, and the no. 161 bus, which connects the holiday resorts of Puerto del Carmen and Playa Blanca, stops at Puerto Calero (www.arrecifebus.com).

INSIDERTIP The marina boasts lots of nice eateries. **Café Milla** (tel: 928 511 641; daily 11am–midnight) on the promenade makes a nice choice for coffee and cake.

✛ 183 E2

i

For more information on Puerto Calero:
🌐 www.caleromarinas.com

⑱ Puerto del Carmen

Don't Miss	Holiday resort with good beaches and long promenades
Why	Lanzarote's largest and liveliest holiday resort is worth seeing
When	In the late afternoon or early evening, when the harbour restaurants are starting to fill up
Time	At least half a day
In Short	Even at the height of the season it is still possible to find space somewhere along the beach in Puerto del Carmen

Tourist hotspot – the largest and loudest holiday resort on Lanzarote awaits guests with plenty of sandy beaches and an infrastructure tailored to meet the requirements of holidaymakers from all over Europe, one that leaves few wishes unrequited. The fact that it is not so long ago that this used to be a fishing village is only really still detectable in the harbour area.

Don't expect a lot of cultural sights in Puerto del Carmen. Hotels, holiday apartments and numerous restaurants dominate about 10km (6mi) of the coastline. There is something for every taste. In the first row of buildings next to the sea, it can be quite loud, but a few hundred metres away from the beach there are also quieter places to stay – most of which have the added advantage of being less expensive. The sports and entertainment possibilities are also extensive. Diving schools have their bases right next to the water, by Hotel Fariones there is a large public sports centre with tennis and squash courts.

The old fishing harbour on the western edge of town has a nice atmosphere. It's lined by cafés and restaurants where guests spill right out onto the street on summer evenings.

A very lively spot is La Lonja, the former fish hall, which now houses a restaurant on two floors. Those who like things to be a bit quieter will find something to their taste in the streets away from the harbour basin.

The resort's main artery is Avenida de las Playas, which connects the various beach districts and extends almost as far as the airport. Nowhere else on Lanzarote has such a high con-

centration of restaurants, bars and clubs. Along the beaches, the Avenida only has buildings on one side, thus enabling you to stroll along the palm-lined promenade with a wonderfully unobstructed view of the sea.

To the east of the harbour district is the almost 1km (0.5mi) long Playa Grande, a golden-yellow sand beach. In the peak season, despite thousands of sun chairs, it struggles to cope with the onslaught of bathers. A rocky stretch of around 1km (0.5mi), punctuated by two sandy coves, makes the break between Playa Grande and the town's second beach, the Playa de los Pocillos, which, at 1.2km (0.75mi) in length, is slightly bigger than its neighbour. The Plaza de las Naciones, a large square that opens out to the sea is regularly used for events and festivals. Adjacent to Pocillos beach is a third sandy beach, Playa Matagorda, which despite its proximity to the airport runway is surrounded by a large number of hotels and apartment complexes. From here a pedestrian promenade provides a connection to Arrecife. Plane spotters in particular get their money's worth here (p. 82).

Built close to the water: In Puerto del Carmen everything centres around the sea.

INSIDER TIP Sit down in one of the **harbour restaurants** in the late afternoon. While the sun goes down you can watch the boats coming in.

✝ 183 E/F2   ⓘ

At Your Leisure

19 San Bartolomé

Tourism has made little impact on this small town in the centre of the island. Nonetheless, the numerous recently restored historical buildings make it an interesting place to visit. On the Plaza León y Castillo, the main square located away from the thoroughfare, is an eminent ensemble, comprising of the church, town hall and theatre. The most important tourist attraction though is the Museo Etnográfico Tanit, a private museum housed in a beautiful 18th-century townhouse. The exhibits, including antique furniture and early agricultural tools, reveal a lot about the everyday life on the island in days gone by. An eye-opener is the property's former wine cellar.

✝ 180 C3
Museo Etnográfico Tanit
✉ Calle Constitución ☎ 928 520 655
🌐 www.museotanit.com
🕐 Mon–Sat 10–2 🎫 €6

20 Monumento al Campesino

This bizarre, 15m-high (50ft) Cubist monument marks the very centre of the island and was designed by César Manrique as a tribute to the Lanzarote *campesino* (field worker) for having overcome so much adversity. It is constructed of water tanks from old boats and is said to represent a farmer and his dog. The much-photographed traditional white buildings beneath it are a small part of an old village, restored to house a restaurant (p. 100) and the Casa Museo del Campesino. The latter is home to a farming and craft museum where you can watch

The old wine cellar at the Museo Etnográfico Tanit

artisans at work. The potter's workshop is particularly worth a look.

✚ 180 C3 ☎ 928 520 136
🌐 www.turismolanzarote.com
🕐 Daily 10–5:45 ◆ Free

22 Bodegas El Grifo

Established in 1775, this charming bodega is the oldest wine cellar in the Canaries, and is still hard at work today. There is an atmospheric museum located in the original wine cellars with an exhibition of old wine presses, machinery and tools. A small wine tasting is included in the price of entry.

✚ 180 C3
✉ Carretera La Geria-Mozaga (LZ30)
☎ 928 524 951 🌐 www.elgrifo.com
🕐 Daily 10:30–6 ◆ €6

23 Museo Agrícola El Patio

Established in 1845, the Museo Agrícola El Patio is one of the oldest farms on the island still surviving in its original form. It's now a splendid open-air museum in landscaped gardens that kids will find interesting, too.

The farmhouse was built in the early 19th century and was inhabited until 1949, when it was the biggest farm on the island, employing 20 workers. Looking very photogenic are the two restored windmills, in which grain used to be ground to make *gofio* flour. Mills were also powered by donkeys and dromedaries.

A long, wooden building between the two windmills houses the rest of the Ethnographic Museum and gives a fascinating insight into rural life during the last two centuries.

Don't miss the atmospheric wine museum with its antique bottles and equipment; in the adjacent bodega you can knock back a glass of rough home-made wine and nibble a small tapas (included in the admission price). At its height the farm used 15 camels; now there's just one, a tourist curiosity, corralled with a donkey.

✚ 180 C4 ✉ Tiagua ☎ 920 529 134
🕐 Mon–Fri 10–5, Sat 10–2:30 ◆ €6.50

Seen from far and wide: The Monumento al Campesino, a monument to the farmers of the island

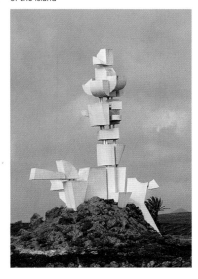

Where to...Stay

Expect to pay per double room, per night:

€ under €60
€€ €60–€100
€€ €100–€150
€€€€ over €150

PUERTO DEL CARMEN

Bungalows Velazquez €€–€€€
This offers a very central, first-row location, directly on the waterside promenade, on the rocky stretch between Playa Grande and Playa de los Pocillos. Next to it is the La Ola restaurant, a large and well-frequented restaurant – meaning the bungalows nearby do not enjoy complete peace and quiet.
✚ 183 E2
✉ Avenida de las Playas 8
☎ 928 513 800
⊕ www.bungalowsvelazquez.com

Lani's Beachfront Suites de Luxe €€€€
This new designer hotel leaves nothing wanting in terms of location and comfort. It has just 25 suites; all of them are right by the sea. The bathing area in front of the complex is relatively small, but the Playa Grande is just a few minutes away. Guests have to be at least 16 years old.
✚ 183 E2
✉ Avenida de las Playas 26
☎ 928 596 068 ⊕ www.lanissuites.com

Los Jameos Playa €€€
A four-star establishment, Los Jameos Playa belongs to the German Seaside-Gruppe and is totally focused on the needs of its mainly German-speaking guests. It is on a traffic-limited road on the eastern side of the Playa de los Pocillos. The large main building with its colonial design elements is extremely attractive, as is the large pool area surrounded by palm trees. Active guests can choose from a large selection of sports. Besides tennis and squash courts, there is also a modern fitness studio. There is a large wellness area with a sauna, massage offers and beauty treatments.
✚ 183 F2

✉ Calle Marte 2 (Playa de los Pocillos)
☎ 928 511 717
⊕ www.los-jameos-playa.de

PUERTO CALERO

Costa Calero €€€€
If you don't want the bright lights of Puerto del Carmen right outside your window but you do want easy access to its attractions within walking distance (Puerto Calero quay-side is a three-minute walk away), then this may be just the spot for you. The 4-star Costa Calero is modern, with a large atrium. A special bonus is the spa area with its sea-water pool and Roman bath.
✚ 183 E2
✉ Puerto Calero
☎ 928 849 595
⊕ www.hotelcostacalero.com

Hesperia Lanzarote €€€
Located on the seafront very close to the marina, its main strengths are its spa and wellness centre and its gourmet restaurant, La Caleta (it also offers three other restaurants and no fewer than three bars in the evenings). The location, at the far end of Puerto Calero, is away from it all, and if you want to be pampered in peace this is as good a place as any on the island. There are four pools, a fitness room, tennis and squash courts and a putting green. You can enjoy the beautiful view not only from the pool but also from the balcony of your room.
✚ 183 E2
✉ Urbanización Cortijo Viejo
☎ 828 080 800
⊕ www.nh-hotels.de

ARRECIFE

Arrecife Gran Hotel & Spa €€€€
The only high-rise building on the island, the Gran Hotel has a very chequered history. Once reviled as an eyesore and, following a fire, threatened with demolition, it has since established itself with its five star accoutrements as the best hotel in the capital. Rooms and public areas are cutting-edge modern and the main attractions are the state-of-the-art spa and the

The Casa Gaida is situated on a small side street in tiny La Asomada.

stunning views from the 17th-floor Altamar restaurant (p. 100). It's also worth noting that while few tourists use this hotel at present there is a good beach right outside which has just been re-landscaped.

✠ 186 B2
✉ Parque Islas Canarias
☎ 928 800 000
⊕ www.aghotelspa.com

Hotel Villa Vik €€€€

This villa is in one of the city's most prestigious suburbs, lying just about 1km (0.6mi) west of the Gran Hotel: It's not right on the coast but is close to El Cable beach. Head out on foot down the waterside promenade and you'll reach the centre of Arrecife or nearby Playa Honda in no time at all.

The decor is very elegant, blending contemporary and classic styles, with antiques in public areas and bedrooms. You can expect a high standard of cooking, and the bar is a relaxed place to hang out. The service is very personal; they will even pack and unpack your suitcases!

With only 14 rooms, the villa exudes an almost private character. Adults only.

✠ 181 E2
✉ Calle Hermanos Diaz Rijo, Urbanización La Bufona
☎ 928 815 256
⊕ www.vikhotels.com

LA ASOMADA

Casa Gaida €€€€

Although Casa Gaida is situated well inland it enjoys panoramic views of the southern coast overlooking Arrecife, Puerto del Carmen and Puerto Calero, with Fuerteventura in the distance. The house sits within a 14ha (34-acre) estate and is some 200 hundred years old, featuring beautiful traditional interiors of wood and lava stone. It has a fully fitted kitchen and luxurious lounge and dining room with sweeping views. The swimming pool is solar heated and completely private.

✠ 183 C3
✉ Camino La Caldereta 52
☎ 928 832 531, 696 982 882
⊕ www.casagaida.com

MOZAGA

Caserío de Mozaga €€€
Caserío de Mozaga was built at the end of the 18th century. It has been lovingly restored and is now a pristine small hotel beautifully decorated in a simple style with traditional furniture. There are 8 double rooms, 2 of which have a private lounge. All are en suite and offer an Internet connection, mini bar, satellite TV and hairdryer. The restaurant is particularly attractive and serves top-quality, appetising Spanish cuisine.
✛ 180 C3 ✉ Malva 8 ☎ 928 520 060
🌐 www.caseriodemozaga.com

SAN BARTOLOMÉ

Finca de la Florida €€
A cross between a *casa rural* and a small mainstream hotel, the Finca de la Florida lacks some of the old-fashioned charm of a traditional *casa rural* but it does have many more facilities and is suited to families for whom a beach on the doorstep is not a priority. There are 15 double rooms (plus one suite) with mini bar, air-conditioning and hairdryer. Facilities include a swimming pool, a tennis court, mountain bikes, gym and sauna, mini-golf, table tennis and a children's playground. Weekly treks are also organised (subject to numbers). The restaurant (open to the public) is well regarded for its typical Canarian and international cuisine, and enjoys views across the vineyards. After dinner there is a comfy lounge with an open fire where you can have a drink.
✛ 180 C3
✉ El Parral 1, San Bartolomé
☎ 928 521 124
🌐 www.hotelfincadelaflorida.com

Where to...
Eat and Drink

Expect to pay for a three-course meal for one, excluding drinks:

€	under €15
€€	€15–€25
€€€	over €25

PUERTO DEL CARMEN

Bodega €€–€€€
Bodega, located in the Old Town of Puerto del Carmen is also known as La Cascada. Good Spanish cuisine is served here accompanied by a respectable house wine. The menu includes Secreto ibérico, Iberian pork from pigs fattened on acorns. Tomatoes, peppers and other ingredients come from the restaurant own farm.
✛ 180 B1
✉ Calle Roque Nublo 3, Old Town
☎ 928 512 953
🌐 www.restaurante-lacascada.com
🕐 Daily 1pm–midnight

La Cañada €€€
One of the resort's longest-established and most fêted restaurants, La Cañada has been under the same owner-chef for 20 years. The setting is formal but rustic and the menu is extensive. Specialities include for example fish prepared in a salt crust, and grilled lamb chops.
✛ 180 C1
✉ Calle César Manrique
☎ 928 510 415
🕐 Mon–Sat noon–midnight

La Casa Roja €€
The "Red House" on the old harbour has a beautiful terrace right over the water from where you can admire the colourful fishing boats. Views like this don't come cheap, but it's a good bet if you want a romantic spot for dinner.
✛ 180 B1
✉ Avenida del Varadero 22
☎ 928 515 866
🕐 Daily 10–11:45

La Cofradía de Pescadores La Tiñosa €€€
The best address for fresh fish is the restaurant run by the fishing cooperative, located directly on the breakwater. At the entrance a sign indicates the catch of the day, and those with a large appetite should opt for the mixed fish platter.
✛ 180 B1
✉ Plaza del Varadero
☎ 660 433 578 🕐 Daily 12–11

MÁCHER

La Casa del Parmigiano €€–€€€
If you fancy something Italian – the trattoria next to the sports centre Los Fariones is one of the best around. Produced in-house the ravioli contain a delectable filling and the thickly topped pizzas are always crisply backed. Apart from good Rioja wines, the wine menu also has lots of Italian wines from Tuscany. You need to make a reservation if you want a table on the outside terrace.
🞜 183 E3
✉ Calle Alegranza 1 ☎ 928 512 731
🌐 www.lacasadelparmigiano.es
🕐 Daily 1–11.30

La Tegala €€€€
This impressive designer restaurant is the brainchild of long-time Lanzarote resident, Antonio Hernandez. His bold, modern, yet still very vernacular building is set high on a hill with fabulous 180-degree views through full-length windows from Arrecife to Fuerteventura. The menu is modern Canarian and Spanish with linen tablecloths,

The restaurant in Castillo de San José affords a beautiful view of the harbour in Arrecife

fine china and comfortable leather armchairs. Besides the multiple course gourmet menus, it is possible to sit at the bar and just eat a few tapas and/or enjoy a drink. Whichever, dress to impress!
🞜 183 E3
✉ Carretera de Tías a Yaiza, 60
☎ 928 524 524
🌐 www.lategala.com
🕐 Tue–Sat 2–4:30, 8–11:30, Mon 8–11:30

PUERTO CALERO

Amura €€€€
You can't miss this blinding white building, pointedly set apart from the rest of the quay-side restaurants; it resembles a grand mansion from the Deep South of the USA and is the place to come when you really want to push the boat out. The interior is very stylish in a minimal fashion and the menu is nouvelle cuisine with Mediterranean influences. Fluffily light lobster ravioli and refined suckling pig in a truffle sauce are among the difficult choices. Leave space for the tempting desserts. The Amura should definitely be on your list of restaurants for a special occasion.
🞜 183 E2
☎ 928 513 181
🌐 www.restauranteamura.com
🕐 Daily 1–11

ARRECIFE

Castillo de San José €€–€€€
The modern art gallery upstairs (p. 88) sets the tone for the César Manrique-designed restaurant; a bold statement with stripped wooden floor, black plastic 1960s-style seats (with comfy cushions) and floor-to-ceiling windows giving wonderful sea views. Start with dates wrapped in bacon or monkfish carpaccio, then try the *cherne* (bass grouper), with king prawns or thyme or a steak flambé, and finish off with *gofio* ice cream.
Cool jazz provides the perfect background accompaniment to the quietly elegant atmosphere.
🞜 181 E2
✉ Carretera de Puerto Naos
☎ 928 812 321
🕐 Daily 1–3:45, 7:30–11 (bar 11am–midnight)

Emmax €€

This restaurant-café is set in a typical single-storey Canarian house, but with a modern, stylish interior. The cooking is Italian-influenced Canarian. Try the black pasta with prawns in an orange sauce if available, sea bass is another good choice (there are always fresh fish options).

✛ 181 D2
✉ Avenida Playa Honda 21
☎ 928 820 917
🕐 Wed–Mon noon–midnight

Restaurante (Panorámico) Altamar, Gran Hotel €€€

It's not just the views that you'll enjoy from the 17th floor of this 5-star hotel: Large picture windows and pale wooden floorboards give a real feeling of light and space, and the prices for a hotel of this class are in an acceptable range. One speciality is the rosemary braised shoulder of lamb. The cafeteria next to the restaurant is open during the day – and enjoys the same spectacular view.

✛ 186 B2 ✉ Arrecife Gran Hotel, Parque Islas Canarias
☎ 928 800 000 🕐 Daily 7pm–11

MOZAGA

Casa Museo del Campesino Restaurante €€–€€€

At the Monumento al Campesino (p. 94), created by César Manrique, light meals are available from a small, rustic-looking bodega. The huge restaurant in the basement serves a whole range of Canarian specialities.

✛ 180 C3
✉ San Bartolomé
☎ 928 520 136 🕐 Daily 1–4

Caserío de Mozaga €€€

It's well worth the detour to dine in the old farmhouse. The food is of outstanding quality, combining traditional Canarian and Spanish ingredients. The menu may seem fairly limited, but it guarantees that the dishes are always fresh. Try out the homemade Bienmesabe (a sweet dessert comprising mainly of honey, egg yolk and ground almond). Each plate is a work of art.

✛ 180 C3 ✉ Mozaga, Calle Malva 8
☎ 657 640 514
🌐 www.caseriodemozaga.com
🕐 Wed–Mon 7.30pm–10.30pm

You are spoiled for choice in the Biosfera Plaza shopping centre in Puerto del Carmen.

Where to...Shop

PUERTO DEL CARMEN

The Biosfera Plaza, a short walk uphill from the port or the Hotel Los Fariones, is the best shopping centre in Puerto del Carmen. This attractive, modern mall includes Spanish and international mainstream fashion shops such as Zara, Pull & Bear, Timberland and Footlocker. Arteguise sells handicrafts and souvenirs of every possible sort, Bijou Brigitte fashion jewellery; both are on the first floor (Planta 1). People catering for themselves will find a supermarket on level 3.

If you are looking for organic food, a tiny but well-stocked shop with whole grain bread and vegetables from Lanzarote can be found in the Centro de Terapia Antroposófica in Calle Salinas 12 (in the Tamarindos apartment complex).

Walk downhill towards the beaches and along the main Avenida de las Playas and you will find many small shops selling cameras, watches and discounted electronic goods. The choice and competition mean that prices are as keen here as anywhere on the island, though you will still have to barter to come away with a bargain. Competition to sell is intensive, so take all after-sales or product performance promises with a large pinch of salt.

Mystic, beneath La Perla Hotel, sells aloe vera products, Haitian art, stylish silk clothes, ethnic jewellery and accessories.

Every Friday morning from 10am to 2pm, the Mercadillo de La Tiñosa, a market selling cheese, wine, a lot of handicraft products and knick-knacks, springs up along the harbour (Plaza del Varadero).

On the road from Puerto del Carmen to Macher, Artisdecor sells attractive contemporary and classic Spanish and island pottery, plates, glassware and general household items.

PUERTO CALERO

Puerto Calero is only small, and doesn't have all that many places to go shopping.

But as you might expect, the selection of shops at the marina isn't bad at all. You'll find a few souvenir stores and fashion boutiques alongside the restaurants and excursion providers.

ARRECIFE

Lanzarote's most comprehensive retail therapy is found in the capital. Some of the establishments occupy premises that are over a century old, which adds fun to window shopping. The pedestrianised centre includes a wide range of shops that appeal to both islanders and visitors.

The main street is Calle León y Castillo – you'll find most of the main shops on or just off here (Calle Canalejas has some nice clothes stores). Fashion names you may have heard of include Mango, Vero Moda and Planet, but there are plenty of other local stylish clothes and accessories shops that are worth checking out, such as Jack Jones, Tomás Panasco and La Puerta.

Lots of little designer boutiques have taken root in the Calle José Antonio Primo de Rivera among some long-standing fashion emporia. You'll find the small El Mercadillo shopping centre with its beautiful courtyard on León y Castillo.

A small craft market is held along the promenade on Fridays. Stalls also sell culinary goods in the alleyways around the church on Saturday mornings.

On the main road into Arrecife from Puerto del Carmen is Deiland, the island's biggest mall with around 35 shops, cafés, restaurants, a children's soft play area and a cinema.

AROUND SAN BARTOLOMÉ

Oenophiles should look in at the shop at Bodega El Grifo (p. 95), which has a good range of wine accessories, as well as a full range of bottles for sale. The Monumento al Campesino (p. 94) features a number of artisans' studios, so come here if you are seeking basketware, pottery, embroidery or other island craft souvenirs.

Where to...Go Out

NIGHTLIFE

There are two main areas to go out at night in Puerto del Carmen: The square by the Avenida del Varadero and on the Avenida de las Playas. Good places to start on the Avenida del Varadero (to the west of the town centre) are the Terraza Heineken Harbour, an elegant venue with good music, and the neighbouring Cervecería San Miguel, where they also play good pop, rock, house and classic hits. You'll also find the Lanzarote Palace – a club which boasts a great light and sound system – in this area. With all this on offer, it's not really that necessary to go and check out the Avenida de las Playas at all.
If you do, it's worth stopping off at La Ola (club music with some funk, chill-out and pop) where you can also get some good Asian and Canarian dishes. There are quite a few music bars in the Centro Comercial Atlántico (Avenida de las Playas). Just east of that in the Delicatezza Cocktail Bar (Avenida de las Playas 31), the barman mixes great drinks. At the weekend in the capital of Arrecife, most of the night owls flock to the music bars in the Calle Manolo Millares. Others meet in the new Kopas Lounge, an oasis of cool style at the Marina Lanzarote, to share a drink as they look out at the yachts.

CONCERTS

The charming little Teatro Municipal in San Bartolomé stages concerts and musicals. Occasional concerts are also held in the atmospheric surroundings of the Castillo de San José and the Iglesia de San Ginés in Arrecife (p. 87). For details of all the cultural events in the area, visit www.-turismo lanzarote.com/en/events-calendar.

SPORT

Water Sports
Divers will find some superb diving spots off the coast around Puerto del Carmen. Diving schools can be found in, among other places, Puerto del Carmen on the small Playa de la Barrilla (tel: 928 511 992, www.safaridiving. com) and at the harbour (tel: 928 584 780, www.divelanzarote.com). For parascending and water inflatable rides go to Playa Chica, between the port and the Hotel Fariones.

Deep-sea Fishing and Sailing
Puerto Calero is *the* island's top sailing centre (p. 90), with a mix of locals, whose boats are berthed more or less permanently here, and transatlantic sailors who use Lanzarote as a halfway house between Europe and the Caribbean. Several sailing boats are available for charter or day hire. Puerto Calero is also Lanzarote's deep-sea fishing centre, attracting professionals and holidaymakers in search of the Hemingway experience. You can arrange fishing trips from Puerto Calero with, for instance, the boat from Belduca (tel: 626 502 733; www.belducalanzarote.com).

Bike Hire
You can hire bikes from Renner Bikes in Puerto del Carmen; there you can also book easy or more demanding organised day tours (Ave. de las Playas, Centro Comercial Marítimo, tel: 928 510 612, www.mountainbike-lanzarote.com).

Go Karts
There is one circuit: Gran Karting on the LZ 2 at km 7, about 2km (1.2mi) from the airport (tel: 928 524 956, www.kartinglanzarote.com).

Other Sports
The Centro Deportivo (tel: 928 595 702; www. farioneshotels.com) at the Hotel Los Fariones is open to non-guests for a small fee and includes tennis, paddle tennis and squash courts, a fitness and aerobic centre, mini-golf, table tennis and an attractive swimming pool.

EXCURSIONS

Sea Excursions
There are numerous excursions from Puerto del Carmen and Puerto Calero. Submarine Safaris (tel: 928 512 898; www.submarinesa-faris.com; €55, children €32, 15% reduction for online bookings; free pickup service from most parts of the island) dive up to 50m (165ft) below the waves. A diver attracts fish with food and there are wrecks to be spotted, too.

There are some fantastic diving spots near Puerto del Carmen –
even wreck fans get their money's worth here.

People say Lanzarote does not have any dream beaches. Nonsense! The Playas de Papagayo offer great bathing and a wonderful beach backdrop.

The South and Timanfaya

Stunning contrasts: in the south the light sandy beaches, in the west Timanfaya with its dark volcanic landscapes.

Pages 104–127

Getting Your Bearings

Although Lanzarote is one complete island of contrasts, nowhere highlights it quite as remarkably as the southern part: from the infernal blasted landscape of Timanfaya's *malpaís* to the orderly houses and gardens of Yaiza; the golden Playas de Papagayo to the cinder vineyards of La Geria; the luxury hotels and urban spread of Playa Blanca to the natural phenomena of El Golfo and Los Hervideros. It's a case of black and white wherever you look.

The Fire Mountains of the Parque Nacional de Timanfaya are the main attraction here. If you want an idea of what it looks like on the moon, then this is the perfect place to come: huge expanses of black, sharp-edged lava stone, dark ash fields, giant volcanic cones and not a tree or bush anywhere to be seen... Although the devastating volcanic eruptions took place almost 300 years ago, from 1730 to 1736, large areas of the affected region still resemble a picture of early creation.

What is particularly remarkable is how the people of Lanzarote dealt with the changed conditions, for example by planting vines in the barren lava fields. An exceptional example of the ingenuity of the Lanzaroteños, the result is a cultivated landscape and landscape composition rolled into one that is absolutely astounding. Another example of their artistic powers of creation are the accurately formed salt pans of the Salinas de Janubio.

Seaside tourism on the south coast has the good fortune to benefit from consistently sunny weather all year round, a situation helped by the fact that this is where the island's best beaches are located. Despite the volcanic heritage of the island, these are not dark but almost as light as the beaches in the Caribbean. What is also surprising is that they are not at all spoilt either!

TOP 10
❶ ★★ Parque Nacional de Timanfaya
❹ ★★ La Geria
❻ ★★ Playas de Papagayo

Don't Miss
㉓ Yaiza

At Your Leisure
㉔ El Golfo
㉕ Los Hervideros
㉖ Salinas de Janubio
㉗ Playa Blanc

My Day
Visiting Volcanoes

The Fire Mountains are unquestionably Lanzarote's most spectacular natural wonder. However, the central zone of the national park is not an area you are allowed to enter on your own. What you can do is learn about the volcanic region by taking part in a walking tour with a national park ranger. Make sure you book early, as these complimentary tours are in great demand.

9am: Out with the Ranger

The meeting place for the tour that takes place several times a week is generally Plaza de los Remedios in **23** Yaiza. From there a minibus shuttles everyone to the Montaña Termesana at the south entrance of the national park. During the walk around the volcanic cone, the ranger points out various volcanic features, shows a collapsed lava tunnel and explains the difference between Aa-Lava and Rope Lava. During the trip, the expert staff are happy to answer most questions.

If the guided walk is already fully booked on the day you want to go, another option is the "Ruta de los Volcanes" bus tour (p. 114). It is equally fascinating, but pretty touristy.

Noon: White Village with a lot of Atmosphere

After the tour, Yaiza has a good choice of restaurants for lunch. One

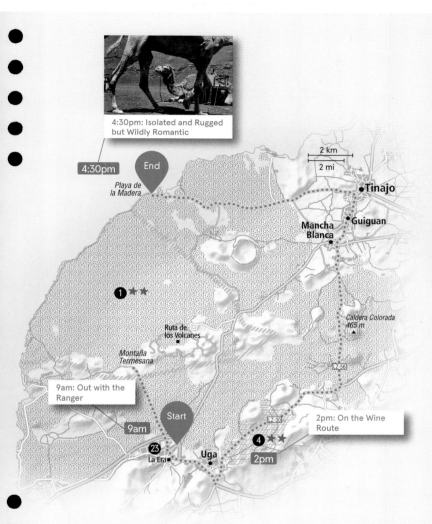

4:30pm: Isolated and Rugged but Wildly Romantic

4:30pm

End

Playa de la Madera

2 km
2 mi

Tinajo

Guiguan

Mancha Blanca

❶ ★★

Caldera Colorada
465 m

Ruta de los Volcanes

Montaña Termesana

9am: Out with the Ranger

9am

LZ-56

Start

LZ-30

2pm: On the Wine Route

❹ ★★

23

La Era

Uga

2pm

wonderful place to eat, for instance, is <u>La Era</u> (p. 126), a 17th-century farmhouse beautifully restored by César Manrique. It is also worth reserving a bit of time to wander round Yaiza – the whitewashed houses are representative of the island's typical rural architecture.

9am

Alternative Programme: On tour with a ranger at Montaña Termesana (above) or presentation of volcanic phenomena near the starting point of Ruta de los Volcanes (upper right). Man becomes a midget: lava bomb near Caldera Colorada (lower right).

2pm: On the Wine Route

Drive from Yaiza to Uga and turn into LZ 30 towards La Geria. This region, which was devastated by the eruptions in the 18th century is a prime example of how a barren piece of land can be transformed into a thriving wine-producing area with a good idea and a lot of hard work. The vines are grown in thousands of funnel-shaped pits protected from the wind by crescent-shaped walls – producing a landscape that is a work of art. Wine tasting is possible at any of the numerous bodegas en route.

3pm: A Big Surprise

About 2.5km (1.5mi) after the Bodega Antonio Suarez, turn left onto the LZ 56 towards Tinajo. On the righthand side of this road, at Km Stone 3.4, you will reach a hikers car park at the foot of Caldera Colorada. A marked nature trail starts here with information points about the volcanoes. Follow the path to the right when it divides after about 100m (328ft). A huge surprise awaits you after ten minutes: a volcanic bomb that looks like some giant hand placed it in the middle of the trail. One really wonders how the 4m (13ft) high chunk of lava actually got there.

4:30pm: Isolated and Rugged but Wildly Romantic

If you still have enough time, stop off at Playa de la Madera. Follow

9am

Noon

3pm

Time for a little break? Then take a break in Yaiza and indulge yourself a bit in "La Era".

the LZ 56 northwards and turn off left in Tinajo at the Unide supermarket into Calle Laguneta. You leave this tarmacked road after driving straight on for about 4km (2mi) to continue on a dirt road (passable for normal cars as well). It ends after 6km (ca. 4mi) at a car park further up from the Playa de la Madera. The bad news first: it is generally far too dangerous to swim here. What makes up for that though is the lava coastline and its spectacular testimony to past volcanic eruptions. Let the ocean wind awaken your senses, and – if the fancy takes you – wander along the bizarre coast for a while on the slag path that starts on the western edge of the beach.

Guided Walk:
Trail round the Montaña Termesana: 4km (2.5mi)
Registration: www.reservasparquesnacionales.es.
As the demand for these tours is high, it is recommendable to reserve the day you want a month in advance.
Walking time: The actual hike takes just 1 hour, but with the transfer and various stops, you should plan to be away for about 3 hours. The tour is led by an English-speaking guide.
Maximum Number of Participants: 8
Minimum Age: 16
Information: Centro de Visitantes Mancha Blanca ☎ 928 118 042

❶ ★★ Parque Nacional de Timanfaya

Don't Miss	Dramatic volcanoes in an apocalyptic landscape
Why	With more than 500,000 visitors each year, the volcanic landscape is Lanzarote's main attraction – and rightly so!
When	Late afternoon when the reddish tint of the volcano acquires a powerful glow
Time	Half a day
In Short	After the visit, you feel like you have been to the moon

The Timanfaya National Park, or Montañas del Fuego (Fire Mountains), as this area is also called, is one of the most spectacular landscapes on Earth, though Earth will probably be the farthest place from your mind as you gaze upon this scorched and contorted terrain. Its brooding craters and blasted badlands resemble a distant planet. If you only stir once from your beach towel on Lanzarote, make sure it's in this direction.

"Badlands"

The vast majority of visitors approach Timanfaya from the south, and this is the best introduction. The volcanic debris or *malpaís* (literally, badlands) begins just north of Yaiza, and El Diablo, an impish César Manrique-designed devil welcomes you to the outer park area. Indeed it may look impossible to do so but there are paths – barely discernible to the untrained non-local eye – which are used by locals and dromedary caravans. You may initially find it a bit disappointing that you are not even allowed to get out of the car on the road that goes through the national park, let alone wander off through the lava on your own.

The reason why the authorities do not allow unsupervised travel within the park is part aesthetic, part environmental, part safety. There is no doubt that the landscape of Timanfaya would certainly lose its other-worldly appeal if there were troops of tourists swarming all over it, but perhaps more importantly it is the fragile landscape

that is in danger. Footprints in the volcanic sands here can take years to disappear and there is always the very real possibility of walkers going right through the thin crust.

There are only two official stopping points in the National Park. The first is at the Echadero de los Camellos ("Camel Park"). This is a chaotic spot, often with dozens of tour buses disgorging passengers into long lines waiting for camels to take them on a short ride up and down the mountain. It's an unusual experience and worthwhile if you haven't ridden a camel before, though this is by no means the most spectacular part of the park. Animal-rights activists constantly point out the, at times, pitiful state of the animals: muzzles made of wire mesh and metal chains sometimes directly against the animals' fur don't exactly bear witness to good animal welfare. Next to where the dromedaries set off is a small museum exhibiting the various kinds of stone and lava found in the national park.

The second official stop is the large car park at Islote de Hilario where there is a restaurant designed by César Manrique. It is front of the building that the tour buses depart from for their tour of the volcanic region. You can walk a little way around the restaurant and take in the views, but you are not allowed to stray far. The area before you,

Manrique's *El Diablo* ("The Devil") greets you at the entrance to Timanfaya National Park

covering just over 50km² (20mi²), was mostly created in the first explosive wave of volcanic eruptions that shook the island between 1730 and 1731, though these continued for a total of six years and devastated an area four times this size (p. 14).

Just in front of the restaurant a park ranger demonstrates that the volcano beneath your feet is still very much alive; a bucket of water is emptied into a tube into the ground and transformed into a scalding geyser; a dry bush is dropped into a fissure and promptly ignites. The <u>temperature</u> at ground level is around 100–120°C (212–248°F), at just 13m (43ft) down temperatures rise to 610°C (1,130°F). The heat is being generated by a live magma chamber some 4–5km (2.5–3mi) below the surface.

From the car park in front of the restaurant coaches depart continuously for the <u>Ruta de los Volcanes</u> (Route of the Volcanoes) tour. The tour is an unforgettable 35-min trip taking in various volcanic phenomena: a bizarrely shaped mini volcano called Manto de la Virgen (virgin's coat), a look into a hollow crater, a stop in a collapsed lava tunnel and after the Valle de la Tranquilidad (Valley of Tranquillity) a drive up to the Montaña Timanfaya, from which the national park takes its name and from which one has a panoramic view across the volcanic landscape.

Equally impressive: doing the bus tour through Timanfaya...

A short commentary in different languages accompanies the tour, together with mood music and special sound effects. The tour ends with the theme tune to *2001: A Space Odyssey* – generally to enthusiastic applause It is only a bit of a shame that one is not allowed to leave the bus at all on the trip.

...and watching the natural geothermal displays

Additional Information about Volcanoes

Around 3km (2mi) north of the National Park entrance, this visitor centre (Centro de Visitantes e Interpretación de Mancha Blanca) is designed to answer all your questions about vulcanology on Lanzarote and further afield.

INSIDERTIP The national park restaurant uses **geothermal heat** from a dormant volcano to cook fish and meat. The quality of the food still leaves considerable room for improvement. It is better to visit one of the good country restaurants in Yaiza (p. 125)

✛ 182/183 C–D4/5

Parque Nacional
☎ 928 173 789
🌐 www.turismolanzarote.com
🕐 Daily 9–5:45, last coach tour 5pm.
Restaurant noon–4:30
🍴 €10 (includes coach tours and geothermal demonstrations), children under 12 years free

Echadero de los Camellos Museum-Information Centre:
🕐 Mon–Fri 9–3
🍴 Free; camel rides €12

Centro de Visitantes e Interpretación de Mancha Blanca:
☎ 928 118 042
🕐 Daily 9–5
🍴 Free

ℹ️

❹ ★★ La Geria

Don't Miss	A wine-growing region in which you sample a bottle or two in the bodegas
Why	Lanzarote's wine route leads through a uniquely formed landscape
When	Late afternoon when the tour buses have left for the day
Time	Half a day
In Short	The vintners are doing a good job

Fine wines in attractive surroundings: In the bodegas (here Bodega Rubicón) you can buy the local wine – and sample it too

Bordering the Parque Nacional de Timanfaya, the wine-growing region of La Geria was born out of the volcanic disaster that befell the island in 1730–36. Realising that vines could not only grow but thrive in these conditions, the resilient island farmers have not only guaranteed themselves a fail-safe crop but have created a unique and visually stunning viticultural landscape (p. 32 and 165).

The black volcanic fields of the valley of La Geria straddle the LZ30 for around 10km (6mi) or so. Along the route, you'll find several wine producers – bodegas – that offer samples to visitors and sell the wines they create. The Bodega La Geria is one of the best known. This atmospheric place is one of the oldest bodegas on the island, having been established at the end of the 19th century. It is the only bodega to offer guided tours without the need to make a reservation in advance (one-hour guided tours: Monday–Friday at 1pm; €8). Somewhat further east, still on the main road (LZ30) near Masdache, is Bodegas El Grifo (p. 95). The wine museum here is worth checking out. It has exhibits of old presses, decanting pumps and other gadgets and gizmos used in winemaking.

The Spanish introduced vines to the Canary Islands, but Lanzarote's characteristic <u>Malvasia</u> grape, which now accounts for 75 per cent of island wines, was brought from Crete in the 18th century. Since then, a unique combination of geology and climate has produced a wine that has won many admirers. Today Lanzarote vineyards are flourishing and produce around two million litres of wine per year, most of which is consumed on Lanzarote and its neighbouring islands.

INSIDER TIP Don't miss **Bodega El Chupadero.** Unlike the other bodegas mentioned above, it's not a wine producer though it does label and market wine from the locality. Moreover, it is home to a super little restaurant (p. 125). The fact that it is "a discovery", albeit only just off the main road, makes it all the more enjoyable.

The well-known Bodega La Geria in the middle of the wine region

✛ 183 D3

Bodega La Geria
☎ 928 173 178
🌐 www.lageria.com

🕐 Guided tour (about 40 min.)
Mon–Fri 2pm (Booking tel: 828 180 500
or bodegalageria@lageria.com)

❻ ★★ Playas de Papagayo

Don't Miss	Beaches to swim, relax and lap up the sunshine
Why	The by far the prettiest beach area on the island
When	When it is cloudy in the central and northern parts of the evening
Time	Half a day
In Short	There are still dream beaches around which have not been blemished by concrete jungles

Half a dozen coves with golden yellow sand – quite unlike one expects on this otherwise dark volcanic island. Another surprise: they are completely unspoilt! If there actually were a label "dream beach", this area would win it. The region around the Playas de Papagayo was christened the

Monumento Natural de Los Ajaches in 1998. You have to pay a fee when you drive into the area (you pay per car). From Playa Blanca, the drive on a fairly dusty and bumpy dirt road lasts about a quarter of an hour.

One of the fantastic beaches at the southern tip of the island

The first beach you arrive at, Playa Mujeres (2km/1.2mi after the pay booth), is usually the most crowded. Playa del Pozo and Playas de Papagayo, the prettiest beaches, are reached after another 3.5km (2mi). Just past here, around the corner of the promontory, are Playa Caleta del Congrio with its campsite and Playa de Puerto Muelas. These are the least attractive but they are relatively secluded and thus popular with nudists.

INSIDER TIP There are two simple cafeterias on the cliff overlooking the Playa de Papagayo. Although the prices are not exactly cheap, they are always buzzing.

ℹ ✛ 182 C2
🏖 Admission to Monumento Natural de los Ajaches: €3 (car)

㉓ Yaiza

Don't Miss	White houses, quiet squares and a smattering of art
Why	A picture-book village by the Fire Mountains which is well worth a visit
When	At lunchtime, to eat in one of the good country restaurants
Time	As long as you want
What Else	César Manrique also played a part in the village's facelift
In Short	Even supermarket architecture does not have to be exclusively functional

The "door to the south of the island" is often referred to as a model village for the traditional rural architecture on Lanzarote. With its whitewashed, sugar-cube houses, Yaiza is indeed an impressive sight.

Yaiza is the capital of Lanzarote's southernmost municipality. Its inhabitants take great pride in adorning their squares

The beautiful village of Yaiza is picturesquely situated to the south of the Fire Mountains.

and streets with plants, their houses are beautifully decorated, and they've even gone to the effort of making the supermarket on the high street aesthetically pleasing. In the centre is the charming small church of Nuestra Señora de los Remedios, dating from the 18th century. The church sits between two elegantly designed squares – the Plaza de los Remedios and the small, peaceful Plazoleta de Víctor Fernández. Galería Yaiza is a small art oasis in which Canarian artists exhibit contemporary works, and it is well worth checking out. The Casa de la Cultura is also mainly dedicated to work by Canarian artists.

A typical street in tranquil Yaiza. The house walls are always neatly whitewashed.

There is something by Manrique in Yaiza too: The artist played a decisive role in the restoration of the La Era finca (p. 126), a pretty 300-year old farmhouse. It is now a restaurant.

INSIDERTIP The Casona de Yaiza (p. 125) serves imaginatively prepared Lanzarotean cooking in a rustic ambience. The Bodega de Santiago (Montañas del Fuego 27, Yaiza; tel: 928 836 204; www.labodegadesantiago.es; ue–Sat 12.30–11, Sun–6pm) on the road to the Fire Mountains is a nice place to sit and enjoy Lanzarotean cheese, goat and lamb. The shady terrace offers a view of the houses in Yaiza and the surrounding volcanic landscape.

ℹ ✝183 D3

Magical Moment

Sundowner in El Golfo

The crowning finale after such an exciting day? The little fishing village of El Golfo (p. 122) is just the ticket. Pick a front-row table at one of the fish restaurants there. Almost all of them are on the waterfront, some of them even have a few chairs in the black sand. Lean back, glass in hand, and relax. Feel the warm breeze against your cheeks, watch the seagulls soar, and finish the day feasting your eyes as the sun disappears into the sea in a blaze of colour.

At Your Leisure

24 El Golfo

The small fishing village of El Golfo on the south-west coast is at once bizarre and picturesque. Built on a lava field right next to the sea, its good fish restaurants make it popular with tourists and islanders alike. Lots of locals have weekend and holiday homes here.

You can witness a peculiar natural phenomenon to the south of El Golfo: Thanks to the growth of algae, the water in the Charco de los Clicos, an enclosed lagoon that's formed in a volcanic crater, is a deep emerald green. Over time, crashing waves have broken away the edge of the crater on the side closest to the sea. The best view of the lagoon is actually from above, on the elevated walkway that's accessible from the village. The lava beach is bordered by an impressively eroded cliff. At the back of the beach, half of the El Golfo volcano has fallen away to create an amphitheatre rich in red and orange hues.

✝ 182 B4

25 Los Hervideros

The name translates as "the hot springs", and although the water has not been hot here since molten lava tumbled into the sea in 1730–36, the Atlantic certainly still boils up, particularly on windy days. Walkways and viewing areas have been cleverly cut into the 15m (50ft)-high lava cliffs to let you witness the waves hammering into the shark-tooth caves and

The Marina Rubicon district near Playa Blanca, is the perfect place to unwind at the end of the day.

whooshing up through blowholes at close quarters. You may get a little wet but it's quite safe. One of the island's most popular pictures is taken from here, contrasting the jet-black lava with the bright oranges and purples of the Montaña Bermeja (Purple Mountain) just inland.

✛ 182 B3

26 Salinas de Janubio

Salt pans, where seawater is gathered in large chequerboard squares, then left to evaporate, were once common on the island. Today this is the last survivor, and reckoned to be the biggest producer in the archipelago. At its height it employed 200 men; only a few people work in this area now. The old windmills that you see were once used to pump water into the pans, before being superseded by electric pumps. There is a restaurant and viewing point from which to contemplate this anachronistic sight. If you manage to see it at dawn or dusk it can be quite magical.

✛ 182 C3

27 Playa Blanca

This small fishing village has developed into one of the three biggest holiday resorts on the island over the last 15 years. Ferries to Fuerteventura depart from the harbour several times a day, while taxi boats shuttle

Playa Blanca: Beach living on the protected Playa Flamingo

back and forth between the Papagayo beaches (p. 170). You can walk west along the pretty waterside promenade to Playa Flamingo, and east to Playa Dorada, and if you still feel like it on to Marina Rubicón. The cosy district around the new yacht harbour is seen as one of the island's flagship tourism projects. The district recreates the style of a traditional Canarian village, in which numerous waterfront restaurants invite you to drop in for a meal. Next to the landmark Hotel Volcán Lanzarote (p. 125) is the Castillo de las Coloradas, a sturdy watchtower built in the 1740s. The latest attraction for divers is the Museo Atlántico, an underwater museum just off the coast, opened in 2017; the Sculpture Park is the work of British artist Jason deCaires Taylor.

✛ 182 B1

Where to...Stay

Expect to pay per double room, per night:

€	under €60
€€	€60–€100
€€	€100–€150
€€€€	over €150

LA GERIA

Apartments Bodega El Chupadero €€

Location, location, location are the three magic words here. Set just off the LZ30 in the heart of the wine country (p. 116), this former winery has converted part of its building into a wonderful wine bar (p. 125) and two holiday homes (one accommodates two people, while the other sleeps up to five). The walls, floors and ceilings are white, and the furnishings are a blend of modern and traditional. Both have a kitchen, living room and dining room. The views across La Geria are magnificent, and when the wine bar closes, the silence is deafening.
✛ 183 D3 ✉ La Geria ☎ 928 173 115
⊕ www.el-chupadero.com

YAIZA

Casa de Hilario €€€

This house, now over 200 years old, is also located on the edge of Yaiza. The hotel is surrounded by a garden and boasts an outdoor pool and a terrace with views of the mountains and the Atlantic. This bewitching Casa was named after Hilario Lanzaroteño who, according to legend, collected fig leaves at the foot of the Fire Mountain (Islote de Hilario) to feed his female camels.

The hotel's nine rooms are grouped around the house's typical Canarian courtyard, the stone walls of which date from 1730. The fascinating garden contains over 30 varieties of palm and some beautiful fruit trees.
✛ 183 D3 ✉ Calle Gen. García Escamez 19
☎ 928 836 262 ⊕ www.casadehilario.com

Casona de Yaiza €€€–€€€€

The boutique-style hotel, set in an early 19th-century house on the edge of the village with views to Timanfaya, has eight bedrooms and suites, all individually designed and furnished in rich Italian Renaissance style. Each room or suite is named after a feature of the Fenauso Valley that can be viewed from the hotel: While the decoration in some rooms is quite restrained, others have rather too many cherubs for comfort. All the bathrooms are very spacious. The hotel has an excellent restaurant (p. 125), and downstairs, in a beautifully restored *"aljibe"* (water cistern), is an art gallery. Outside, guests can relax on the solarium terrace, in the heated swimming pool or in the jacuzzi. Breakfast is included.
✛ 183 D3 ✉ Calle Valle de Fenauso
☎ 928 836 262 ⊕ www.casonadeyaiza.com

UGA

Casa El Morro €€€–€€€€

Built in the 18th century, Casa El Morro is a typical example of the beautiful rural architecture to be found in this wealthy part of the island. It was splendidly restored in 1997, splitting the original estate into several holiday homes, joined by a common patio. There is a lovely swimming pool set among gardens and luxurious terraces with wonderful views over Uga, south towards Femés and towards Timanfaya. The most spacious and attractive of the houses is the two-storey Casa Raquel. It accommodates up to five people and features a private terrace and a balcony. The other houses sleep three or four people each. All houses have a living room, kitchen and dining room, satellite TV, radio, coffee machine, toaster and kettle. The décor is rustic

The rooms of Casa de Hilario surround a patio

throughout with lots of warm teak wood, and the furnishings are cosy and in keeping with the atmosphere.

✠ 183 D3 ✉ Calle El Morro
☎ 928 830 392, 699 417 871
🌐 www.casaelmorro.com

Finca de Uga €–€€

This charming Casa Rural with three separate accommodations is set on the edge of Timanfaya National Park. Rooms are in a traditional-minimalist style with "designer" black-lava garden and magical sunset views to the Fire Mountains.

✠ 183 D3 ✉ Calle La Agachadilla 5
☎ 629 372 220 🌐 www.fincauga.com

PLAYA BLANCA

Casa del Embajador €€€–€€€€

This is a small historic family-run hotel with an entrance right on the promenade. It originally comprised a block of small early 19th-century dwellings, which were bought by an ambassador and converted into a single house. The present owners have made a fine job of restoration and landscaping the grounds in traditional style. The patio where breakfast is served and the outside terrace, with views to Fuerteventura and Isla de Lobos, are particularly attractive. There are 12 large twin/double rooms and one superior suite, each with full sea views, en-suite facilities, satellite TV and mini bar. In the grounds are two tennis courts.

✠ 182 B1 ✉ Calle La Tegala 56 ☎ 928 519 191
🌐 www.hotelcasadelembajador.com

Hotel Volcán Lanzarote €€€

Set just behind the Marina Rubicón is what appears to be an idyllic little whitewashed village with its own church and volcano. On closer inspection it turns out to be a 5-star-luxe-rated hotel, perhaps the most striking on the island. The entrance is through the "church", the "volcano" houses a public area and the hotel's 255 bedrooms are scattered through the Canarian-style "village" bunga-low houses. Furnishings throughout are very tasteful. All rooms enjoy sea views or over-look the main pool area, and have a lounge area. There are four pools in all, plus a

well-equipped spa. The hotel sets great store in its gastronomy, with five restaurants including one serving Japanese cuisine.

✠ 182 B1 ✉ Calle El Castillo 1
(Marina Rubicón) ☎ 928 519 185
🌐 www.hotelvolcanlanzarote.com

Timanfaya Palace €€€

Set just east of the resort, on the seafront near Playa Flamingo, this large 300-room 4-star hotel is built in an attractive Moorish style with pleasant grounds and an airy in-terior. It has three swimming pools, a nudist area, an open-air jacuzzi, sauna and gymna-sium. Sports facilities include a tennis court, mini-golf, archery, shooting and table tennis.

✠ 182 B1 ✉ Calle Gran Canaria 1
(Urbanización Montaña Roja ☎ 928 517 676
🌐 www.hotelh10timanfayapalace.com

Where to...
Eat and Drink

Expect to pay for a three-course meal for one, excluding drinks:

€	under €15
€€	€15–€25
€€€	over €25

LA GERIA

Bodega El Chupadero €€

This little gem, deep in the heart of wine country, is only slightly off the beaten track but feels like a real discovery. Given its location, the name is slightly misleading as no wine is made here, though they do bottle and label local vineyards' produce. It's a comfy whitewashed tapas and snacks bar with bright soft cushions, modern art on the walls, friendly staff and delicious food. Try the smoked salmon.

✠ 183 D3 ✉ La Geria 3 ☎ 928 173 115
🌐 www.el-chupadero.com ⏱ Tue–Sun 11–11

YAIZA

Casona de Yaiza €€€

The cosy rustic restaurant of this boutique hotel (p. 124) is in what was the former wine cellar with typical whitewashed walls inset with dark lava stones. The menu rotates, offering fine Mediterranean and Canarian cuisine and always a good choice of tapas. Specialities include *Paella*, but it has to be ordered in advance.

✈ 183 D3 ✉ Calle Valle de Fenauso 11
☎ 928 836 262 ⊕ www.casonadeyaiza.com
⏰ Fri–Tue 2–10, Thu from 6.30

La Era €€€
The La Era started life in the 17th century as a farmhouse, was beautifully restored by César Manrique and opened as a restaurant in 1970. It is set in a lovely flower-filled courtyard with a series of rustic cosy dining rooms leading off here. However, both the food and service need to put in a bit more effort to be on the same level as the setting.

✈ 183 D3 ✉ Calle El Barranco
☎ 928 830 016 ⊕ www.laera.com
⏰ Tue–Sun noon–midnight

EL GOLFO

Costa Azul €€
If you want to be right next to the crashing waves with the smell of the sea in your nostrils, it has to be Costa Azul. The food, inevitably seafood and fish, is good. Of course, the locals know that, too, and they tend to swarm in at the weekend, which means the terrace is soon full. However, there are lots of good alternatives right next door.

✈ 182 B4 ✉ Playa del Golfo ☎ 928 173 199
⏰ Thu–Tue 11–10

PLAYA BLANCA / MARINA RUBICÓN

Brisa del Mar €€€
On the promenade in front of the restaurant, you have a lovely view of the harbour and across to Fuerteventura. The food is very good, as are the portions. Apart from a large selection of fish dishes, you can also order pizzas.

✈ 182 B1 ✉ Avenida Marítima 111
☎ 928 519 572 ⏰ Daily 11am–11pm

Brisa Marina €€€
One of the best restaurants on the seafront promenade, Brisa Marina occupies a tra-

ditional green-and-white nautically themed building with an attractive terrace, beautifully lit by night. It features a long menu of pasta, grilled meats and fish. Specialities include paella, fish in salt, and fish soup (24 hours' notice required for the latter).

✈ 182 B1 ✉ Avenida Marítima 97–99
☎ 928 517 206
⊕ www.restaurantebrisamarina.com
⏰ Daily 10–9

Café Terraza €
You're spoilt for choice in the area around Marina Rubicón: If you only want a snack or something to drink, this French bistro is the right address. At midday, there is cake, and in the evening when most of the day trippers have gone back to their hotels, people meet here for a glass of wine or a cocktail.

✈ 182 B1 ✉ Marina Rubicón ☎ 928 517 150
⊕ www.cafeterraza.com
⏰ Mon–Sat 10–midnight

Casa Brígida €€€€
Serves innovative Canarian dishes prepared under the watchful eye of well-known island chef, Pedro Santana Camacho. You can choose from a selection of several excellent set menus. The staff are happy to help and give very good advice. Unsurprisingly, this eatery in the marina is always busy.

✈ 182 B1
✉ Puerto Deportivo Marina Rubicón
☎ 928 518 946
⊕ www.restaurantecasabrigida.com
⏰ Tue–Sun noon–4.30, 8–10:30

Casa Roja €€€–€€€€
This red-painted house boasts an impressive location right next to the marina and two beautiful terraces directly overlooking the water. Naturally, the focus is on fish and seafood; specialities include black rice with tuna fish and prawns.

✈ 182 B1 ✉ Marina Rubicón
☎ 928 519 644
⊕ www.lacasaroja-lanzarote.com
⏰ Mon–Sat noon–11, Sun noon–4

L'Artista €–€€
Set slightly back from the main promenade, this cheerful restaurant is in a lovely old

fisherman's house, with a distinctive bright turquoise exterior and attractive colour-washed interior. The menu is typical Italian trattoria fare, home-made pizzas and pastas. On balmy summer nights book a seat on the balcony.

🔶 182 B1 ✉ Calle La Tegala 18
☎ 928 517 578
🌐 www.pizzerialartista.com
🕐 Mon–Sat 12:30–11:30, Sun noon–4

Where to...Shop/ Go Out

SHOPPING

Calle Limones is Playa Blanca's main shopping street. It boasts boutiques, jewellery stores and shops selling everything you need for the beach.
Head to the Avenida Marítima and check out Tienda César Manrique and Mystic, where everything's made from natural materials.
A market selling a selection of creative crafts and tasty produce is held in Marina Rubicón on Wednesdays and Saturdays.
Les Routes des Caravanes, located in the Old School at Yaiza (La Antigua Escuela de Yaiza), sells exotic Moroccan clothes, accessories and household items.
Ahumadería de Uga on the LZ2 is known for its smoked salmon (tel: 928 830 132, it's closed Sun and Mon). They also sell to restaurants and hotels across the island.

NIGHTLIFE

Playa Blanca is a family resort and the nightlife here is pretty low-key as a result. The liveliest district to go out is round the Avenida Marítima. Blue Note in Marina Rubicón is a good place if you want to chill out listening to piano music and live jazz by the sea.
Jazz can also be found at the music bar Cuatro Lunas in the premier hotel Princesa Yaiza; the barman mixes excellent cocktails and serves a refined selection of wines. But be careful – it is not exactly cheap!

SPORT

Water Sports
The attraction per se for divers is the under-water museum Museo Atlántico in the bay of Las Coloradas. Independent diving is not possible, however. You can only visit the museum in the company of one of the local diving schools (e. g. www.divecollegelanzarote.com, tel: 928 518 668).
You'll find catamaran excursions and sailing and windsurfing courses on offer at the marina in Playa Blanca (www.marinarubicon.com). Various fishing trips run from the port at Playa Blanca. Playa Dorada has water bananas and pedalos.

Horse Riding
4km (2.5mi) east of Uga on the main Arrecife road, is a good riding stable. Lanzarote a Caballo (tel: 626 593 737; www.lanzarotea caballo.com),

EXCURSIONS

From the ferry harbour Playa Blanca, Chillout Cruise (tel: 649 023 013, www.chilloutcruise. com) offers daily excursions along the south coast. The boat stops along the way to allow people to swim and snorkel, and has a barbecue on board.
Segway tours that head to the Papagayo beaches or along the promenade are an equally eye-catching way to get around (tel: 657 557 190; www.movingsegway lanzarote.com).

Wind-kissed: It is not surprising that so many pretty windmills were built on this island.

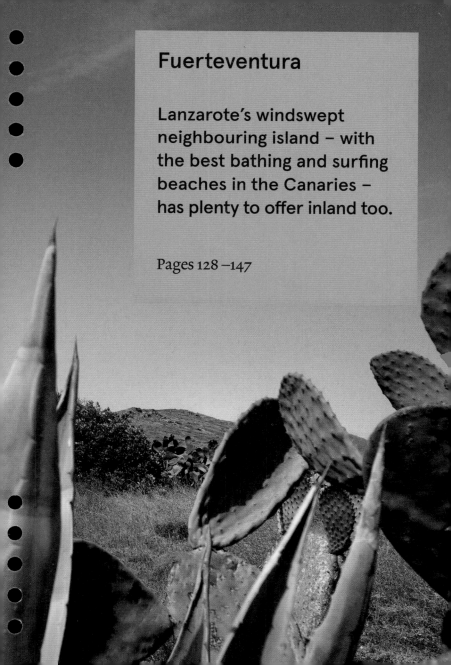

Fuerteventura

Lanzarote's windswept neighbouring island – with the best bathing and surfing beaches in the Canaries – has plenty to offer inland too.

Pages 128 –147

Getting Your Bearings

After the tidy lines of Lanzarote with its green and white houses and manicured fields and gardens, the barren landscapes and long, sandy beaches of Fuerteventura come as quite a contrast. Heading into Fuerteventura's interior is rather like setting the clock back, once you are out in the countryside, time seems to stop altogether.

Corralejo is the busiest resort in the north of the island, not dissimilar in atmosphere to Playa Blanca and, like Puerto del Carmen, it has a Strip of international bars and shopping centres. The town's biggest attraction is the long sandy beach behind which enormous crescent dunes invite you to go on long walks.

If you're feeling more adventurous, hire a car and head down to the old capital of Betancuria (p. 138), passing through historic villages en route. After the Fire Mountains of Timanfaya, the volcanic landscapes may be a little tame, but there's no denying that it has a certain grandeur and in places you can drive for miles without seeing another person, let alone a designer restaurant or boutique hotel: Fuerteventura has had no César Manrique-type figurehead to create tourist attractions or pronounce on matters of design. Despite that, there is still a lot to see in the little towns of La Oliva, Tefía and the former capital Betancuria.

<u>TOP 10</u>
🔟 ★★ Betancuria

<u>Don't Miss</u>
㉘ Corralejo

<u>At Your Leisure</u>
㉙ La Oliva
㉚ Ecomuseo de La Alcogida
㉛ Antigua
㉜ Oasis Park La Lajita

Corralejo
㉘

El Cotillo •   Lajares •
   FV-10   FV-101   FV-1

• Villaverde

㉙ **La Oliva**

• Tindaya   Caldereta •
La Matila •
FV-10   • Tetir

Los Molinos •   • Puerto
de Lajas
FV-221   Tefía •

Ecomuseo de ㉚   Casillas del
La Alcogida   Ángel   FV-3

   Puerto del
   Rosario

Valle de •   • La
Santa Inés   Ampuyenta
   FV-20

Betancuria 🔟 ★   • Triquivijate   FV-2

㉛ **Antigua**

Puerto de •
la Peña   FV-30   • Caleta
   de Fuste

   FV-50
• Toto
Pájara •   • Tiscamanita

Tuineje •   • Pozo Negro
   FV-20   FV-2

FV-605

Carga •
del Camelo

   Gran
• Tarajalejo   Tarajal

㉜
Oasis Park
La Lajita   10 km
• Costa   5 mi
Calma

My Day
on the
Neighbouring Island

Given the fact that the ferry trip takes only 30 minutes, a trip to the neighbouring island is an easy addition to the itinerary. If you want to see more of Fuerteventura than just the harbour town of Corralejo, you should hire a car or take the car you have on Lanzarote across on the ferry.

9am: Arrival on Lanzarote's Sister Island

The harbour town of  **28** Corralejo is not exactly large, and with an infrastructure that is completely focused on tourism, it does not offer much that is of cultural interest. Carry straight on to **29** La Oliva and drive from there past Montaña Tindaya to Tefía located further south.

10am: Pure Rural Idyll

If you would like to know what life was like for people living in the countryside on the Canaries well into the last century, the 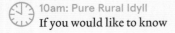 **30** Ecomuseo de La Alcogida in Tefía is the perfect place to find out. With a site plan (and an admission ticket) from the reception, you can set off on your own to explore the open-air museum and peer into the little farmers' cottages. Grazing goats and clucking hens underline the rural atmosphere of the museum village.

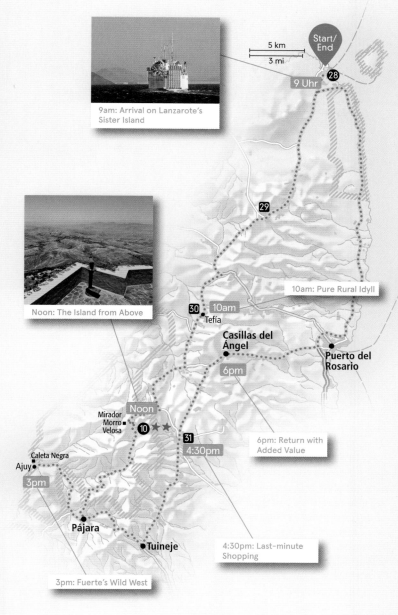

9am: Arrival on Lanzarote's Sister Island

Noon: The Island from Above

5 km
3 mi

Start/End

28

9 Uhr

29

10am: Pure Rural Idyll

30 10am
Tefía

Casillas del Ángel

6pm

Puerto del Rosario

Noon

Mirador Morro Velosa ■ **10** ★★ **31** 4:30pm

Caleta Negra
Ajuy ●

3pm

6pm: Return with Added Value

Pájara

●**Tuineje**

4:30pm: Last-minute Shopping

3pm: Fuerte's Wild West

From La Oliva make your way to the Ecomuseo de La Alcogida in Tefía (upper left). When you have had enough rural idyll, then continue on up and away to the mirador (upper right).

 Noon: The Island from Above

From the Tefía plane a narrow mountain road winds up to the Betancuria Massif. Visible from afar, exposed on a mountain peak, is the Mirador Morro Velosa. From the lookout platform, at a height of 675m (2,215ft), there is a magnificent view of the north of Fuerteventura, beyond which you can see the contours of Lanzarote. Your next destination, the island's old capital ❿ ★★ Betancuria, is already awaiting you below.

 1pm: Colonial Flair in the Mountains

Betancuria still breathes the flair of the colonial era. The historic centre around the parish church of Santa María has been beautifully spruced up. Opposite the church, in the Casa Santa María, a lovingly restored manor house, the multimedia show by German photographer Reiner Loos is well worth seeing.

In the centre, there are lots of enticing restaurants – in the Bodegón Don Carmelo, just a few steps away from the church square,

Noon

1pm

1pm

The pretty Betancuria (both ills. above) entices visitors to stroll and stop for a meal.

for example, you can order a very decent selection of tapas.

3pm: Fuerte's Wild West

To the south of Betancuria a winding road takes you from the "oasis village" of Vega de Río Palmas to a pass and then back down to Pájara. From there, you should definitely make a stop at Ajuy on the west coast. Although it is generally impossible to swim from the dark

sand beach, because of the high waves, you can take a short walk along the white limestone cliffs to Caleta Negra and then walk down steps carved into the cliff to an enormous sea cave – albeit only when the sea is calm enough.

4:30pm: Last-minute Shopping

Drive back to Pájara and via Tuineje to **31** Antigua. On the northern edge

3pm

Ready for a little adventure? The path takes you over rough and smooth to the caves near Ajuy.

of town is a picture-book windmill, which you can also visit inside. Molino de Antigua (p. 143) has a cheese museum and a pretty botanic garden; in the well-assorted handicraft shop, you can look for a typical souvenir from Fuerteventura – how

about a piece of goat's cheese rolled in *gofio*?

6pm: Return with Added Value
You just have to make time for them on the way back! From Antigua it is a relatively short drive via

4:30pm

6pm

Mill Idyll. If you want to, you can have a closer look before continuing on to the "desert landscape" near Corralejo.

6pm

Evening atmosphere on Corralejo's waterfront. Perhaps there is enough time for a sundowner before you take the ferry.

Casillas del Ángel to Puerto del Rosario and from there along the east coast back to the ferry. But on the way, just a few miles before you reach Corralejo, high crescent-shaped dunes on each side of the road demand your attention. Drive onto the curb on the right and wander through this impressive sea of sand for a few minutes (p. 140).

Tour
Journey Distance: c. 155km (96mi)
Ferries between Lanzarote and Fuerteventura shuttle back and forth between 7am and 8pm every one to two hours. Not all rental companies allow you to take your hire vehicle from one island to the next, one exception being, e.g. **Cicar** (☎ 928 822 900 ◑ www.cicar.com).

Bodegón Don Carmelo
✉ Calle Alcalde Carmelo Silvera 4, Betancuria
☎ 928 878 391 ◑ Sat–Thu 11–6

⑩ ★★ Betancuria

Don't Miss	Colonial flair in the shade of the date palms
Why	To have a stroll and something to eat
When	Not too late as things start being put away towards the end of the afternoon
Time	Two to three hours
What Else	An abbey without a roof
In Short	Fuerteventura's most beautiful village

Betancuria, the island's former capital, is the most beautiful place on Fuerteventura. The church and the handsome 16th and 17th-century colonial houses bear witness to the splendour of a bygone age. Conveniently enough, the town is also a good place to stop for lunch.

The island's conqueror, Jean de Béthencourt (p. 21), founded his capital here in 1405, well away from the coast, with the intention of avoiding pirate attacks. Unfortunately, the

The Iglesia de Santa María houses one of the oldest wood carvings in the Canary Islands.

raiders were undeterred and in 1593 they destroyed the church and took 600 islanders as slaves. The village remained the capital until 1834 but thereafter became a sleepy backwater until tourism gave it a fresh lease of life.

Santa María Sends Greetings

Rebuilt in 1620, this is the most beautiful church Iglesia de Santa María on the island, with naïve-style pastel-painted side altars, a baroque high altar, Gothic arches, a wine-glass pulpit, and a *mudéjar*-influenced (Moorish) ceiling. The figure of Santa Catalina (on an altar in a side aisle) is regarded as one of the oldest wood carvings in the Canaries. There's much more to the Casa Santa María – a lovingly restored, sixteenth-century manor house located opposite the church – than its relaxing café and well-known restaurant (p. 146). Part of the building – the largest structure in the village – is home to the beautiful terraces, court-yards and colonial-style rooms of the Museo Artesanía. Visitors to the museum can watch artisans at work and learn about the history

Picturesque Ruin: Convento de San Buenaventura

and culture of the island from an audio-visual show. Shops sell some good island souvenirs, and the cactus garden is a lovely place for a stroll.

Museums and Masonry

The Museo Arqueológico y Etnográfico is primarily dedicated to exhibiting archaeological artefacts harking back to the time of the Canary Islands' original Berber inhabitants.

Liturgical objects are on show in the Museo de Arte Sacro. The exhibits are currently being housed in the Santa María church.

Set 200m north of the Iglesia de Santa María in a gully just off the main road is the roofless ruin of the Convento de San Buenaventura. This Franciscan abbey was founded by monks who came over with the Norman conquerors.

INSIDER TIP The best spot for a break is the café in the **Casa Santa María.** Other cafés and restaurants are found in and around Betancuria (p. 146).

✝ 184 D3   *i*

Casa Santa María
✉ Plaza Santa María 1 ☎ 928 878 282
🕑 Mon–Sat 11–4 💰 €6

**Iglesia de Santa Maria,
Museo de Arte Sacro**
🕑 Mon–Sat 10–12:30, 1–3:30 💰 €1.50

Convento de San Buenaventura
✉ Calle Presidente Hormiga, 13,
Betancuria

Museu Arqueológico y Etnográfico
✉ Calle Roberto Roldán (main road)
🕑 Currently closed for renovation

㉘ Corralejo

Don't Miss	Little town, large dunes
Why	As it is only a short trip from Lanzarote to Corralejo, it seems an obvious option
When	In the morning, after the arrival of the ferry
Time	Two hours – or longer with a walk through the dunes
In Short	A trip into the desert

At first glance Corralejo seems to be a copy of Playa Blanca on Lanzarote – there is little difference between the two resorts as far as the tourist infrastructure is concerned. Both seaside resorts can boast great beaches – but only Corralejo can lay claim to stunning sand dunes.

Tourists will enjoy visiting the old part of town with its squares and narrow streets, nearly all of which lead down to the waterfront. The centre is made up of a small marketplace with cafés, restaurants and all the shops you'll need. It's relatively peaceful here during the day, but can get pretty lively in the evening during the holiday season. The small promenade is a good place for a stroll, and boasts several restaurants and cafés. The new Corralejo runs along the Avenida Nuestra Señora del Carmen, lined with apartment complexes and shops. Don't expect to see any great sights here, they are all located outside the main centre.

No End of Beaches

You'll find several beaches and sandy bays near Corralejo, but the very best beaches – featuring magnificent golden sand – are located further to the south-east. They begin immediately after the town border and stretch over 7km (4.3mi) towards the south. All of the beaches offer fantastic views out over Lobos and Lanzarote. Windsurfers and kiteboarders should head to Flag Beach.

A Sea of Sand

On the other side of the road from the beaches, Corralejo's white sand dunes cover an area of around 27km² (10mi²).

This area was declared a <u>national park</u> (Parque Natural Corralejo) in 1982, too late to stop the two hotels that were already built here, but it has prevented further attempts to scar this otherwise pristine landscape. Just a short walk on the other side of the main road and one could imagine that you have landed in the desert world of the nearby African continent.

Daily life in Corralejo: Tourists hardly ever venture into some corners of this harbour town.

Westwards

The little holiday resort <u>El Cotillo</u> is primarily visited by individuals not interested in glittering seaside promenades and chic shopping centres. The beaches are not as full here and at the Muelle de Pescadores in the old harbour, there are some wonderful fish restaurants. To the south of the little centre is the Castillo de El Tostón, an 18th-century <u>watchtower</u> – identical in construction to the <u>Castillo de las Coloradas</u> (p. 123) – used by the townspeople to watch out for pirates. In the north of El Cotillo, you can climb up a lighthouse. It gives you a broad view of the south coast of Lanzarote and of the small island of Lobos in the strait in between the two islands.

INSIDER TIP In the **Café Latino** (p. 146) on the promenade, you can see everything that is going on in the harbour basin.

✛ 185 E5

Magical Moment

Just Like the Sahara

Brave the desert! At Corralejo you can roam through the expanse of shifting sand. Every day, the huge dunes are continually tousled by the wind and given a slightly different shape. The best way to experience them is to take off your shoes, pace barefoot through the sand and climb to the top of the delicately formed ridges. When the evening sun bathes the crescent-shaped tips in a reddish light, you will feel like you have been catapulted into a different, magical world …

29 La Oliva

La Oliva is no more than a large village but it has a number of notable buildings. It is most famous for its grandiose Casa de los Coroneles (House of the Colonels), a large, castellated, colonial-style house dating back to 1650. It was home to the island governors from 1709 to 1859 and is an arts and cultural centre today (open Tue–Sat 10–6). Another impressive structure is the Iglesia de Nuestra Señora de la Candelaria, built in 1711, with a striking black lava-stone bell tower. Its interior is very attractive with features similar to the church at Betancuria (p. 138).

The Centro de Arte Canario (CAC) is a cool contemporary space devoted to Canarian art.

✝ 185 E4
Centro de Arte Canario
✉ Calle Salvador Manrique de Lara (opposite Casa de los Coroneles)
☎ 928 868 233 ◐ Mon–Sat 10–5 ✦ €4

---

30 Ecomuseo de La Alcogida

This open-air museum, set in typical empty red-dust countryside, shows rural life as it was some 50 to 100 years ago. There are houses and farms to visit. Allow around an hour to see everything. At the main entrance, you receive a site plan which will help you to find your way around the extensive complex. The houses range from a simply-furnished, modest house to a well-to-do family house, a farm with a working donkey-powered mill, the miller's house and craftwork demonstrations.

✝ 185 D4 ☎ 928 175 434
◐ Tue–Sat 10–6 ✦ €5

---

31 Antigua

Like its close neighbour, Betancuria, this old *(antigua)* village was established in 1485 by settlers from Normandy and Andalucía, and it too was the capital of the island at one time, although today, Antigua is little more than a well-kept village. In its pretty main square is the diminutive church of Nuestra Señora de Antigua, built in 1785. The interior is worth seeing.

Just north of the village is the Molino de Antigua. The centrepieces of this beautiful complex are a reconstructed windmill and a cheese museum full of interesting information about Fuerteventura's most important agricultural product. In

A good address for regional art; the Centro de Arte Canario in La Oliva

If you have time, head to the Playa de Cofete on the Jandía peninsula.

the botanic garden surrounding the building, endemic plants rub shoulders with cacti and succulents from all over the world. About 10km (6.2mi) south of Antigua near Tiscamanita is a <u>mill centre</u>; this region was once the island's granary.

Flamingos in the Oasis Park

✠ 185 D3
Centro de Interpretación de los Molinos
✉ Calle la Cruz 13, Tiscamanita (Tuineje)
☎ 928 164 275 🕐 Tue–Sat 10–6 💰 €2

32 Oasis Park La Lajita

It's a long way south (85km/90mi from Corralejo), but if you like animals and nature, it's worth a visit. Oasis Park is Fuerteventura's largest, oldest, most beautiful tourist attraction. With its three good restaurants, it's a great place to spend the whole day. The name "Oasis Park" is used to market three separate attractions: The <u>Zoo Park</u>, the <u>Camel Safari</u> and the <u>Jardín Botánico</u>, located 700m away. All three destinations lie on the main road from Tarajalejo to Jandía.

This expansive recreational park, originally founded as a plant nursery in 1985, lives up to its name with its palm groves and subtropical ornamental plants. In the meantime, there is also a large area in which indigenous plants appear next to the cacti.

You can still tell that Oasis Park was established as a botanical garden in 1985 – even today it looks less like a zoo than an oasis of a vivid greenery and vibrant plants set in the middle of a dusty desert. It also boasts an attractive area with 2,300 different varieties of cactus.

One of the best features is the location of the enclosures, set along narrow, shady tracks with dense foliage, brightly coloured plants and running water. There are hundreds of reptiles, primates, mammals and birds. The sea lion, parrot and crocodile shows are fun for kids and the birds of prey show is entertaining and informative.

Camel breeding is a speciality of the park and the herd is the largest in the Canaries at 220 strong. You can take camel rides, and a visit to see the baby camels is recommended.

The African Savannah area has giraffes, antelopes and endangered African animals including rhinoceroses.

✠ 184 C2
✉ Carretera General de Jandía
(FV2km 57.4), La Lajita ☎ 928 161 102
🌐 www.fuerteventuraoasispark.com 🕐 9–6
💰 Park: €33 adults, €19.50 children;
Camel Safari: €12 adults, €8 children

Where to...
Eat and Drink

Expect to pay for a three-course meal for one, excluding drinks:

€   under €15
€€   €15–€25
€€€   over €25

CORRALEJO

Ambaradam €
Just off the top end of Avenida Grandes Playas, this Italian-owned and run café is a stylish, relaxed oasis, perfect for a snack or full meal after visiting the market. They specialise in breakfasts, sweet and savoury pancakes and serve up to 14 different types of bruschetta. Attentive friendly young staff, good music, Italian football on TV.

➕ 185 E5
✉ Avenida Grandes Playas s/n
☎ 604 215 369
🕐 Mon–Sat 8am–1:30am

Antiguo Café del Puerto €€
This is the sort of place where you will be made welcome at any time of the day or night, whether you want to drink a *café con leche* or a beer while watching the boats on the seafront, or to put together a meal from a good choice of tasty tapas in its attractive, pastel-washed, typically Spanish dining room. The staff are friendly and obliging.

➕ 185 E5 ✉ Calle La Ballena
☎ 928 537 024
🕐 Daily 11am–11.30pm

Café Latino €–€€
Set right on the front row of the promenade, with tables in a striking black pumice cactus garden, Café Latino is popular at most times of the day. International snacks make up much of the menu but there are tapas and interesting local dishes such as avocado, cheese and palm honey.

➕ 185 E5
✉ Avenida Marítima 11
🕐 Daily 9pm–late

Factoria €€€–€€
Set right on the seafront, but just away from the main hubbub, this little pizzeria is one of the friendliest places in Corralejo. They do serve steaks and fish but specialise in pizzas.

➕ 185 E5
✉ Avenida Marítima 38 ☎ 928 535 726
🌐 www.restaurantelafactoria.eu
🕐 Daily 10:30am–11pm

VILLAVERDE

El Horno €€
The large barbecue at the entrance to this attractive rustic restaurant – decked in green gingham tablecloths and farming bygones – tells you that the speciality of the house is grilled meats. Apart from steaks the restaurant also serves typical Canarian dishes, such as kid and rabbit: You can try *gofio* ice cream for dessert. The dining area has a rustic flair with stimulating element in the form of a little fountain.

➕ 185 E5
✉ Carretera General 44
☎ 928 868 671
🕐 Thu–Tue 12.30–11, Sun 12:30–4:30

Hotel Rural Mahoh €€
Choose from one of the most interesting Canarian menus on the island while relaxing in one of its most charming settings. Start with croquettes, stuffed peppers for the main course, then the lamb chops and as to round it off the fig ice cream with hot chocolate sauce.

➕ 185 E5
✉ Sitio de Juan Bello, Carretera Villaverde-La Oliva (on the main road)
☎ 928 868 050 🌐 www.mahoh.com
🕐 Daily 1pm–midnight

BETANCURIA

Casa Santa María €€€–€€€€
A wonderfully appointed 17th-century farmhouse in a prime location just opposite Betancuria's parish church. You enter Casa Santa María's café through a dark, atmospheric bar hung with hams and huge cowbells. Two lovely sunny

courtyards – decorated with vintage storage pots and filled with olive trees, yucca plants and subtropical ornamental plants. Antiques abound though don't overpower, and the food is expensive. One of the specialities served is braised kid.

✛ 185 D3 ✉ Plaza de Santa María
☎ 928 878 282
🌐 www.casasantamaria.net
🕐 Mon–Sat 11–5

Val Tarajal €€

This traditional dark-wood restaurant has few frills except for a giant 4m-long (13ft) *timple* (a Canarian ukulele-like instrument, p. 52) on one wall. All the usual Canarian favourites are on the menu, though some, like *puchero* and *sancocho*, are only available on Sundays and public holidays.

✛ 185 D3 ✉ Calle Roberto Roldán 6 (main road) ☎ 630 884 945 🕐 Tue–Sun 11–5

VEGA DE RÍO PALMAS

Casa de la Naturaleza €–€€

This restaurant, just outside Vega de Río de las Palmas, is reached down a small street leading from the church. It is not far from a beautiful hiking trail through a gorge to the hermitage Ermita de la Peña (the path is signposted towards Ajuy). Before or after the walk, you can enjoy a little break in the Casa de la Naturaleza. Relax in the pretty garden while you eat a snack. The local goat's cheese is always a good choice.

✉ Plaza Iglesia ☎ 928 175 464
🌐 www.casanaturaleza.net
🕐 Tue–Sun 10–5

Excellent cuisine is another appealing feature of Casa Santa María.

From Mirador del Río there is a breath-taking view of
La Graciosa, the small island just off the coast of Lanzarote.

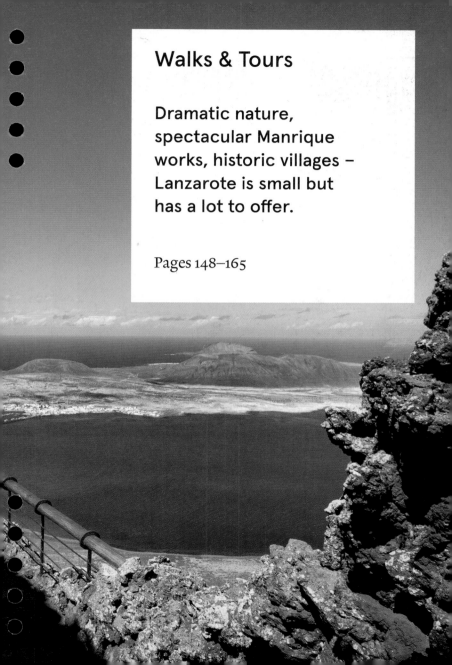

Walks & Tours

Dramatic nature,
spectacular Manrique
works, historic villages –
Lanzarote is small but
has a lot to offer.

Pages 148–165

Teguise

What?	Walk
When?	If you don't mind the hustle and bustle of the market, you can also do this tour on Sunday, although on a Sunday, of course, quite a few things are closed or only open for a limited time
Distance	about 2km (1.25mi)
Time	1½ hr
Start/End	San Miguel A 181 D4

The walk around Teguise leads you down small streets of snow-white houses and past the Iglesia Nuestra San Francisco.

Teguise is a perfect town for a walking tour, with history and character oozing from the fabric of most of its perfectly preserved buildings, which are protected by planning controls. It is small, easy to navigate and traffic free.

1–2

The church of Nuestra Señora de Guadalupe on Plaza de la Constitución is the logical place to begin the tour of this historic town. The church originally dates from 1420. It was almost completely destroyed during a vicious pirate attack in the 1600s and was ravaged by a blazing fire at the start of the 20th century. Parts of the tower are all that survive of the original building today.

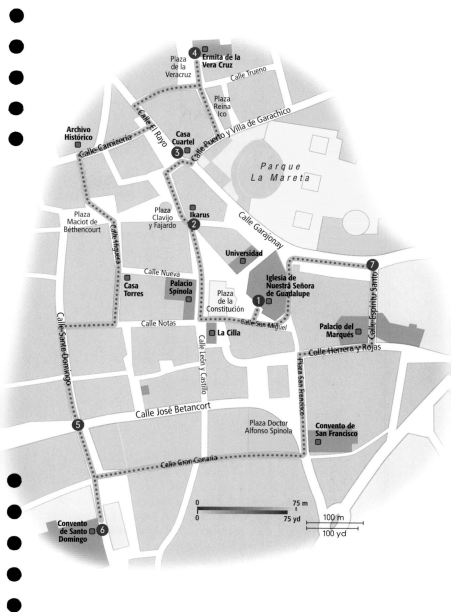

Ever-popular: The Sunday market in Teguise

While you're on the Plaza de la Constitución, Teguise's main square, have a look at the Caja Canarias, a sturdy stone house dating from 1680. Formerly known as La Cilla ("the tithe barn"), it was used in medieval times to store a tax – amounting to one tenth of all the island's crops – that was given to the church. The Palacio Spínola opposite, built between 1730 and 1780 (p. 52), is now home to the Timple Museum.

The Malvasia shop is located in another 17th-century house in the north-west corner of the square. Look out for the wooden cross next door: There are fourteen of these dotted around the town to mark out the Stations of the Cross. They're used in the *Semana Santa* (Holy Week) procession at Easter time.

2–3

Enter the beautiful square of Plaza 18 de Julio and see the statue of a lady carrying a pitcher of water. Examine the handsome row of buildings on the right-hand side of the square (which becomes Plaza Clavijo y Fajardo). The one occupied by Ikarus is about 250 years old and was once home to the Justice of the Peace. It has been superbly restored by the current owners and plays host to a restaurant today.

La Bodeguita del Medio next door once functioned as a mortuary – very different from its current function as a lively tapas bar (p. 73).

Its neighbour, <u>Galeria La Villa</u>, is one of the few old houses in the town to have retained its central patio area. You can go right inside past the Moroccan shop that now occupies the front.

The big two-storey house directly opposite was built in the early 1700s. A former building on the site housed the town's first hospital (Hospital del Espíritu Santo; established 1473).

3–4

In the next square, the typical 18th-century Canarian house, painted white with a dark wooden balcony, is known as the <u>Casa Cuartel</u> (Barracks). In front of it, turn right along Calle

Those looking for scarves and other fashion accessories will discover a lot of possibilities at the Sunday market.

Puerto y Villa de Garachico, then left into Plaza Reina Ico. Straight ahead is the simple chapel of the <u>Ermita de la Vera Cruz</u>, founded in 1841. It holds a statue of Christ which came from Portugal in the 17th century. Unfortunately, it is rarely open to the public, though you may be able to get a key if you ask next door at the Escuela de Artesanía (Artisan's School).

4–5

Take Calle Dr Alfonso -Spínola and turn left into Calle el Rayo, then first right into Calle Carniceria, the street which once housed the town's butchers.

On the right-hand side are the town archives, the <u>Archivo Histórico</u>, set in an 18th-century building. If you speak a little Spanish they will be only too pleased to answer any queries you may have about the town's history. Turn into Calle Correo and cross Plaza Maciot de Béthencourt into Calle Higuera.

The most eye-catching building in the alley is the <u>Casa Torres</u>, a splendid 18th-century house with carved wooden shutters. At the end of Calle Higuera, turn right into Calle Notas to find a charming former cinema. It's home to Emporium Antiques today. On the corner just past here, turn left into the rather quiet Calle Santo Domingo. At the end, cross the Calle José Betancort – the town's narrow main street that sees more traffic than anywhere else in Teguise – before going straight on and walking down the wide Calle Santo Domingo.

5–6

Part of the square on the left-hand side has been freshly designed and somewhat enhanced with a white entrance arch. The building behind is the Casa Spínola, another property owned by the town's wealthiest family. It once belonged to the Dominican Order whose former monastery is just across the street. The <u>Convento de Santo Domingo</u> (p. 53), built in the 17th century, is now used as a modern art gallery. The building next door is now the town hall. Have a look inside and you will see that it's retained the original cloister arcade.

6–7

Retrace your steps and turn into Calle Gran Canaria. Directly ahead, the Castillo de Santa Bárbara (p. 54) sits high on the hill in the distance. Calle Gran Canaria ends at the Convento de San Francisco, now home to the Museo de Arte Sacro (p. 54). Continue left past the church and turn right into Calle Herrera y Rojas. The Palacio del Marqués, on the left, is the oldest house in Teguise and it has an exquisite garden which is now the Patio del Vino, open for refreshments (p. 54 and 73).

The Calle Espíritu Santo turns left behind the Palacio del Marqués. The municipal theatre or Teatrillo ("Little Theatre") stands right on the corner. It occupies the nave of the old church of Espíritu Santo, which was built in 1730 and has been a theatre since 1825.

Calle Espíritu Santo leads to the Parque La Mareta, a wide, open space that is the centrepiece of the Sunday market. It was formerly a 9m/29.5ft deep (40m/131ft diameter) tank that provided the city with drinking water.

The Castillo de Santa Bárbara provides a spectacular view of Teguise.

7–1

Turn left, take the steps and turn left again into Callejón de la Sangre at the rear of the church. It takes its name (Street of Blood) from the 16th century when pirate raids were frequent, and in 1586 many townsfolk were slaughtered here. Keep to the right and you are back in the Plaza de la Constitución in front of the church.

INSIDER TIP The rustic café-Bar **Tahona** (p. 73) near the Convento de Santo Domingo has a charming courtyard which invites you to linger.

North

What?	Drive
When?	Whenever you feel like getting to know the north of the island better
Distance	58km (36mi)
Time	about 6 hours
Start/End	Taro de Tahíche (Fundación César Manrique roundabout) ✛ 181 E3

This full-day drive will show you the best of north and central Lanzarote. The roads are fast and straight in the north – only a few of the roads get a little bumpy. The trip takes in a fantastic mountain panorama and beautiful views of the sea.

This tour of the north shows that Lanzarote has much more in the way of spectacular scenery that just its Fire Mountains. The north is also indelibly stamped by the hand of the great Lanzarote artist César Manrique, and if you haven't already got the lowdown on him then it's a good idea to visit the Fundación César Manrique (p. 58) right at the start of the tour. This would make it a long day out, so if you can do it on another occasion it may be better – because to visit Manrique's home you need time.

1–2

The roundabout we begin from is marked by a huge silver wind mobile, designed by César Manrique. Head north on the LZ10 towards Teguise. Tahíche and neighbouring Nazaret are two of the island's more fashionable places to live, as you can see from some of the many small properties just off the roadside. Continue on to Teguise with excellent views of the countryside. Ahead of you to the right, high above Teguise, stands the Castillo de Santa Bárbara (p. 54). If you set off early and have enough time, spend a while visiting the town. Otherwise, just stop off here for a quick coffee and come back again another day to discover what Teguise has to offer.

Mirador del Río

LZ-202

Las Rositas
Yé **5**
LZ-203

Guinate
609 m
▲Monte
Corona
Los Molinos

LZ-201

LZ-201
LZ-204

Máguez
LZ-205

Las Cuevas

Haría **4**
Boca Tiesto

LZ-10

Mirador de Haría
LZ-206
*Peñas del
Chache*
▲
671 m
**Mirador de
los Helechos**
Tabayesco

Arrieta

LZ-10

3 **Ermita de
las Nieves**

LZ-1

**Parque
Eólico**

El Cangrejo

Mala

Los Valles

2

6
**Jardín
de Cactus**

LZ-405

El Mojón
Guatiza

Teguise
LZ-404
7

**Castillo de
Santa Bárbara**
Teseguite

3 km

Nazaret

2 mi

Urbanización
Oasis de Nazaret

LZ-10

LZ-1

Las Cabreras

Tahiche

LZ-34

**Fundación
César Manrique** **1**

LZ-1

Continue on the LZ10 which begins to climb and wind. Los Valles is a very well-tended pretty little village. It sits on the edge of a basin and the fields are cultivated into large squares, giving a very neat and geometric feel to the whole landscape. Traditional low houses with small windows, women in the fields wearing traditional bonnets *(sombreras)*, and old men wearing black felt hats or cloth trilbies complete a very rural bygone scene. You can take it all in from the Mirador de los Valles.

2–3

Continue for another 3km (2mi) or so, then turn off right to Parque Eólico. Here you'll find the huge wind turbines that you may have seen from elsewhere on the island. You're not allowed to enter the Parque Eólico, but the complex, which began operating in 1993, can be admired from outside. It's one of the largest wind farms in the Canaries. You can see right down to the coast near Arrecife from here.

For great views of the opposite coast, turn off left after another 1km (0.5mi) to the Ermita de las Nieves (Hermitage of the Snows). Snow is rather unlikely but it may be blowing a gale. Below lies the beach of Famara (p. 69), with the regular shaped roofs of its holiday homes creating quite a striking pattern. To the right looms the Risco de Famara (Famara cliffs) and beyond are Lanzarote's northern islands. The military installations at Peñas del Chache are out of bounds, which is a shame as they occupy the island's highest point (671m/2,201ft). Return to the main road and head out towards Haría.

3–4

From here it's downhill all the way to Haría, and it is a spectacular descent with two *miradores* (lookout points) along the way. The first is Mirador los Helechos, offering an excellent panorama due north to "the Valley of a Thousand Palms" and due east to the fishing village of Arrieta, which comes later on this trip. There is a restaurant here that is overpriced and often overrun by coach parties. The second lookout point, the Mirador de Haría, provides an excellent view into the town.

Haría is a beautiful little town (p. 65) that's spread out in a wide valley. It's best on a Saturday when craftspeople from all over the island gather to exhibit their wares. Leave your car in the car park outside El Cortijo de Haría restaurant (p. 73). This is a good place to eat and the centre of the village is literally just around the corner.

Haría's palm tree-studded valley looks like a fertile, green oasis.

4-5

After you've had a look round Haría, head to the Mirador del Río on the LZ201, which passes through the neat little village of Máguez. Just before Yé, the LZ202 forks off left to the Mirador del Río. This, the mother of all *miradores*, is a truly brilliant creation by César Manrique (p. 18). The view is breathtaking and the building – which comes complete with giant panoramic windows – is architecturally fascinating. Next, pass Yé and head to the south. The landscape is now dominated by the mighty Monte Corona, the tallest volcano on the island at 609m (1,998ft). Its debris, the Malpaís de la Corona, covers this whole north-west corner of the island. Beneath it lie two of the island's finest tourist attractions, Jameos del Agua (p. 55) and the Cueva de los Verdes (p. 61).

5–6

You'll see more and more fantastic coastal views as you head into the valley. Continue your descent, which eventually meets the coast at Arrieta. Turn right at the roundabout marked by a César Manrique wind mobile if you want to visit one of the town's fish restaurants, otherwise stay on the main road (now the LZ1) heading towards Arrecife.

Do you wish to get to the top? Then follow the road to Mirador del Rio.

6–1

A few kilometres past Guatiza, a village surrounded by opuntias and home to the Jardín de Cactus (p. 63), a garden which is well worth seeing, you reach Tahíche. That is where you turn left to get back to the start point of the excursion.

7 Optional Extension

If you're in no hurry to get home, take the next right to Teseguite when you rejoin the LZ1 south of the Jardín de Cactus. You'll almost immediately come across some strangely shaped rock formations on both sides of the road. Thanks to the combined effects of quarrying and the wind, the rock has formed isolated columns and blocks the size of boats. Some rocks have holes where the soft stone has eroded away. In Teseguite you'll find Arte Cerámica, one of the island's best and friendliest art galleries. The road emerges onto the LZ10 just north of Teguise. In Teguise, you can round off the day in one of the many good restaurants (p. 72f.).

INSIDER TIP As you drive along, you will see a number of restaurants and cafés that would make a good place to stop, including for instance the restaurant **Mirador de los Valles** or the café in **Jardín de Cactus** (p. 64).

South

What?	Drive
When?	Whenever you feel like following the winding roads
Distance	57km (35mi)
Time	about 6 hours
Star/End	Mácher roundabout (LZ2) ✛ 167 E3

This drive through some of Lanzarote's most beautiful and timeless scenery will show you both natural and man-made wonders. The final leg, through the vineyards of La Geria, is quite extraordinary. Like its wines, this is a landscape to be savoured in a leisurely manner.

1–2

The tour begins north of Puerto de la Cruz at the big Mácher roundabout. Drive towards Yaiza on the LZ2 with its view of the Ajaches Mountains, and turn off left after 7km (4.3mi) shortly after the petrol station towards Femés. You first drive through the pretty little hamlet of <u>Las Casitas de Femés</u>

Neat village churches like this one in Uga can be found all over the island.

where you should keep an eye out for the very last house on the right-hand side. Astonishingly, in addition to its display of nautical paraphernalia, it also has a small US attack helicopter parked in its front garden. In winter the landscape around here is very green, and the fields are reminiscent of alpine meadows. The road continues to climb and reaches

its zenith at the volcanic peak of Atalaya de Femés at 608m 1,995ft). Sitting in a saddle of the mountain, the little village of Femés looks right down to Playa Blanca, the Isla de Lobos and Fuerteventura. The church here, the Ermita San Marcial del Rubicón, was founded in the 15th century and was one of the first on the island. It was destroyed in the 16th century by pirates, and the current church dates from 1733 (open only for weekend masses). San Marcial is the island patron saint and the Plain of El Rubicón lies below you. It was here that the island conqueror Jean de Béthencourt landed in the summer of 1402 and made a peace pact with the last of the island's Guanche kings, Guadarfía. Continue down to Playa Blanca and stop for a coffee on the seafront.

2–3

Return north on the main road, but at the first roundabout, instead of taking the main LZ2 road, take the LZ701, which runs parallel to it. After 8km (5mi) you can pull over to the left and enjoy the view over the Salinas de Janubio salt pans (p. 123). Alternatively, wait until you have just passed the front of the salt pans and pull in on your left at the *mirador* restaurant where you can dine or have a drink right next to picture windows overlooking the salt pans.

Keep on the same road and after 1.4km (1mi) you come to a black sand beach (no swimming here) where you will sometimes find the locals looking for limpets.

A green crater lake set against a dark sand beach: the Charco de los Clicos

Keep following the road around the shoreline, and take a break to explore the grottoes of Los Hervideros (p. 122). As you drive on past here the Montaña Bermeja (Purple Mountain) is a curious sight with its bright purples and orange hues, quite out of place in the almost monotone black landscape.

As you get closer to El Golfo a bizarre profile of jagged, torn rock looms directly ahead of you. Take the short detour left to follow the Charco de los Clicos sign to see the striated rocks here and to enjoy the view of the beach from this angle.

Return to your car and then drive round the corner, following the El Golfo sign to the village itself and the cliff path that gives the best view of its famous lagoon (p. 122).

3–4

Return the way you came, out of El Golfo, and continue straight ahead at the roundabout through the centre of Yaiza, one of Lanzarote's best-kept villages (p. 119). Look left at the village's eastern end to see the unusual pink façade of the Finca de las Salinas, once one of the island's best rural hotels. A windmill just to the left of the roundabout has been truncated and converted into a learning centre by the island government. Go straight ahead on the LZ2 back towards Arrecife, with the village of Uga – home to the pleasant Bodega Uga – on your left. Uga is most famous for its popular Ahumadería (smokehouse) and shop, which provides much of the island with smoked salmon (p. 127). Turn left onto the LZ30. This road climbs and gives an excellent view back down to Uga on the left. The large open circular area is the old *mareta* (reservoir/water tank).

4–5

The LZ30 is Lanzarote's most picturesque and most memorable road, cutting through the heart of La Geria (p. 116) and affords fabulous views of volcanoes and vineyards. To the left, the mountains of Timanfaya National Park provide an epic backdrop to the surreal sight of a thousand horseshoe-shaped vine shelters.

Several Bodegas lie along the road. The first is the Bodega La Geria, which is well worth a visit (p. 116). Continue another 100m (110yds) and look for a small track to the right with the sign of a knife and fork. This leads to the Bodega El Chupadero which boasts a charming little wine bar (p. 117).

Back on the main road the next bodega is Antonio Suarez. After another 2–3km (1–2mi) turn right towards La Asomada.

Very merry! The wine cellar of Bodega Rubicón in Yaiza is full of barrelled treasures.

5–1

Pass through La Asomada back to the Mácher roundabout on the main LZ2 road.

INSIDER TIP If it's lunchtime you won't get a fresher meal of fish than at **El Golfo** (p. 122), but you may prefer to wait until you get to **Yaiza** to eat in a country restaurant (p. 119).

As if one beautiful island were not enough, Lanzarote offers you the opportunity to take day trips and discover the neighbouring islands. How about a little bike tour of La Graciosa for example? The boat will take you there.

Practicalities

This is where you'll find important information prior to your trip, such as the best means of travel and other tips.

Pages 166–176

BEFORE YOU GO

Advance Information
Websites
www.holaislascanarias.com
The Canarian government's official "Welcome website" provides a short introduction to all the Canarian islands.

www.turismolanzarote.com
On this page, the *Cabildo* (island government) provides information about the most important sights.

www.cactlanzarote.com
Here you will find the current opening times and admission fees to the tourist centres operated by the island government.

www.gazettelanzarote.com
the website of *Lanzarote Gazette*, an English-language weekly magazine.

Spanish Tourist Offices
6th floor, 64 North Row
W1K 7DE London
tel: +44 020 73 17 20 11
www.spain.info/en_GB

Callaghan House, 13-16 Dame Street
D02 HX67 Dublin
+353 016 350 200
www.spain.info/en

2 Bloor Street West, Suite 3402
4W 3E2 Toronto-Ontario
tel: +1-416-961-4079
www.spain.info/en

60 East 42nd Street
Suite 5300 (53rd Floor)
New York, NY 10065-0039
tel: +1-212-265-8822
www.spain.info/en_US/

Consulates and Embassies
British Consulate
Calle Luis Morote, 6–3°
35007 Las Palmas, Islas Canarias, Spain
tel: +34 928 262 508
www.gov.uk/world

U. S. Consulate
Edificio ARCA, C/ Los Martínez Escobar 3, Oficina 7, 35007 Las Palmas
Islas Canarias, Spain
tel: +34 928 271 259
https://es.usembassy.gov

Consulate of Ireland
Calle León y Castillo, 195
35004 Las Palmas, Islas Canarias, Spain
tel: +34 928 297 728
www.dfa.ie/irish-embassy/spain

Embassy of Australia
Torre Espacio, Paseo de la Castellana, 259D
28046 Madrid, Spain
tel: +34 913 536 600
https://spain.embassy.gov.au

Canadian Embassy
Torre Espacio, Paseo de la Castellana, 259D
28046 Madrid, Spain
tel: +34 913 828 400
www.canadainternational.gc.ca/spain-espagne/

Currency & Foreign Exchange
As in the rest of Spain, the Canary Islands have adopted the euro. Notes are in denominations of 5, 10, 20, 50, 100, 200, 500; coins come in 1, 2, 5, 10, 20 and 50 cents and 1 and 2 euros. Major **credit cards** are widely accepted in the resorts, but don't rely on these elsewhere.

Health
Insurance: Citizens of the EU and certain other countries receive free medical treatment in Spain with the relevant documentation, although private medical insurance is still advised and is essential for all other visitors. Prescription and non-prescription **drugs** and medicines are available from pharmacies, usually distinguished by a large green cross. Outside normal hours, a notice on the door of each pharmacy should give the address of the nearest duty pharmacist.

International Dialling Codes
dial 00 followed by:

UK:	44	USA:	1
Ireland:	353	Lanzarote:	34

Emergency Numbers

Police (Policía Nacional:	☎ 112
Fire (Bomberos):	☎ 112
Ambulance (Ambulancia):	☎ 112

National Holidays

1 Jan	New Year's Day
6 Jan	Epiphany
Mar/Apr	Good Friday
1 May	Labour Day
30 May	Canary Islands' Day
15 Aug	Assumption of the Virgin
12 Oct	Hispanic Day
1 Nov	All Saints' Day
6 Dec	Constitution Day
8 Dec	Feast of the Immaculate Conception
25 Dec	Christmas Day

Staying in Touch
Post
The state post offices are generally open from Mon–Fri 9am–2pm, Sat 9am–1pm. Beside the state-run postal service *Correos,* there are also private service providers on the Canaries with their own stamps (*sellos*) and letterboxes. It is therefore important to make sure you use the right letter box when you send your postcards. State letter boxes are yellow and often have a slot marked *extranjeros* for mail abroad. A postcard to the UK or northern Europe will usually take about 7–10 days.

Telephones
Mobile/cell phones (*móvil*) will automatically choose the appropriate partner network when you arrive. Since 2017 roaming charges are not due under a safeguard (fair use) limit. Lanzarote's network is very well developed.

Internet Access
Many hotels provide Wi-Fi for their guests, but the service is not always free of charge. You can usually surf free of charge in many cafés and restaurants. Look at the entrance for the "WiFi" sign and, where applicable, ask for the password (*clave, contraseña*).

Time
Unlike the rest of Spain, the Canary Islands observe Greenwich Mean Time (GMT). Summer time (GMT+1) operates from the last Sunday in March to the last Sunday in October

Travel Documents
Travellers need a passport. National driving licences and motor vehicle registration certificates are recognised. Dogs and cats travelling from the EU need an EU Pet Passport as well as a microchip with their identification number. At least 30 days need to have passed since the rabies vaccination, and not more than a year.

If your pet is travelling from outside the EU, for example USA, Canada, or Australia, the same rules apply as above, and a licensed vet must also complete a non-commercial EU health certificate for the Canary Islands within ten days of your travel date.

When to Go
Lanzarote's subtropical, well-balanced climate means that it is an **all-year-round travel destination**, and even in the coolest months of the year in January and February you can still bathe in the sea. The peak season is the winter, especially Christmas, but the Easter period is also very popular.

GETTING THERE

By Air
There are numerous charter flights throughout the year from London and other European cities. If you can get a cheap flight to Fuerteventura, but not Lanzarote, do so then take a ferry (see below) from Corralejo to Puerto del Carmen or Playa Blanca.

Airport Connections
Bus line 22 connects the airport with Arrecife (journey time, about 10 mins; the bus leaves approx. every 30 mins), there are good connections to Costa Teguise.
Line 161 heads to Puerto del Carmen (10–15 mins) and Playa Blanca (40 mins) every 30 mins. The services are more limited on Sundays and public holidays. https://arrecifebus.com/index.php?lang=en.

By Boat

Once a week there is a car ferry from Cádiz to Lanzarote; the journey takes two days. The passage is relatively expensive and only really of any interest to people planning to spend an extended period on the island and keen to take their own car along.

GETTING AROUND

Buses

Island buses (*guaguas*) travel to most places on Lanzarote. **Arrecife Bus** (www.arrecife bus.com) offers a dense network of buses between the main towns, but there are few to no buses to the smaller and more remote places. Timetables are available at the large bus stations and tourist offices. Frequent travellers should buy a Bono Bus card to obtain discounts of up to 50% on normal tickets. The buses are very punctual.

Taxis

Taxi drivers are obliged to switch the taxi-meter on. The trip from the airport to Puerto del Carmen costs about 22 euros, and to Playa Blanca about 45 euros.

Car Hire

Compared with prices in Central Europe, car hire rates on Lanzarote are quite reasonable. Depending on the supplier and the hire time, you pay between 20 and 30 euros a day for basic models. Owing to the lower taxation on petrol here, filling up is also much cheaper than on the mainland.

Regardless of whether you book from home, at one of the international car hire companies or at a local rental company on Lanzarote, mileage is never limited. The major **car hire companies** (Avis, Europcar, Hertz...) have offices at the airport, but lots of local com-panies (the largest is Cicar, www.cicar.com), have offices directly in the arrival hall. Find out what is included in the **insurance cover** and how high your excess is in the case of damage. One of the few providers who offer full insurance without excess is Sunny Cars (www.sunnycars.de). As the driver you have to be at least 21 years old and in possession of a credit card.

The roads are in a good to very good condition. The high level of traffic around Arrecife and Puerto del Carmen often results in traffic jams. Parking space is limited, especially in Arrecife and Puerto del Carmen.

Speed limits are 90kph (56mph) on the open road, 100kph on dual carriageways and motorways, and 40kph (25mph) in urban areas.

Drive on the right-hand side of the road. The legal **alcohol limit** is 50mg alcohol per 100ml blood. Fines, especially for speeding, are very high in Spain and col-lection agencies make sure that they are paid, even from abroad.

Boat

The harbours of **Puerto Calero** and **Playa Blanca** offer extended excursions along the east and south coasts. There is a fantastic boat trip from Órzola to Caleta del Sebo on **La Graciosa**.

Boats shuttle to and from the neighbouring island every day. The crossing takes 20 min-utes (www.biosferaexpress.com and www.lineasromero.com). The ferry from Playa Blanca to Corralejo (Fuerteventura) does not need much longer; business is shared between the Naviera Armas (www.navieraarmas.com) and Fred Olsen (www.fredolsen.es) shipping companies.

If you want wheels on Fuerteventura, then arrange for your hire car to be brought to the Corralejo harbour. Most hire companies will not allow cars to be taken from one island to another. One exception is the Canarian company Cicar (www.cicar.com), as long as the car is brought back to the island on which it was hired.

Island Hopping

First-time visitors to the Canary islands can fit in two or three islands on one holi-day. Many tour operators offer holidays on more than one island. You can depend on a very good network of flight and ferry connections. Fuerteventura makes a very nice day trip (see above). It is best to travel to the other Canary Islands by air; the Iberia daughter Binter flies several times a day to Gran Canaria and Tenerife, from which there are connecting flights to La Palma, La Gomera and El Hierro (www.bintercanarias.com).

ACCOMMODATION

From a middle-class hotel to a luxury resort with a pool, there is an enormous choice of hotels, apartment complexes and holiday homes.

Most people book a package deal through a travel agent, opting for just breakfast, half-board or all-inclusive. Self-caterers and individual travellers, who wish to organise their holiday independently can find lots of accommodation options on Internet portals (e.g. www.booking.com). As long as you don't need the beach on your doorstep, plenty of pretty country hotels and fincas await further inland. Regardless of whether you want a package or individual solution, make sure you book in good time if you wish to go during the peak season in winter (especially over Christmas).

Prices
Expect to pay per double room, per night (breakfast not included):

€	under €60
€€	€60–€100
€€€	€100–€150
€€€€	over €150

FOOD AND DRINK

Classic Canarian cuisine may not become your favourite food – it is hearty country-style cooking, based on what the land and waters provide – but it is part of the cultural experience and you should give it a try.

You can find Canarian food in many country restaurants, while in the tourist centres you will find that the cuisine tends to be of a more Spanish and international character. As yet, Lanzarote cannot boast any star-studded gourmet restaurants, but the island does have a large selection of good hotel and excursion restaurants.

Prices
Expect to pay for a main course, excluding drinks and service:

€	under €15
€€	€15–€25
€€€	€25–€30
€€€€	over €30

Regional Fish and Meat Dishes
Hearty soups and casseroles are an essential part of Canarian cooking. *Sancocho* and *zarzuela*, both hearty fish stews, have earned a certain acclaim. Meat and fish are generally *a la plancha*, grilled, and served with *papas arrugadas*, potatoes in a salt crust, and a *mojo picón* or *moja verde* sauce. The green *mojo* accompanies fish and the red *mojo* meat. Almost all of the meat is imported; besides beef steaks and pork chops, you will also find lamb and marinated rabbit on the menu; goat meat does tend to be from the island. **Vegetarian food** is served in Asian and Italian restaurants as well as in some of the trendier restaurants in Teguise among other places. The Canarian side dish *gofio*, a flour made grinding toasted barley, maize or wheat, was a staple food even at the time of the Guanches.

Specialities from the Spanish Mainland
Although the island has been Spanish for over half a century, the cuisine from the mainland has only started to establish itself in the last few decades. Naturally, every tapas bar will have serrano ham and tortillas. In these stand-up bars, you can also try tuna fish salad, fish croquettes, meatballs and goat's cheese with olives. And, of course, there is also the Spanish national dish, paella.

Café solo, Carajillo, Sangria & Co.
Coffee culture on the islands has developed in the same way as the Canarian cuisine. While just 10–15 years ago, it was difficult to get anything other than the traditional *café solo* (the Spanish espresso) and the *café con leche* (milk coffee), Cappuccino and Latte macchiato are now matter of course. *Barraquito* (an expresso layered with condensed milk and frothy milk and *carajillo* (espresso with a shot of brandy)

are another two of the Spanish-Canarian coffee variations on offer.

Although Lanzarote has a long wine-making history, the locals often prefer to drink a fresh draft beer with their meal. The local brands are Tropical (from Gran Canaria) and Dorada (from Tenerife), and you order either a *caña* (small glass) or a *jarra* (big glass).

Lanzarote's most well-known wine comes from the La Geria region; this wine together with the produce of the smaller wine-growing areas in San Bartolomé, Tinajo and Haría, bears a protected *Denominación de Origen*, designation of origin. Among the market leaders are the El Grifo and La Geria bodegas, both of which press acceptable table wines which can be found on the menus in many restaurants. Wine connoisseurs, however, usually opt for the imports from the Spanish mainland. The Sangria though tastes good almost everywhere.

Mealtimes and Tipping

People generally eat later than in Central Europe. Lunchtime is from around 1pm and dinner from 9pm. Hotels and tourist restaurants have adapted to the needs of their guests however and serve dinner from 7pm. Many places offer a good value *menú del día*: It consists of three very average courses with bread and a drink. VAT and service are included in the price, but a small tip of around 5% is still expected. It is important to remember that you do not round up the amount when paying or give the tip directly to the waiter or waitress. Leave the tip on the plate on which you received the change.

SHOPPING

In the tourist centres, there are *Centros comerciales* (shopping centres) on almost every corner, and there you will find supermarkets, boutiques and restaurants all under one roof. The offer is mainly focused on the requirements of the tourists.

The largest shopping centre on the island is Deiland on the road between Arrecife and Puerto del Carmen. It is mainly the Lanzaroteños who come here to stock up on groceries and everyday items (www.deilandplaza.com). The handicraft markets held in in Puerto del Carmen (Sat), Costa Teguise (Wed), Marina Rubicón (Wed, Sat) and Haría (Sat) are of interest. Here you can discover attractive souvenirs between the bric-a-brac and kitsch. The Sunday market in Teguise is also a tourist magnet.

Island Wares

Typical souvenirs are culinary objects. Top of the list: a little glass of *mojo* sauce, a package of *gofio* or a jar of the cactus jam produced on the island. You can even take vacuum-packed goat's cheese on the plane, one of the best comes from the Quesería El Faro and is available in many supermarkets. Wine connoisseurs will find a selection of island wines along the La Geria wine route. You can buy skin care products and other aloe vera products directly from the aloe vera farm (on the LZ 204).

Craft articles are very popular, and they can be found on the markets and in many boutiques and souvenir shops. These include earthenware, wickerwork and handicraft, as well as fashion jewellery made of olivine (also called peridot), an olive-green mineral found in lava stone. The semi-precious stones are imported and made into among other things pendants, rings and ear clips by local gold- and silversmiths. You are not allowed to take any stones with streaks of olivine you find on Lanzarote, or any other stones for that matter, off the island.

Opening Times

Most shops are open Mon–Sat from around 9–1 and 4–8. It is only in the tourist centres that the shops open all day without a lunchtime break, often staying open until 10pm and also opening on Sat and Sun.

Low Tax Rate

Compared with other European countries, including the Spanish mainland, VAT is very low. The sum passed on to the customer varies tremendously from one shop to another. Alcoholic drinks and cigarettes, however, are generally cheaper. You also get a better rate for perfume and cosmetics.

ENTERTAINMENT

You can find interesting information about Lanzarote, leisure tips and an event calendar in the island magazine *Lanzarote37* (www.lanzarote37.net), which is published every four weeks. Tourist centres provide details of fiestas, sports programmes and events, and the island authorities provide information on www.culturalanzarote.com about what is on.

Nightlife

Bars and clubs: Puerto del Carmen is the nightlife capital of the island. Music bars and discos are mainly centred around the old harbour and along the Avenida de las Playas. Costa Teguise is the second liveliest place, with the focus centring around the Pueblo Marinero. In Puerto Calera people meet to unwind in the Buda Bar at the marina. If you want to party with the locals: at the weekends, the nightlife in Arrecife mainly buzzes around the Gran Hotel. Live musicians (jazz etc) often perform by the pool bar at the Gran Hotel itself.

Classical and Modern

The holiday resorts are not famous for their heady cultural delights, but one highlight is the International Music Festival of The Canary Islands in January and February (www.festival decanarias.com). This series of classical concerts is held in collaboration with the neighbouring islands, venues on Lanzarote being i. a. Los Jameos del Agua, the Teatro Municipal in San Bartolomé and the Teatro El Salinero in Arrecife.

Sports

The large **La Santa** hotel on the west coast is an absolute haven for active people: Guests to the resort can participate in around thirty varieties of sport. Cycling, aerobics and athletics are the house specialities (www.club lasanta.com). In the holiday resorts on the coast, almost everything naturally focuses on **water sports**. Here you can **swim**, **snorkel** and go out on **boat excursions**. The best **diving resorts** are on the east coast around Puerto del Carmen and on the south coast to the east of Playa Blanca, the main attrac-

tion there being the Underwater Museum (Playa Blanca). **Surfing and kiteboarding** are very popular, particularly at Playa de las Cucharas (**Costa Teguise**) and around Famara on the west coast, where the conditions are world class. Besides the water activities, **hiking** through the volcanic countryside has also become very popular. The paths and trails may not be on a par with hiking islands such as Tenerife and La Palma, but there are still some very attractive and well-marked routes available. Alternatively, join a guided trek. **Hiking and trekking tours** through the Parque Nacional de Timanfaya are offered from the local *Centro de Visitantes*. Check out such sites as www.blackstonetreks.com for more information about guided island walks. The conditions are also ideal for **cyclists**. You can rent **mountain bikes**, **racing bikes** and now increasingly **E-bikes** from all holiday centres. You'll find **golf courses** by Costa Teguise (tel: 928 590 512, www.lanzarote-golf. com) and north-east of Puerto del Carmen (tel: 928 514 050, www.lanzarotegolfresort.com). Both of these links boast eighteen holes.

EVENTS CALENDAR

January/February

Cabalgata de Los Reyes: Cavalcade of the Magi (Parade of the Three Wise Men) on 5–6 January.

Festival de Música de Canarias: a big classical music festival organised in collaboration with the neighbouring islands.

Carnaval: highlights of the street carnivals are in Arrecife the selection of the carnival queen, the street parade on Easter Monday and El Entierro de la Sardina The Burial of the Sardine) on Ash Wednesday. Check out www.lanzarote.com/carnival for dates

May/June

Ironman Lanzarote: The Triathlon organised by the Sporthotel La Santa is Lanzarote's biggest sport event.

Corpus Christi: Celebrations are held all over the island but the finest sights are in Arrecife and in Teguise, where beautiful flower-patterned carpets of coloured salt are created around the main church.

July/August
Fiestas de la Virgen del Carmen: Homage is paid to the patron saint of fishermen in many coastal towns on 16 July.
Fiestas de San Ginés: In Arrecife one of the largest island festivals is in honour of the city's patron saint, San Ginés.

September
Fiesta de la Virgen de los Dolores: A traditional pilgrimage on 15 September is led to the parish church in Mancha Blanca to give thanks for salvation from the eruptions of 1824.

December
Rancho de Pascua: Christmas Eve starts off in the parish church of Teguise with a mass and a street festival.

USEFUL WORDS AND PHRASES

Spanish (*español*), also known as Castilian (*castellano*) to distinguish it from other tongues spoken in Spain, is the language of the Canary Islands. The islanders' version has a sing-song quality more reminiscent of the Spanish spoken in Latin America than the mainland.

Greetings and Common Words

Do you speak English?	**¿Habla inglés?**
I don't understand	**No entiendo**
I don't speak Spanish	**No hablo español**
Yes/no	**Sí/no**
OK	**Vale/de acuerdo**
Please	**Por favor**
Thank you (very much)	**(Muchas) gracias**
You're welcome	**De nada**
Hello/goodbye	**Hola/adiós**
Good morning	**Buenos días**
Good afternoon/ evening	**Buenas tardes**
Good night	**Buenas noches**
How are you?	**¿Qué tal?**
Excuse me	**Perdón**
How much is this?	**¿Cuánto vale?**
I'd like...	**Quisiera/me gustaría**

Emergency!

Help!	**¡Socorro!/¡Ayuda!**
Could you help me please?	**¿Podría ayudarme por favor?**
Could you call a doctor please?	**¿Podría llamar a un médico por favor?**

Directions and Travelling

Aeroplane	**Avión**
Airport	**Aeropuerto**
Car	**Coche**
Boat	**Barco**
Bus	**Autobús/guagua**
Bus stop	**Parada de autobús**
Station	**Estación**
Ticket (single/ return)	**Billete (de ida/de ida y vuelta)**
I'm lost	**Me he perdido**
Where is...?	**¿Dónde está...?**
How do I get to...? the beach the telephone the toilets	**¿Cómo llego a...?** **la playa** **el teléfono** **los servicios**
Left/right	**Izquierda/derecha**
Straight on	**Todo recto**

Accommodation

Do you have a single/double room available?	**¿Tiene una habitación individual/doble?**
With/without bath/toilet/ shower	**Con/sin baño/lavabo/ ducha**
Does that include breakfast?	**¿Incluye el desayuno?**
Could I see the room?	**¿Puedo ver la habitación?**
I'll take this room	**Cojo esta habitación**
One night	**Una noche**
Key	**Llave**
Lift	**Ascensor**
Sea views	**Vistas al mar**

Days

Today	**Hoy**
Tomorrow	**Mañana**

Yesterday	**Ayer**
Later	**Más tarde**
This week	**Esta semana**
Monday	**Lunes**
Tuesday	**Martes**
Wednesday	**Miércoles**
Thursday	**Jueves**
Friday	**Viernes**
Saturday	**Sábado**
Sunday	**Domingo**

Numbers

0	**cero**
1	**una/uno**
2	**dos**
3	**tres**
4	**cuatro**
5	**cinco**
6	**seis**
7	**siete**
8	**ocho**
9	**nueve**
10	**diez**
11	**once**
12	**doce**
13	**trece**
14	**catorce**
15	**quince**
16	**dieciséis**
17	**diecisiete**
18	**dieciocho**
19	**diecinueve**
20	**veinte**
21	**veintiuno**
22	**veintidós**
30	**treinta**
40	**cuarenta**
50	**cincuenta**
60	**sesenta**
70	**setenta**
80	**ochenta**
90	**noventa**
100	**cien**
101	**ciento uno**
110	**ciento y diez**
120	**ciento y veinte**
200	**doscientos**
300	**trescientos**
400	**cuatrocientos**
500	**quinientos**

600	**seiscientos**
700	**setecientos**
800	**ochocientos**
900	**novecientos**
1,000	**mil**
5,000	**cinco mil**

Restaurant

I'd like to book a table	**Quisiera reservar una mesa**
A table for two please	**Una mesa para dos, por favor**
Could we see the menu, please?	**¿Nos trae la carta, por favor?**
What's this?	**¿Qué es esto?**
A bottle/ glass of...	**Una botella/ copa de...**
Could I have the bill please?	**¿La cuenta, por favor?**
Service charge included	**Servicio incluido**
Waiter/waitress	**Camarero/a**
Breakfast	**Desayuno**
Lunch	**Almuerzo**
Dinner	**Cena**
Menu	**La carta**

Menu Reader

a la plancha	grilled
aceite	oil
aceituna	olive
agua	water
ajo	garlic
almendra	almond
anchoas	anchovies
arroz	rice
atún	tuna
bacalao	cod
berenjena	aubergines
bistec	steak
bocadillo	sandwich
café	coffee
calamares	squid
cangrejo	crab
carne	meat
cebolla	onion
cerdo	pork
cerezas	cherries

cerveza	beer
champiñones	mushrooms
chocolate	chocolate
chorizo	spicy sausage
chuleta	chop
conejo	rabbit
cordero	lamb
crema	cream
crudo	raw
cubierto(s)	cover (cutlery)
cuchara	spoon
cuchillo	knife
embutidos	sausages
ensalada	salad
entrante	starter
espárragos	asparagus
filete	fillet
flan	crème caramel
frambuesa	raspberry
fresa	strawberry
frito	fried
fruta	fruit
galleta	biscuit
gambas	prawns
gazpacho andaluz	gazpacho (cold soup)
guisantes	peas
habas	broad beans
helado	ice cream
hígado	liver
huevos fritos/ revueltos	fried/ scrambled eggs
jamón serrano	ham (cured)
jamón York	ham (cooked)
judías	beans
judías verdes	french beans
jugo	fruit juice
langosta	lobster
leche	milk
lechuga	lettuce
legumbres	pulses
lengua	tongue
lenguado	sole
limón	lemon
lomo de cerdo	pork tenderloin
mantequilla	butter
manzana	apple
mariscos	seafood
mejillones	mussels
melocotón	peach
melón	melon
merluza	hake

mero	sea bass
miel	honey
naranja	orange
ostra	oyster
pan	bread
papas arrugadas	Canarian-style boiled potatoes
patata	potato
patatas fritas fries	
pato	duck
pepinillo	gherkin
pepino	cucumber
pera	pear
perejil	parsley
pescado	fish
pez espada	swordfish
picante	hot/spicy
pimientos	red/green peppers
piña	pineapple
plátano	banana
plato principal	main course
pollo	chicken
postre	dessert
primer plato	first course
pulpo	octopus
queso	cheese
rape	monkfish
relleno	filled/stuffed
riñones	kidneys
salchicha	sausage
salchichón	salami
salmón	salmon
salmonete	red mullet
salsa	sauce
seco	dry
solomillo de ternera	fillet of beef
sopa	soup
té	tea
tenedor	fork
ternera	beef
tocino	bacon
tortilla española	Spanish omelette
tortilla francesa	plain omelette
trucha	trout
uva	grape
verduras	green vegetables
vino blanco	white wine
vino rosado	rosé wine
vino tinto	red wine
zanahorias	carrots
zumo	juice

Road Atlas

Key to Road Atlas

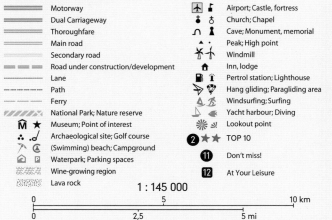

Motorway	Airport; Castle, fortress
Dual Carriageway	Church; Chapel
Thoroughfare	Cave; Monument, memorial
Main road	Peak; High point
Secondary road	Windmill
Road under construction/development	Inn, lodge
Lane	Pertrol station; Lighthouse
Path	Hang gliding; Paragliding area
Ferry	Windsurfing; Surfing
National Park; Nature reserve	Yacht harbour; Diving
Museum; Point of interest	Lookout point
Archaeological site; Golf course	TOP 10
(Swimming) beach; Campground	Don't miss!
Waterpark; Parking spaces	At Your Leisure
Wine-growing region	
Lava rock	

1 : 145 000

0	5	10 km
0	2,5	5 mi

Oceáno Atlántico

Caletón Caloco
Isla de Montaña Clara
Punta del Agua
Pla

La Gra

Caleta

Punta

Caleta

Punta de las Carreras

Monta

Punta del Pobre
Playa de la Cocina
Punta Ma

Las Bajas

Punta Guerra

El Rebolaje Machin
La Isleta
Punta Prieta
Santa Sport
La Costa
Los Risquetes
La Santa
Los Lajares
Casas de
El Melián
Casas de
la Caldera
Punta los Cuchillos
**Playa
Teneza**

Caldera Trasera
293 m
Sóo
**Ermita San Juan
Evangelista**

Bajamar

Playa de San Juan
**Playa de
Famara**

**Caleta
de Famara**
14
Urbanización
Famara

Urbanización
Vista Graciosa
Casa del Molino

Las Laderas

El Cuchillo

178

LZ-67
LZ-401
LZ-410
LZ-402
180

A

B

C

5

4

3

2

I

D Roque del Infierno o del Oeste   **E**   **F**

Caletón Oscuro
de Montaña Clara
Punta de la Camella
256 m
Punta del Agua
Punta Gorda
Montaña
Bermeja
Playa Lambra
157 m
Playa de las Conchas
Punta del Hueso

La Graciosa **17**
Pedro Barba
Agujas Chicas
257 m
Punta de Pedro Barba
Caleta del Morro de Abajo
Agujas Grandes
266 m
Punta de la Baja
Punta del Bajío
Caleta de
Pedro Barba
Caleta del Burro   Montaña del Mojón
185 m
Punta de las Carreras
La Sociedad
Punta Fariones
Montaña Amarilla   Caleta
172 m   de Sebo
Punta
Corrales
*Playa
Salinas
del Río*
El Río
Playa de la Cantería
El Embarcadero
Bahía del Salado
Playa de la Cocina   Playa Francesa   La Punta
Salinas
del Río
Batería
479 m
Mirador del Río
Orzola **16**
Caletón Blanco
Caletón Blanco
Bajo
de los Sables
Punta Marrajos
Playa del Risco
15
Pardelas Park (Las Pardelas Park)
Punta de Palo
Casas de
Bajo Risco
La Bahía
Vega
Chica
LZ-202
Cerro Llano
Las Tababitas
Punta Prieta
LZ-202
Las Rositas
Casas
La Breña
Malpaís de la Corona
3
Ye
Mirador de Guinate
Punta de Lomo Blanco   Guinate
Monte Corona
609 m
Los Molinos
LZ-21   *Caleta del Mero*
Los Helechos
581 m   LZ-201
Casas Las Escamas   *Playa Mojón Blanco*
Máguez
Las Cuevas
LZ-204
Punta Escamas
Punta Ganada
LZ-205
La Atalaya
392 m
Boca Tiesto
8
Cueva
de los Verdes
3 Jameos del Agua
Punta Usaje
El Palmar
Los Picachos
Playa La Seba
El Cortijo
Montaña Ganada
585 m
Haría
Casa Museo
César Manrique
268 m
Casas del Canto
Punta de
Mujeres
Punta Mujeres
Punta Mujeres
12
LZ-10
Las Bajas
Valle de Temisa
Tabayesco
Juguetes del Viento
Galería
de Famara
*Mirador
de Haría*
LZ-207
Arrieta
Playa de San Juan
*Playa de
Famara*
Los Helechos
Peñas del Chache
671 m
LZ-10
487 m
Playa de la Garita
*Urbanización
Famara*
Molino
Ermita de
las Nieves
Parque
Eólico
El Cangrejo
Mirador de Los Valles
Peña del Silvo
394 m
Mala
Playa del Seifío
Riscos de Famara
Risco de las Nieves
Los Arrabales
Los Loberas
Los Valles
Ermita de San José
Ermita del Val
Charco del Palo
181   F   **179**
Ermita de
11
Jardín
de Cactus
Playa de Charco del Palo

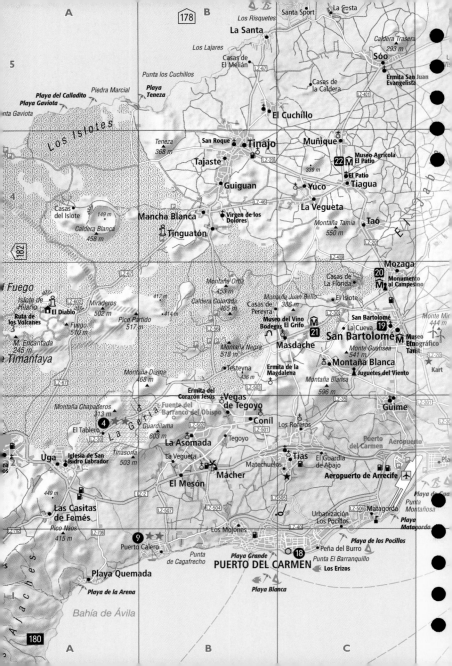

Océano

Atlántico

Playa de la Madera

Punta del Paletón

Paletón
22 m

Baja de la Piedra Dorada

Playa del Cochino

1 ★ ★

Parque Nacional

Montañas del

Los Cangrejos

Montaña Halcones
105 m

Playa del Paso

de Timanfaya

Isla
Hila

Ruta
los Vol

Punta
del Jurado

Montaña Rajada
374 m

M. E
245

**Las Casas
de El Golfo**

24 ⚑

Casas de
Juan Perdomo

de Tima

El Golfo

Montaña de la Vieja Gabriela
226 m

Playa de
Montaña Bermeja

LZ-704

23

Los Hervideros ★ **25**

LZ-703

Yaiza

LZ-2

**Nuestra Señora
de los Remedios**

LZ-701

26

Salinas de Janubio

La Hondura

Las Hoyas

Punta del Volcán

Laguna de Janubio

La Degollada

Playa de Janubio

LZ-701

**Las
Breñas**

Atalaya de Femés
608 m

LZ-702

Punta Gorda

LZ-702

**Ermita de San
Marcial de Rubicón** ✦ **Femés**

Punta Piedra Alta

**Cortijo
de la Mareta**

LZ-2

El Convento

Casas de Masión

El Rubicón

Punta Gorda
Atlante del Sol

Los Charcones ★

El Terminillo

*Hacha Grande
561 m*

Punta Ginés

Cortijo
de la Punta

El Veril Atravesado

Montaña Roja
194 m

Montaña
Baja

Las
Coloradas

Castillo
del Agua

**Castillo de
las Coloradas**

★ **Museo Atlántico**

Faro de Pechiguera ⚓
Punta de Pechiguera

**27 Playa
Blanca**

Punta Límones

Punta
de Águila

*Playa de las
Coloradas*

Playa Mujeres

6 ★

*Playas de
Papagayo*

Playa de Puerto

a Madera

Los Isl...

180

Teneza 368 m

San Roque

Tinajo

Muñique

Museo Agrícola
El Patio

22 M

LZ-30

El Patio

339 m

Tajaste

Guiguan

LZ-46

Yuco

Tiagua

La Vegueta

Taó

Mancha Blanca

Virgen de los
Dolores

Montaña Tamia
550 m

LZ-20

Casas
del Islote

149 m

Tinguatón

Caldera Blanca
458 m

1

Nacional
...s del Fuego

Montaña Ortiz
453 m

Casas de
La Florida

El Islote

20

Monumen...
al Camp...

M

Mozag

anfaya

Islote de
Hilario

El Diablo

Miraderos
502 m

LZ-602

Caldera Cojorada
465 m

417 m

Montaña Juan Bello
386 m

Casas de
Pereyra

LZ-67

Ruta de
los Volcanes

Fuego
510 m

Pico Partido
517 m

414 m

Museo del Vino
Bodegas El Grifo

La Cueva

San Bartolomé

San Bartolomé

21 M

19

4

M

...a Rajada
374 m

M. Encantada
245 m.

LZ-56

LZ-30

de Timanfaya

LZ-67

Montaña Negra
518 m

Masdache

Monte Guatisea
541 m

Montaña Blanca

Montaña Dizma
468 m

Testeyna
436 m

Ermita de la
Magdalena

Juguetes del Viento

LZ-503

Montaña Blanca
596 m

Ermita del
Corazón Jesús

Vegas
de Tegoyo

LZ-35

Güime

Montaña Chapaderos
313 m

Fuente del
Barranco del Obispo

4

La Geria

Conil

LZ-502

Los Roferos

LZ-501

Puerto
del Carmen

Aerop...

23

El Tablero

Guardilama
603 m

LZ-30

Tegoyo

Yaiza

Uga

Iglesia de San
Isidro Labrador

La Asomada

Tías

El Guardia
de Abajo

3

Nuestra Señora
de los Remedios

Tinasona
503 m

La Vegueta

Matechuelos

Aeropuerto de Arrecife

449 m

El Mesón

Mácher

LZ-505

Las Casitas
de Femés

LZ-2

LZ-507

LZ-504

Urbanización
Los Pocillos

LZ-506

Matagorda

P...

Pla...
Ma...

de Femés
8 m

Pico Naos
415 m

LZ-702

LZ-708

Los Mojones

LZ-40

Playa de los Pocillos

181

9

Puerto Calero

Punta
de Cagafrecho

Peña del Burro

Femés

18

Punta El Barranquillo

Los Erizos

Playa Quemada

Playa Grande

PUERTO DEL CARMEN

Playa de la Arena

Playa Blanca

2

Bahía de Ávila

Los Alaches

Punta Gorda

...
51 m

I

Playa de Puerto Muelas

183

D

E

F

Océano Atlántico

Los Molino

Ecomus

Cu

Parque Natural
de Betancuria

Lla
Co

Va
Sant

Mirador Morro V

Betancu

10 ★

Puerto de la Peña

FV-621

Toto

FV-30

Pájara

Montaña de la Fuente
496 m ▲

FV-605

Melindraga
619 m ▲

Cardón
691 m ▲

Tarajale

★ **Oasis Park La Laji**

32

FV-20

Parque de la Pared

Istmo de la Pared

Costa
Calma

Playa de Cofete

de Jandía

Natural

Playas de Sotavento

Risco del Paso

Macizo de Jandía

FV-2

Esquinzo

Jandía

⚓ Morro Jable

A   B   C

Isla de los Lobos
Parque Natural

Corralejo
28

Parque Natural de las Dunas de Corralejo

El Jable

El Cotillo
Castillo de Tostón
Lajares
FV-109
FV-101
FV-1
FV-10
Villaverde
Roja
312 m
La Oliva **29**

Tindaya
Caldereta

La Matila
FV-207
FV-10
Aceitunal
686 m
Puerto de Lajas
Los Molinos
FV-221
Ecomuseo de La Alcogida **M**
30
Tefía
Tetir
FV-3
Cuchillo del Cabo
Casillas del Ángel
Puerto del Rosario
FV-20
Llanos de la Concepción
FV-30
La Ampuyenta
Valle de Santa Inés
Cuchillo de Palomares
Aeropuerto de Fuerteventura (FUE)
FV-2
Mirador Morro Velosa ★
FV-416
Tegú 645 m
Triquivijate
Betancuria **10**
Antigua **31**
Cuchillete de Buenavista
FV-30
Morro Janana 670 m
FV-20
FV-50
Caleta de Fuste
FV-621
Gran Montaña 708 m
Toto
Carbón 606 m
Tiscamanita
Montaña de la Fuente 496 m
Tuineje
Pozo Negro
Malpais Grande
Pájara
FV-30
Telindraga 619 m
FV-20
FV-2
...ón ...m
Carga del Camelo
La Entallada
Fuerteventura

Gran Tarajal
FV-4
Tarajalejo
★
Oasis Park La Lajita

185

Arrecife

350 m
350 yd

186

Index

A

accommodation 71, 96, 124, 171
airports, airport services 169
air travel 169
Alegranza 70
aloe vera 11
Antigua, Fuerteventura 143
Arrecife 8, 86
  accommodation 96
  Castillo de San Gabriel 87
  Castillo de San José 88
  eating out 99
  Gran Hotel 96
  harbour 86
  Iglesia de San Ginés 87
  Museo Internacional de
    Arte Contemporáneo
    (MIAC) 88
  shopping 101
Arrieta 158, 160
  eating out 74
arrival 169
arts & crafts 172
Atalaya de Femés 163

B

Berber 21
Betancuria, Fuerteventura
  138
  cactus garden 139
  Casa Santa María 138
  Convento de San
    Buenaventura 139
  eating out 146
  Iglesia de Santa María 138
  Museo Arqueológico y
    Etnográfico 139
Béthencourt, Jean de 21
Béthencourt, Maciot de 22
boat & ferry services 69, 170
bodegas 73, 98, 101
  Bodega de Santiago 120
  Bodega El Chupadero 117,
    125, 165
  Bodega La Geria 116, 165
  Bodegas El Grifo 95, 101,
    116
bus services 170

C

cactus gardens
  Fuerteventura 139
  Lanzarote 63
Caleta del Sebo 70
Caletón Blanco, Órzola 69
camels 11, 145
  Camel Park 113
  camel rides 113, 145
Canarian cuisine 171
  gofio 29
  mojo rojo 29
  mojo verde 29
  papas arrugadas 29
  tapas 29
car hire 170
carnival 11, 38
Casa de los Volcanes 56
Casa Museo del Campesino
  94
Casa Santa María, Betancuria
  138
Castillo de San Gabriel,
  Arrecife 87
Castillo de San José, Arrecife
  88
Castillo de Santa Bárbara,
  Teguise 54
Centro de Arte Canario,
  La Oliva 143
César Manrique House 156
Charco de los Clicos 122, 164
Charco de San Ginés 88
Chinijo Archipelago 70
climate & season 24, 169
clubs 173
cochineal beetle 35
consulates & embassies 168
Convento de San Buena-
  ventura, Betancuria 139
Convento de San Francisco,
  Teguise 54
Convento de Santo Domingo,
  Teguise 54
Corralejo
  beaches 140
  eating out 146
  national park 141
  sand dunes 140, 142
Corralejo, Fuerteventura 140
Costa Teguise 68
  accommodation 71
  eating out 74
  Playa de las Cucharas 68
  shopping 74
Cueva de los Verdes 61, 159
currency 168
cycling 75, 102, 173

D

desalination plants 27
diving 75
drugs and medicines 168

E

eating out 98, 125, 146
Echadero de los Camellos 113
ecology 24
Ecomuseo de La Alcogida,
  Fuerteventura 143
El Golfo 15, 121, 122, 164, 165
  eating out 126
El Morro del Jable 69
El Rubicón 163
emergency telephone
  numbers 169
entertainment 173
Ermita de las Nieves 158
events calendar 173

F

Famara 67, 75, 158
Femés 163
festivals and events 8, 102, 173
fincas to rent 72
Fire Mountains 7
fishing 102, 127
food and drink 28, 171–
  see also: canarian cuisine
  bodegas 73, 98, 101, 116,
    120, 125, 165
  Malvasía 34, 117
foreign exchange 168
Fuerteventura 129–147
  Antigua 143
  Betancuria 138
  Corralejo 140
  eating out 146
  Ecomuseo de La Alcogida
    143
  La Oliva 143
  Oasis Park La Lajita 145
Fundación César Manrique
  20, 58, 156

G
galerías (water tunnels) 27
getting around 170
gofio 29
go karting 102
golf 173
Gran Hotel, Arrecife 96
Guanches 21
Guatiza 160

H
Haría 65
    accommodation 72
    shopping 74
Hayworth, Rita 55
health 168
hiking 16, 150, 173
history 21
horse riding 127
hot springs 122
Humboldt, Alexander von 21
Hussein, King 60, 68

I
Iglesia de San Ginés, Arrecife 87
Iglesia de Santa María, Betancuria 138
Internet access 169

J
jameos 16
Jameos del Agua 16, 55, 75, 159
Jardín de Cactus 63
juguetes de vientos 59

K
kiteboarding 75, 140, 173

L
La Asomada 165
    accommodation 97
La Caleta 69
La Geria 116, 161, 165
    accommodation 124
    eating out 125
LagOmar, restaurant 75
La Graciosa 70
La Oliva
    Centro de Arte Canario 143
La Oliva, Fuerteventura 143

Las Pardelas Park, Órzola 69
Los Hervideros 122, 164
Los Valles 158
    accommodation 71
Lucha Canaria 41

M
Mácher
    eating out 99
Magalef, Luís Ibáñez 90
malpaís 16, 112
Malvasía 34, 117
Manrique, César 7, 11, 18, 55, 58, 69, 71, 72, 94, 112, 159
markets 8, 52, 66, 74, 75, 101, 127
mealtimes 172
menu reader (phrase guide) 175
Mirador de Haría 158
Mirador del Río 69, 159
Mirador los Helechos 158
Miró, Joan 60
Montaña Bermeja 123, 164
Montaña Clara 70
Monte Corona 61, 159
Monumento al Campesino 94, 95, 101
Monumento Natural de Los Ajaches 118
Mozaga
    accommodation 98
    eating out 100
Museo Agrícola El Patio 95
Museo Arqueológico y Etnográfico, Betancuria 139
Museo Atlántico 127
Museo de la Piratería, Teguise 54
Museo del Timple, Teguise 52
Museo Internacional de Arte Contemporáneo (MIAC), Arrecife 88
music venues 102, 173

N
national holidays 169
Nazaret 156
    eating out 72
nightlife 8, 75, 102, 127, 173

O
Oasis Park La Lajita, Fuerteventura 145
opening hours 172
Opuntia 35
orchella lichen 21
Órzola 69
    Caletón Blanco 69
    eating out 73
    Las Pardelas Park 69

P
Palacio Spínola, Teguise 52
Parque Eólico 158
Parque Nacional de Timanfaya 112
Parque Natural Corralejo 141
Peñas del Chache 158
Picasso, Pablo Ruíz 60
Playa Blanca 123, 163
    accommodation 125
    eating out 126
Playa Caleta del Congrio 118
Playa de la Cantería 69
Playa de las Cucharas, Costa Teguise 68
Playa de los Pocillos, Puerto del Carmen 93
Playa del Pozo 118
Playa de Puerto Muelas 118
Playa Mujeres 118
Playas de Papagayo 118
postal services 169
prickly pear 35
Puerto Calero 90
    accommodation 96
    eating out 99
    shopping 101
Puerto del Carmen 92
    accommodation 96
    eating out 98
    Playa de los Pocillos 93
    shopping 101

R
Ramírez, Pepin 19
Risco de Famara 69, 158
Roque del Infierno 70
Rubicón 22
Ruta de los Volcanes 114

S
sailing 102
Salinas de Janubio 123
salt pans 123
San Bartolomé 94
  accommodation 98
  shopping 101
shopping 101, 127, 172
souvenirs 172
sports and activities 75, 173
  cycling 75, 102, 173
  diving 75, 102, 127
  fishing 102, 127
  go karting 102
  golf 173
  hiking 16
  horse riding 127
  kiteboarding 75, 140, 173
  parascending 102
  sailing 102
  Segway tours 127
  surfing 67, 173
  windsurfing 75, 127, 140
submarine trips 102

T
Tahíche 156
tapas 29
Taro de Tahíche 20, 58, 156

taxis 170
Taylor, Jason deCaires 89
  sculpture park 123
Teguise 52, 150, 156
  Castillo de Santa Bárbara 54
  Centro de Arte 54
  Convento de San Francisco 54
  Convento de Santo Domingo 54
    eating out 72
  Iglesia de Nuestra Señora de Guadalupe 54
  Museo de la Piratería 54
  Museo del Timple 52
  Palacio Spínola 52
  shopping 74
telephones 169
Teseguite 160
Timanfaya 14
time differences 169
tipping 172
tours and excursions 102, 173
  Canary Trekking tour 17
  driving tour, North 156
  driving tour, South 161
  Teguise walking tour 150
travel documents 169
Treaty of Alcáçovas 22

U
Uga 11, 127, 165
  accommodation 124
useful words and phrases 174

V
Valley of a Thousand Palms 158
Vega de Río Palmas
  eating out 147
Villaverde
  eating out 146
Volcán de la Corona 61
volcanic activity 14, 56, 112

W
websites 168
windmills 95, 123
windsurfing 75, 127, 140
wine 7, 8, 32, 116, 161
wrestling 41

Y
Yaiza 119, 164, 165
  accommodation 124
  eating out 125
Yé
  accommodation 72

Picture Credits

AA/A. Steve Day: 6 (Nr. 7), 17 (centre), 19, 57, 87, 159, 161

AA/Cliff Sawyer: 6 (Nr. 3), 55

AA/James A. Tims: 6 (Nr. 2), 17 (bottom), 18, 27, 40 (top right), 52, 54, 88, 94, 143

akg-images: 22, British Library 23, Album/ Miguel Raurich 40 (top left), Hedda Eid 50/51

AWL Images: Sabine Lubenow 82/83 (top)

DuMont Bildarchiv/Gerald Hänel: 6 (Nr. 1, 4), 20, 24, 30, 32, 33, 42/43, 48, 64, 68, 70, 81 (bottom left), 104/105, 113, 115, 116, 117, 119, 121, 136/137 (top), 147, 150, 165

DuMont Bildarchiv/Sabine Lubenow: 5 (top), 6 (Nr. 5, 6, 10), 10, 12/13, 14, 15, 17 (top), 28, 31 (top left, top right), 35, 40 (bottom), 53, 58, 59, 63, 72, 76/77, 81 (bottom right), 85, 86, 109, 110/111 (top), 114, 118, 120, 123, 126, 127 (bottom), 128/129, 133 (bottom), 134, 135 (bottom left, bottom right), 136/137 (bottom), 137, 138, 139, 141, 142, 144, 145, 148/149, 166/167

DuMont Bildarchiv/Olaf Lumma: 5 (bottom), 31 (bottom), 37, 51 (bottom), 56, 62, 65, 95, 111, 133 (top), 152, 155, 160, 164

Dumont Bildarchiv/Th.P. Widmann: 41

DuMont Bildarchiv/Hans Zaglitsch: 36, 135 (top)

Fotolia: traveldia 25

Getty Images: Lonely Planet 6 (Nr. 9), UIG/ Geography Photos 26 (top), Lonely Planet 90, Victor Ovies Arenas 110/111 (bottom)

huber-images: Sabine Lubenow 38

laif: Gerald Hänel 6 (Nr. 8), 10, hemis.fr/ Pierre Jacques 39, Stefan Volk 49, Gerald Hänel 61, hemis.fr/Marc Dozier 66, Hedda Eid 67, hemis.fr/Marc Dozier 71, robert-harding/John Miller 93, Gerald Hänel 110, Michael Amme 122

Lookphotos: age fotostock 9, Brigitte Merz 89, 99

mauritius images: Walter Bibikow 48/49 (bottom), Chromorange/Manfred Dietsch 50, Alamy/Helmut Corneli 82, Alamy/Colin Palmer 82/83 (bottom), Alamy/Doug Hall 83, Alamy/P Tomlins 84 (top), Alamy/Wilf Doyle 91, Alamy/Jorge Tutor 97, Alamy/ Doug Houghton 100, Alamy/Charles Stirling 103, Westend61/Martin Siepmann 124, age fotostock/Ana del Castillo 136, Alamy/ RichStock 136/137 (bottom), Alamy/Chavi Nandez 153

picture-alliance: Chromorange/Manfred Dietsch 47 (bottom), Bildagentur-online 48/49 (top), Peter Schickert 84 (bottom),

Shutterstock: irabel8 26 (bottom), Marc Lechanteur 51 (top),

VISUM: Bjoern Goettlicher 81 (top)

© VG Bild-Kunst, Bonn 2018: 6 (Nr. 1, 3, 5), 18, 19, 20, 42/43, 48, 48/49, 50/51, 51 (bottom), 53, 55, 56, 57, 58, 59, 63, 64, 71, 72, 95, 99, 113, 148/149

On the cover: Top: Getty Images, Sabine Lubenow / LOOK-foto
Bottom: age fotostock / Lookphotos
Back: Getty Images, Danita Delimont

Credits

2nd Edition 2019
Fully revised and redesigned

Worldwide Distribution: Marco Polo Travel Publishing Ltd
Pinewood, Chineham Business Park
Crockford Lane, Chineham
Basingstoke, Hampshire RG24 8AL, United Kingdom.
© MAIRDUMONT GmbH & Co. KG, Ostfildern

Authors: Rolf Goetz, Paul Murphy
Editor: red.sign, Stuttgart
Revised editing and translation: Sarah Trenker, Lietzow
Design: CYCLUS · Visuelle Kommunikation, Stuttgart
Project manager: Dieter Luippold
Programme supervisor: Birgit Borowski
Chief editor: Rainer Eisenschmid

Cartography: © MAIRDUMONT GmbH & Co. KG, Ostfildern
3D illustrations: jangled nerves, Stuttgart

Printed in Poland

Despite all of our authors' thorough research, errors can creep in.
The publishers do not accept any liability for this. Whether you
want to praise us, alert us to errors or give us a personal tip –
please don't hesitate to email or post:

MARCO POLO Travel Publishing Ltd
Pinewood, Chineham Business Park
Crockford Lane, Chineham
Basingstoke, Hampshire RG24 8AL
United Kingdom
Email: sales@marcopolouk.com

FSC
www.fsc.org
MIX
Paper from
responsible sources
FSC® C018236

My Notes

SPIRAL GUIDE

DUBAI

AA
Publishing

Contents

the magazine 5
+ Meet the Maktoums
+ What is the United Arab Emirates
+ The Godolphin Story
+ Architecture
+ Dubai in Numbers
+ Food + Outdoor Dubai
+ Events + Shop Until You Drop
+ Fantasy Islands

Finding Your Feet 25
+ First Two Hours
+ Getting Around
+ Accommodation
+ Food and Drink
+ Shopping
+ Entertainment

Deira 33
Getting Your Bearings
+ **In a Day**
+ **Don't Miss**
+ Palm Deira
+ The Souks + Dubai Creek
At Your Leisure + 3 more places to explore
Where to... + Stay + Eat and Drink + Shop + Be Entertained

Bur Dubai 55
Getting Your Bearings
+ **In a Day**
+ **Don't Miss**
+ Sheikh Saeed Al Maktoum House + Dubai Museum
+ Bastakiya + BurJuman Centre + Creekside Park
At Your Leisure + 5 more places to explore
Where to... + Stay + Eat and Drink + Shop + Be Entertained

East Jumeirah 79
Getting Your Bearings
✦ In a Day
✦ Don't Miss
✦ Jumeirah Mosque ✦ Dubai World Trade Centre
✦ Emirates Towers ✦ Zabeel Park ✦ Majlis Ghorfat
Um Al Sheef ✦ Nad Al Sheba and Goldophin Gallery
At Your Leisure ✦ 5 more places to explore
Where to... ✦ Stay ✦ Eat and Drink ✦ Shop ✦ Be Entertained

West Jumeirah 105
Getting Your Bearings
✦ In a Day
✦ Don't Miss
✦ Burj Al Arab ✦ Madinat Jumeirah
✦ Wild Wadi ✦ Mall of the Emirates
✦ Dubai Marina ✦ Dubailand
At Your Leisure ✦ 3 more places to explore
Where to... ✦ Stay ✦ Eat and Drink ✦ Shop ✦ Be Entertained

Walks and Tours 135
✦ Fujairah
✦ Al Ain
✦ Al Maha
✦ Jumeirah Beaches
✦ Hatta
✦ Bur Dubai
✦ Desert Driving

Practicalities 155
✦ Before You Go
✦ When You Are There

Useful Words and Phrases 161
Atlas 163
Index 173

Written by Robin Barton
Page layout by Liz Baldin at Bookwork Creative Associates Ltd.
Copy edited by Marilynne Lanng at Bookwork
Creative Associates Ltd.
Verified by Lindsay Bennett
Indexed by Marie Lorimer

Published by AA Publishing, a trading name of Automobile
Association Developments Limited, whose registered office is
Fanum House, Basing View, Basingstoke, Hampshire, RG21 4EA.
Registered number 1878835.

ISBN-10: 0-7495-4996-3
ISBN-13: 978-0-7495-4996-1

The contents of this publication are believed correct at the time of
printing. Nevertheless, AA Publishing accepts no responsibility for
errors, omissions or changes in the details given, or for the conse-
quences of readers' reliance on this information. This does not
affect your statutory rights. Assessments of the attractions, hotels
and restaurants are based upon the authors' own experiences and
contain subjective opinions that may not reflect the publisher's
opinion or a reader's experience. We have tried to ensure accuracy,
but things do change, so please let us know if you have any
comments or corrections.

A CIP catalogue record for this book is available from the
British Library.

Cover design and binding style by permission of AA Publishing

Colour separation by Keenes, Andover
Printed and bound in China by Leo Paper Products

Find out more about AA Publishing and the wide range of services
the AA provides by visiting our website at www.theAA.com/travel

A02409
Maps in this title produced from map data supplied by Global
Mapping, Brackley, UK. Copyright © Global Mapping/ITMB

the magazine

Meet the Maktoums

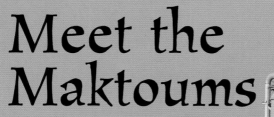

One family runs the city-state of Dubai like a high-powered corporation: the Maktoums. The President of the emirate is Sheikh Mohammed bin Rashid Al Maktoum. With members of his family controlling key businesses and sharing similar ambitions, Sheikh Mohammed is at the helm of the world's fastest-growing city.

Dubai's Maktoum dynasty dates from 1833 when a tribal group moved from neighbouring Abu Dhabi and settled around Dubai's Creek, a site that was to become the foundation for Dubai's fortunes. At that time, the area that is now the United Arab Emirates (UAE) was ruled by disparate tribal families but, under the leadership of Sheikh Maktoum bin Buti, the Dubai people focused on building their community through trade, fishing and pearling.

A number of crucial decisions aided Dubai's progression from a desert village to the metropolis it is today. First, the Maktoums welcomed immigrants. Traders from Persia (modern Iran) and India were encouraged to relocate to Dubai. Business boomed in the markets (souks) alongside the Creek as Dubai became a stopover on the trade and spice shipping routes.

Commercial taxes were abolished under Sheikh Maktoum bin Hasher (ruled: 1894–1906) and many of the divers and workers in the pearl industry were also exempted from tax.

But it was under Sheikh Saeed bin Maktoum Al

Maktoum ("bin" means "son of") that Dubai's development moved up a gear. He ruled from 1912 to 1958. In the first two decades of the 20th century Dubai's population doubled to about 20,000 but the city was hit by the global recession of the 1930s. However, the diversity of its economy kept Dubai afloat.

In 1958 Sheikh Rashid bin Saeed Al Maktoum became Dubai's ruler, bringing a clear and compelling vision for the future of the city. The Sheikh and his advisors formulated a bold strategy fuelled by the commodity that the world was consuming at an ever-increasing rate: oil.

Dubai's oil reserves were limited and by 2004 accounted for a dwindling 6 per cent of the economy. But, although oil-rich Abu Dhabi's largesse with its wealth was a boon to the whole region (►box, page 8), Dubai capitalised on the good fortune in its own business-savvy way.

Knowing that Abu Dhabi would need to import heavy industrial equipment to build refineries, platforms and rigs, Sheikh Rashid had Dubai's Creek dredged at a cost of $850,000 in 1960. The new deep-water port allowed larger cargo ships to dock and it wasn't long before Abu Dhabi was paying to unload its industrial shipments at Dubai's new port.

Sheikh Rashid's next investments were in Dubai's international airport, the Maktoum bridge over the Creek and the Jebel Ali Port. The airport began life as a single, sandy runway in the 1960s but soon had enough capacity for hundreds of weekly flights. Sheikh Rashid's shrewd planning paid off: 24 million passengers passed through the

Sheikh Zayed

Of course, the Maktoums don't have complete control over Dubai's affairs. The emirate is just one of seven under the flag of the United Arab Emirates and the emirate that holds the presidency of the UAE is Abu Dhabi. Abu Dhabi is the world's fourth largest exporter of oil and represents about 90 per cent of the UAE's total wealth. It also has the largest population and is, since Dubai devolved responsibility for defence to Abu Dhabi, UAE's main military force. For 38 years one inspirational figure led Abu Dhabi: Sheikh Zayed bin Sultan Al Nahyan, who died in 2004 aged 86. He bound the disparate emirates together during a crucial period in 1970 before leading the United Arab Emirates into an unparalleled phase of development. With a vast income from its oil resources Abu Dhabi funded civic projects across the UAE, offering cut-price power, water, schools and hospitals. From the time he took over in 1966 to today, life expectancy has increased from 45 years to 72 years. Sheikh Zayed is certainly regarded as the father of the modern United Arab Emirates. They even named Dubai's main road after him.

شارع آل مكتوم
Al Maktoum Rd

airport in 2005. Jebel Ali Port, which was completed in 1979, is the world's largest man-made port. More than $2.5 billion was pumped into the project but it seemed like it was destined to remain half empty. But the introduction of a free-trade zone at the port and problems at the far end of the Gulf between Iraq and Iran encouraged tankers to use Jebel Ali. "Build it and they will come", was the maxim of Sheikh Rashid.

As Dubai's infrastructure expanded quicker than its population and services, Sheikh Rashid's moved to attract people to live, work and holiday in Dubai. The first skyscraper, the Dubai World Trade Centre in 1979, enticed the first wave of businesses to relocate to Dubai. Today, there are whole communities dedicated to bringing people and their work to Dubai. Dubai's first luxury hotel, the Intercontinental, opened on the bank of the Creek in 1975 and the 1980s saw dozens more hotels open for business travellers and, eventually, holidaymakers. The UAE's population grew from

180,000 in 1968 to 2.62 million by 1997 (30 per cent of whom are Emiratis) and then 4 million by 2003.

In 1990, Sheikh Rashid was succeeded by his son Sheikh Maktoum and on his death in 2006 his younger brother, Sheikh Mohammed, took over. Sheikh Maktoum built on his father's legacy, building housing and important infrastructure such as parks, libraries, roads and other facilities. But his brother, Sheikh Mohammed was widely seen as the more ambitious member of the family, asserting that he was planning "20, 30 years ahead." Dubai's oil will run out in the near future and Sheikh Mohammed wants to have established Dubai as world-class financial centre and holiday hotspot by then. Already, 5 million visitors holiday in Dubai annually and with the construction of attractions such as Dubailand, that figure is going to double in the next few years.

Sheikh Mohammed bin Rashid Al Maktoum

WHAT IS THE
UNITED ARAB EMIRATES?

The United Arab Emirates, despite thousands of years of heritage and generations-old families, is one of the world's youngest countries, formed in 1971 from a federation of the seven former Trucial States – Abu Dhabi, Dubai, Sharjah, Ajman, Umm Al Quwain, Ras Al Khaimah and Fujairah. On 2 December, 1971 the United Arab Emirates was born (Ras Al Khaimah, the dissenting emirate, joined in 1972).

The UAE line the southeastern corner of the Arabian peninsula. To the west Abu Dhabi borders Saudi Arabia and Qatar and to the east Fujairah borders Oman. Each emirate is governed by its ruling family but some decisions are made collectively. Sheikh Khalifa bin Zayed Al Nahyan, ruler of Abu Dhabi inherited the presidency of the UAE in 2004 on the death of his father Sheikh Zayed bin Sultan Al Nahyan.

Abu Dhabi
Abu Dhabi is the largest emirate, both in terms of its influence and economy and size. It is the capital of the country.

Dubai
Second only to Abu Dhabi in size and influence, Dubai is arguably the international face of the UAE.

Sharjah
It is the most traditional emirate, with the strictest Islamic laws, and is the protector and promoter of the UAE's cultural heritage.

Ajman
Famous for its seafaring history. Visitors can still see wooden dhows being built.

Umm Al Quwain
The second-smallest emirate, it depends on farming and fishing for income.

Ras Al Khaimah
Ras Al Khaimah is the most scenic corner of the UAE and several new roads thread their way through the mountains to Fujairah.

Fujairah
The only emirate on the east coast, it is a favourite spot for weekending urbanites, thanks to its scenery and beaches.

Above: Sheikh Zayed with his entourage – his influence is still felt throughout the UAE despite his death in 2004

The Godolphin Story

There's an Arab proverb that says that the finest wind in creation is the one that blows between a horse's ears. It's even finer if the wind is rushing between the ears of a race horse for Emiratis, and Sheikh Mohammed bin Rashid Al Maktoum in particular loves horse racing. But Sheikh Mohammed's interests lie far beyond hosting the world's richest horse race at Nad Al Sheba every year: he also founded the Godolphin stable which has premises in Dubai and in England. From these two bases thoroughbred horses are sent out to conquer the world's most prestigious races – and they have been hugely successful, with 55 per cent of all Godolphin's horses winning at least one race.

Godolphin produced its first international champion in 1994, although the stable's first runner was at Nad Al Sheba in 1992. Sheikh Mohammed's horses have raced in 14 countries on 113 racecourses ridden by 152 different jockeys. In just ten years he has created one of the world's top three racing stables. You might be surprised that this could be achieved in the desert just outside Dubai, but visiting the Godolphin stables is like stepping into a parallel universe. Although the horses race on dirt in Dubai, the stable area is lavishly irrigated and you could almost be in the English country-side. From the Dubai stables the Sheikh's horses compete at Nad Al Sheba near by, where the Dubai World Cup, the richest race in the world with prize money in 2005

Above: The Dubai World Cup is one of the largest trophies in the world

Five Great Godolphin Horses

Balanchine Balanchine put Godolphin on the map and proved that Dubai's mild winters were perfect for raising thoroughbreds. She was the first Godolphin filly to win a Group One race, in 1994.

Lammtarra Lammtarra is a legend in European racing circles, winning three of the most sought-after trophies, including the English Derby in 1995.

Dubai Millennium Bred to be Godolphin's top horse at the turn of the millennium, Dubai Millennium was undoubtedly one of the best racehorses of all time. He died in April 2001 but despite his short career was one Godolphin's most successful horses.

Street Cry Street Cry has been Godolphin's highest earning horse, winning £3.5 million in his career. He proved himself by winning the 2002 Dubai World Cup.

Dubawi One of the few foals sired by Dubai Millennium, Dubawi represents the future of Godolphin. The horse began its campaign in 2004 and was retired to stud in 2005 after an injury.

Above:
Thoroughbred winners and hopefuls from the Godolphin stables
Below:
Champions of the future?
Horses train at Al Quoz stables

toppng $15 million, is held every spring. But the real prize is the trophy, an 18-carat, gold-plated cup weighing 5,236g (185 ounces) and standing 73cm tall (29 inches). The cup, one of the largest trophies in the world, was made by British jewellers Garrard and is displayed in a room of its own in the Godolphin Gallery.

However, Sheikh Mohammed's ambitions reach beyond Dubai and his Godolphin stables at Newmarket are the base for his European campaigns on the turf courses of England, Ireland and France. Few horses can run well on both dirt and turf, but Dubai Millennium was one such horse. Godolphin's horses tyically spend the winter in Dubai and the summer at Newmarket. It's an enviable routine.

The Godolphin Arabian

The Maktoum family's racing stable is named after the Godolphin Arabian, the horse from which many of the genes for most of today's modern racehorses derive. The Godolphin Arabian was born in Yemen in 1724 and taken to France as a gift, where Edward Coke, an Englishman, spotted the colt and brought it to England. When Coke died the horse was sold to the 2nd Earl of Godolpin and acquired its name. He sired 80 foals before he died in 1753 near Cambridge – his grave is in Wandlebury Ring, Babraham. England.

Dubai is the city of the superlative: the biggest mall, the highest tower, the most expensive hotel suite, they're all here. "Build it and they will come", has been the maxim of Dubai's rulers since the 1970s, and the emirate is becoming an architectural wonderland.

ARCHITECTURE

When compared to the world's other great cities, Dubai's developers have one overwhelming advantage: an abundance of empty land. They don't have to shoehorn their designs between other buildings, or negotiate a political minefield to get their proposal approved. Instead, desert real estate is a blank slate and architects are encouraged by the political will of Dubai's leader, Sheikh Mohammed, to create increasingly amazing landmarks for his city. Some of the city's projects are worth the airfare to Dubai alone, even if you're not an architecture student. The Burj Dubai – *burj* translates as "tower" – is the most recent of these wonders, but the list also includes the Dubai Creek Golf and Yacht Club, the Emirates Towers on Sheikh Zayed Road, the Madinat Jumeirah hotel and entertainment complex and, of course, the Burj Al Arab hotel.

Dubai is not shy about advertising its architectural ambitions. "The Future is Now", "We Build Cities", "History Rising" and "The World Has A New Centre" are just some of the slogans plastered on billboards around building sites. The next decade will see some of the most radical construction projects in the world realised, including the three Palm Islands, Hydropolis (the world's first underwater hotel) and Dubailand, an extraordinary collection of theme parks covering an area larger than Manhattan.

The famous Emirates Towers (below left) will soon be dwarfed by Burj Dubai (right)

The Burj Dubai

The intense competition between some world cities to have the world's tallest building is the reason why, even with the tower rising from the desert floor day by day, the developers of the Burj Dubai won't say how high the final structure will be. But it is bound to be not far short of 1km (0.5 miles). When it is completed, the top floors will sway up to 1.6m (5 feet) from side to side in the desert winds. That this amazing pinnacle of a skyscraper – almost ethereal but formidably futuristic at the same time – is rising out of barren desert just makes it seem even more like a hazy mirage. Eventually, the Burj Dubai will be surrounded by commercial and residential developments, parks and entertainment facilities, but that will be after the tower is completed in 2008. A total of 60 lifts, including some of the fastest in the world, travelling to the 120th floor in one minute, will transport people up and down the tower. The project will cost $8 billion and is being led by Chicago-born architect Adrian Smith, who admits to being partly inspired by the Emerald City in *The Wizard of Oz*. His dazzling, dizzying creation certainly looks like it has come from a sci-fi fantasy.

Traditional Architecture

Most of modern Dubai dates from the late 1970s onwards, but there are still places where you can see the traditional architecture of the region. Early settlers, many of them Bedouin nomads, would have pitched animal-skin tents and palm frond shelters (called *barasti*) before putting up rudimentary houses made from coral plastered with a lime-based paste. When descendents of the Maktoum family arrived in the 19th century more solid buildings were made from mud blocks. Later gypsum, stone, coral and shells were used, while interiors were furnished with teak and sandalwood. Designers and builders had to fight a constant battle against the desert's heat and light. Ventilation was essential and, in an age before electricity and air conditioning, a clever system of wind towers was used. A wind tower – you can see them in Bastakiya (► 64) – funnelled air down into the room below. Sunlight was another enemy and shade was created by narrow alleys and entrances angled to block direct light.

In 2005 and 2006 the working and living conditions of the 250,000 labourers attracted attention. Many arrive from India, Pakistan and Sri Lanka in the hope of sending money back to their families. However, in many cases, they first have to repay the loan for their journey to Dubai and on a monthly salary of about 700Dh (US$170) that can take a long time; their passports and visas are often retained by their employer. Often they share a room with up to 25 others and will work in temperatures of up to 50°C (122°F). Dubai's government has vowed to clean up and regulate unfair and dangerous working practices for its immigrant workers.

Where to see Traditional Buildings

Bastakiya (► 64–65) This Bur Dubai neighbourhood on the bank of the Creek is being painstakingly restored and includes a wealth of traditional buildings.

Majlis Ghorfat Um Al Sheef (► 90–91) Dubai's future was discussed at this small meeting house.

Sheikh Saeed Al Maktoum House (► 60–61) At the mouth of the Creek, this house was built in 1896 and exemplifies local building techniques of the time.

Heritage House (► 45) See how affluent Emirati families lived at this restored home in Deira. The function and decoration of each room is explained.

Hatta Heritage Village (► 147) Village life is demonstrated at this recreated village in the mountains an hour's drive from Dubai.

stay one step ahead of the prevailing trends. For many years the sail-shaped Burj Al Arab was Dubai's most luxurious hotel. However, while it remains a technological marvel from the outside, its over-the-top interior now looks dated and it has been superseded by glamourous new hotels such as Grosvenor House West Marina Beach at Dubai's Marina development and Park Hyatt Dubai on the Creek.

Top Five Hotels for Design

Park Hyatt Dubai – a Moorish-styled urban oasis with white-washed blocks and blue domes. View it at its best from the Creekside Park

Shangri-La – the conventional exterior doesn't prepare you for the soaring, contemporary lobby of this Sheikh Zayed Road hotel

Emirates Towers Hotel – occupies one of the two futuristic Emirates towers on Sheikh Zayed Road and is a central fixture of Dubai's skyline

Madinat Jumeirah – a complex including two luxurious hotels in a mock-Arabic design

Burj Al Arab – iconic from the outside, a garish hallucination on the inside

Above left: a traditional building
Above: The luxury hotel Madinat Jumeirah

Below: New skycrapers being built

Hotel Babylon

There is no greater concentration of opulent hotels in the world than in Dubai. Lavish beach resorts, sleek business hotels and remote desert hideaways; whatever you need, it's in Dubai. With dozens of new hotels being built, competition for guests is fierce and designers try to

PEOPLE

1.3 MILLION	population of Dubai (2004)
275,000	population of Dubai (1980)
4.3 MILLION	population of United Arab Emirates (2004)
100,000	annual population increase of Dubai
60%	proportion of Dubai's population from India or Pakistan
20%	proportion of Emiratis in the total population of Dubai
11%	proportion of visitors to Dubai who are British
65%	proportion of female university students in United Arab Emirates
250,000	number of construction workers in Dubai
700 DIRHAMS	average monthly salary of a construction worker

MONEY

8.3%	Dubai's annual employment growth, the highest in the world
20%	of Dubai's income is from oil
272.5 MILLION DIRHAMS	the amount spent by British tourists on their credit cards June–August 2005, the highest spending by any nationality
110 BILLION DIRHAMS	Dubai's gross domestic product in 2004
15 MILLION	the number of tourists expected to visit Dubai annually by 2010
40	the number of new Airbus A380 super-size airliners ordered by Emirates airline
$100 BILLION	value of current development projects in Dubai (2006)

TOURISM

6,000 TONNES	amount of snow used in Ski Dubai
50	the number of shopping malls in Dubai
73	football pitches – the extent of the surface area of Mall of the Emirates
800M/2,625 FEET	minimum height of Burj Dubai
$800 MILLION	budget of Burj Dubai

FOOD

Emirati cuisine is rather bland and few restaurants serve local dishes in Dubai itself. However, Arabic food, largely based in Lebanese cuisine, is tasty and easily found in the city's restaurants and is well worth trying.

There are particular flavours that are especially Middle Eastern, including rose water, dried fruits (from lemons to dates), pulses such as chickpeas and beans, pistachios, saffron and coriander. Chilli and pepper are not common components of Middle Eastern cooking, although many spices were introduced to Dubai because of the city's position on the east–west trade routes. To get a flavour of the Middle East try any of the following foods.

Falafel – balls of crushed chickpeas and sesame seeds deep fried

Hummous – crushed chickpeas, garlic and sesame seeds

Tabbouleh – parsley, tomato, mint, onion and cracked wheat

Fattoush – mixed vegetables and toasted pitta bread with a sauce

Shwarmas – spit roasted, especially lamb, served in a pitta bread

Baba Ghanoush – a dip made from grilled aubergine (eggplant) with onion, tomato, green pepper and garlic

Foul Madamas – broad beans, lemon, hummous, olive oil and garlic

Muhallabia – a milk dessert scented with rose petals

And if you are determined to taste traditional Emirati food, visit the Sheikh Mohammed Centre for Cultural Understanding in Bastakiya (▶ 65), Bur Dubai. Meals are served to visitors reclining on white cushions and include Emirati dishes that are rarely tasted in the city's restaurants.

An array of Middle Eastern dishes will tickle the taste buds

OUTDOOR DUBAI

With sweltering heat and 90 per cent humidity, summertime in Dubai is no place to be outdoors. But the cooler winter brings a surprising range of outdoor activities to the city.

There are major sporting events every month from October to March. The world's richest horse race takes place at Nad Al Sheba every March, while camel racing takes place weekly during the winter months. Motorsports fans welcomed the arrival of the Dubai Autodrome in 2005, one of the first areas of the Dubailand development to open. The blue riband motor event at present is the Desert Challenge, a six-day desert rally for motorbikes, trucks and four-wheel-drive cars. Golf, tennis and rugby are also enormously popular spectator sports with A-list golfers teeing off at the Dubai Desert Classic in March and tennis players hitting the courts for the Dubai Tennis Championships in February.

There's more to the outdoor life in Dubai than just watching sport though. The emirate's first golf course opened in 1988, bringing swathes of green to the desert landscape, and seven other courses have followed.

Things get much more adventurous than a round of golf and it's not hard to get an adrenaline rush here. Kite surfing is a fast-growing water sport. You can also go water-skiing, windsurfing, jet skiing and sailing along the coast. The Dubai Marina is the hub of water sports in Jumeirah but many of the beachfront resorts will provide their own activities.

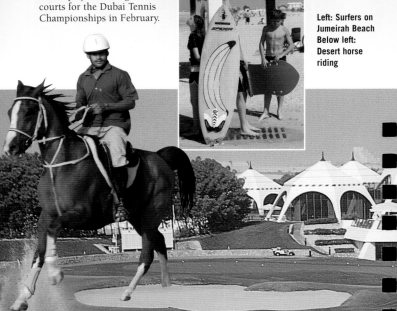

Left: Surfers on Jumeirah Beach
Below left: Desert horse riding

Right: Exploring the desert with a dune safari

Offshore, visitors can also go game fishing or scuba diving, while those who prefer to explore the Arabian Gulf can hire fully-crewed yachts and motor boats. Scuba divers will see the most marine life on the Indian Ocean side of the Emirates – Fujairah is the leading diving spot – but wreck diving is the major attraction for divers on Dubai's Gulf coast.

For some enthusiasts the desert is one vast theme park, with ever more inventive ways of getting up and down the dunes being offered to visitors. One new sport is sandboarding – a local variation on snowboarding – although some say that the drive up to the top of the dune is more thrilling. Dune driving is an extremely popular weekend pursuit with locals heading out into the desert in four-wheel-drive vehicles to power up and down dunes. Most outdoor activity operators offer a variety of dune safaris, with overnight trips involving camel rides, Bedouin camps and belly dancers. Other ways of playing on the dunes include desert horse riding quad bikes and dune buggies.

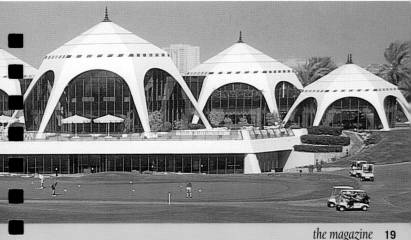

Sticking with the four-wheel-drive theme, "wadi bashing" are drives on the dry river beds that wind through the mountain ranges.

For trekking head for the hills around the town of Hatta, on the Oman border, or to the emirate of Ras Al Khaimah, where the Hajar mountains provide some rugged routes in some of the highest mountains in the United Arab Emirates.

You might think that wildlife-spotting opportunities would be few and far between. But the Ras Al Khor Wildlife Sanctuary at the end of the Creek (and now surrounded by roads and building sites) is where more than a thousand flamingoes choose to spend the winter. Another conservation area, the privately run Al Maha resort, has large populations of oryx and gazelles.

Below: The Emirates Golf Club; a sporting oasis

EVENTS

The Dubai government has introduced a large number of annual events, ranging from high-profile sporting competitions to month-long shopping festivals. Sports competitions dominate the calendar but cultural events are slowly catching up, with film and jazz festivals being established. Muslim celebrations, such as Ramadan, are also widely observed in Dubai.

Events Calendar

JANUARY

Dubai Shopping Festival If shopping is a religion for many in Dubai, then this month-long festival of consumerism has the largest number of devotees. From mid-January to mid-February shops in every mall discount stock by up to 80 per cent but the main attractions are the daily prize draws, raffles and competitions. Prizes are often sports cars or cash; in 2005 the Dubai City of Gold offered 1kg (2.2 pounds) of gold as a prize every day and 100kg (220 pounds) on the last day to one lucky winner. During the festival you stand a good chance of finding a bargain in the malls. The Shopping Festival has a long list of associated events including music shows in the outdoor auditoriums and children's activities. www.mydsf.ae

Dubai Marathon The coolest month of the year is when fun runners and competitive runners take to the roads for Dubai's marathon. www.dubaimarathon.org

FEBRUARY

Dubai Desert Classic One of the highlights of the city's sporting calendar, this golf competition usually takes place at the Emirates Golf Club and attracts many of the sport's big names, with the help of a large cash prize. It has been a part of Europe's PGA Tour since 1989. www.dubaidesertclassic.com

Dubai Tennis Open Dubai's most established tennis tournament is held at the Aviation Club's courts. Competitors usually include a number of top seeds, including Tim Henman and Roger Federer in previous years, serving for the $1 million prize money. The event is a treat for tennis fans, with low ticket prices, mild weather and the close proximity of the tennis stars. www.dubaitennischampionships.com

Dubai International Property Week This exhibition covers property investments world-wide, but all Dubai's main developers are present. People considering buying property in Dubai make the trip for this event. www.dubaipropertyshow.com

Maktoum Sailing Trophy Round One of the spring sailing series takes place off Mina Seyahi. Rounds continue into April. Various classes of yacht enter and the event offers more spectating opportunities than powerboat racing which starts in January. www.dimc-uae.com

MARCH

Dubai International Boat Show This is your opportunity to see the world's most expensive yachts and cruisers close up. It is the largest such event in the Middle East and takes place at the Dubai International Marine Club. www.boatshow.dwtc.com

Dubai International Jazz Festival Performers, from solo artists to big bands, are booked for this three-night festival (www.dubaijazzfest.com). Shows are held in a number of venues but primarily in Dubai's Media City. www.chilloutproductions.com

Dubai World Cup The highlight of Dubai's social and sporting calendar, the Dubai World Cup is the world's richest horse race and draws all the Emirati elite to the Nad Al Sheba racecourse. The World Cup race itself, always held on a Saturday, is the climax of the Dubai Racing Carnival, which starts in January with weekly races. Tickets to the World Cup are hot property and will need to be booked in advance. www.dubairacingclub.com

JUNE

Dubai Summer Surprises With the success of the Dubai Shopping Festival in the winter, it was only a matter of time before the same trick was tried in the summer. And it's worked: whether it's because air-conditioned malls are simply the most comfortable places to be during the summer, the month-long Summer Surprises shopping festival has boosted visitor numbers during the off-peak season. Bargains abound as with the winter festival. www.mydsf.com

Dubai Traditional Dhow Race The sight of dozens of dhows in full sail is majestic. This is the culmination of a six-race series. www.dimc-uae.com

SEPTEMBER

Ramadan Shops change their opening times and restaurants may not serve alcohol during this month-long religous fast. The dates vary each year.

OCTOBER

Eid Al Fitr The starting date of Eid Al Fitr varies according the date of Ramadan's conclusion. The three-day festival is the liveliest and longest holiday for Muslims.

NOVEMBER

UAE Desert Challenge The Desert Challenge is the Emirates' premier off-road driving race with bikes, cars and trucks powering over the dunes. It is usually one of the stages in the Rally World Cup. www.uaedesertchallenge.com

DECEMBER

Dubai International Film Festival In its second year, in 2005, the Dubai International Film Festival screened a number of international films. www.dubaifilmfest.com

Dubai Rugby Sevens Seven-a-side rugby is enormously popular with Dubai's expat Britons, Australians and South Africans and this is the three-day highlight of their year and a great excuse for sinking a few beers. The Rugby Sevens tournament is one of the liveliest weekends of the year. www.dubairugby7s.com

SHOP UNTIL

Commerce has always been the lifeblood of Dubai and the city makes no excuses for coming up with ever more tempting ways of parting you from your money. No other city in the world has the concentration of shopping malls that Dubai has, and more open each year, but currently there are about 50 to choose from.

changers: it's all here. In terms of shops – pretty much every international clothing brand is represented here, ranging from the most revered designers to off-the-peg stalwarts such as Topshop and Zara. Some of the malls are large enough to swallow a department store whole, with Saks Fifth Avenue from the US and Harvey Nichols from the Britain appearing in different malls. And, as if shopaholics needed any more encouragement, two annual shopping festivals see prices slashed by up to 80 per cent.

A shoppers paradise – but which of Dubai's 50 malls will you choose?

The most modern malls – and few are older than 15 years – have an extraordinary range of facilities and entertainment as well as retail outlets. Indoor funfairs, mother and baby rooms, imulti-screen cinemas, left luggage areas, money

Be warned though: prices outside these two periods are no longer guaranteed to be lower in Dubai than elsewhere. A random international price check reveals that everyday clothing items and even electronics cost roughly the same as they do in the UK and more than they do in the US. Yes, there is an enormous range of shops, but bargains are thin on the ground today.

Unless, of course, you make your way into the old souks of Bur Dubai and Deira. These historic street markets are where you may be able to negotiate favourable prices. The most important souks, the Spice Souk and the Gold Souk, are

YOU DROP

on the Deira side of the Creek. Here, all that glitters really is gold. Gold is the one commodity that remains outstanding value for money in Dubai but even if you aren't interested in purchasing jewellery (priced by weight) it's worth window-shopping here simply to see shopfronts glowing with the precious metal. The Spice Souk offers more down-to-earth pleasures: hessian sacks full of spices and dried foods fresh off the dhows. Part of the enjoyment here is

squeezing down the narrow alley and asking shopkeepers what is in each sack: you'll find myrrh, frankincense, saffron and a huge selection of other fine spices.

Other items that can offer good value in Dubai include made-to-measure suits and carpets imported from Turkey, Pakistan and Iran – but haggle hard to get the best price. The prices of electronics such as digital cameras and computers need to be compared carefully with prices at home, but you might make a saving. The Dubai Duty Free shopping area at the airport is one of the largest in the world and is a good place to spend any lingering dirhams.

TOP FIVE MALLS

BurJuman Centre
Fashionistas should make a beeline for the BurJuman Centre in Bur Dubai where the latest frocks from the likes of Chanel and Dior hang in glitzy boutiques. A Saks Fifth Avenue department store anchors the designerwear but there are hundreds more clothes shops.

Deira City Centre
This crowd-pleasing favourite of Deira dwellers has popular, mainstream shops including Debenhams and a Carrefour supermarket. A new wing, Bin Hendi, brings designer sass to the mall. The Magic Planet, a modern funfair

and entertainment zone, is reason enough to drop in to Deira City Centre.

Ibn Battuta
Tour 14th-century China, Persia, India, Egypt, North Africa and Andalusia as you shop; each zone has a particular feature, such as a full-size Chinese junk in the China. If that's not diverting enough, the mall houses Dubai's first IMAX screen.

Mall of the Emirates
Mall of the Emirates is the biggest and best mall in Dubai – until the next mega-mall opens. If nothing catches your eye in the 400 shops, you can go to the cinema, amuse the children in the Magic Planet entertainment zone or learn to ski in real snow.

Mercato
It has to be seen to be believed: Mercato's Italian Renaissance-style façade hides a small but interesting selection of shops, with independent fashion boutiques thriving in the mock-Venetian interior.

Fantasy Islands

The announcement of the construction of the first Palm Island in 2001 gathered column inches in newspapers worldwide. Bold and impossibly ambitious, the idea put Dubai on the map and signalled the emirate's intentions.

By 2003 the foundations of the Jumeirah Palm were in place and in 2006 the island began to open for business. It is connected to the mainland by the palm's trunk. More than 25 resort hotels, three types of residential villa, as well as marinas, shopping malls, restaurants and entertainment complexes will be contained on the island's trunk and its 17 fronds. As soon as work was underway on the Jumeirah island, the local developer Nakheel announced two more Palm Islands would be sprouting from Dubai's coast, off Deira to the east and Jebel Ali to

the west – and it had other, equally outlandish projects in the pipeline.

While the reasoning behind the man-made islands is simple enough – with a coastline limited by nature, the only way to sell sought-after seafront property was to create the seafront by building an island offshore – the execution of the project is far more complicated. The process begins with dredgers dropping sand into position underwater. Rocks from 16 quarries across the UAE are placed on the sand outline; divers ensure that the rock placement is correct. If all this filling material, for one island, were placed end to end, a wall 2m-high (6.5 feet) and 0.5m-thick (1.66 feet) would stretch around the world three times. The cost of the land reclamation is about $1 billion per island, but each island will add 120km (74 miles) to Dubai's shoreline. The results of 50 research studies suggest that the groundwork will remain solid.

The outer crescent of each island is a breakwater, able to withstand a 4m (13-foot) wave. Inside the crescent are over 5,000 residents ranging from beachfront villas to canalside town houses and apartments. Properties have already sold out though so investors will have to look to the next project: The World – 300 islands shaped like different countries.

Above: An artist's impression of Jebel Ali and the other Palm Islands

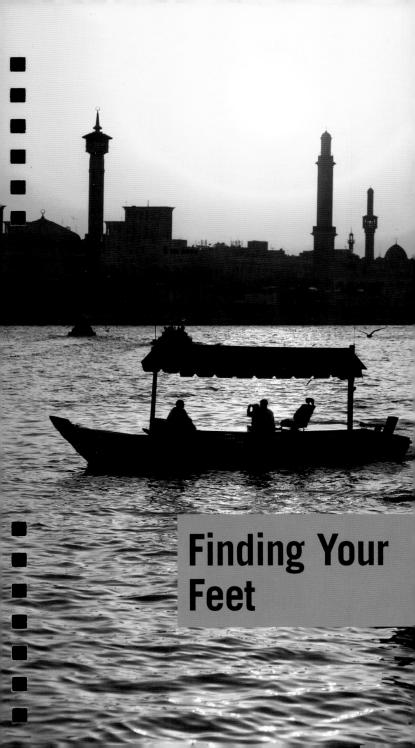

Finding Your Feet

First Two Hours

Dubai International Airport (Code: DXB)

- Dubai International Airport (tel: 224 5555; www.dubaiairport.com) is on Garhoud road on the Deira side of the Creek, about 5km (3 miles) from the city centre. A new international airport is under construction at the opposite end of Dubai in Jebel Ali, but for the near future the highly acclaimed DIA will be the main gateway to the city.
- The 24-hour Department of Tourism and Commerce Marketing **information desk** in the arrivals lounge, provides maps, hotel information and answers queries (tel: 224 5252; www.dubaitourism.ae).
- The vast majority of flights arrive at Terminal 1.
- There is a helpdesk for **visitors with special needs** in the departure hall. Requests for a wheelchair or other assistance for arriving passengers should be made through your airline.
- **Customs** will allow you to bring 2,000 cigarettes, 400 cigars and 2kg (2.2lbs) of tobacco into Dubai. Non-Muslims can also import 2 litres of wine or spirits.
- Although unobtrusive, customs officials do monitor the arrivals' hall. Prohibited items include all drugs and "publications, photogaphs, paintings, cards, books and sculptures that do not adhere to religious morals". Restricted items include weapons and ammunition, ivory and pearls, foodstuffs (including pork, fruit and vegetables), alcohol, medical and pharmaceutical items (including some drugs legal in the West).

Getting to Dubai

- Before you leave the arrivals area, the right side of the hall is lined with 12 **car rental operators,** including Avis (tel: 224 5219; www.avis.com) and Hertz (tel: 224 5222; www.hertz.com). You cannot re-enter this part of the arrivals hall once you have passed through the sliding doors. Cars can be picked up from the airport. When driving out of the airport, turn right for central Dubai (signposted Deira).
- The best way to travel into the centre of Dubai is to take a **taxi** from the stand outside the arrivals hall. A surcharge of 30Dh is added to journeys from the airport (the surcharge for all non-airport journeys is 3Dh) but all taxi drivers use their meters and the trip to Deira or Bur Dubai should cost about 60Dh in total. You will pay more to go to Jumeirah or the Marina area and further afield. The journey to Deira should take around 10 minutes. Other journey times will depend on traffic.
- Guests at Dubai's main international hotels can expect a **complimentary shuttle bus** service to the hotel or a car and driver to meet them, but this should be arranged in advance.
- There is no specific airport shuttle into the city centre but the 410 **bus goes** to Deira and the 402 service goes to Bur Dubai. Both buses operate 24 hours a day and depart the aiport every 30 minutes (tel: 800 4848; www.dm.gov.ae).

Admission Charges

The cost of admission for museums and places of interest featured in this guide is indicated by the following price categories:
Inexpensive 1–5Dh
Moderate 6–15Dh
Expensive more than 16Dh

Getting Around

Orienting Yourself

- Dubai is an easy city to navigate, given that much of it is strung out along one main highway, Sheikh Zayed Road. The older parts of the city, Bur Dubai and Deira on either side of the Creek, retain narrow, convoluted routes with one-way systems. The airport is on the Deira side of the Creek; to cross the Creek drivers have to use Garhoud Bridge for Sheikh Zayed Road or Maktoum Bridge for Bur Dubai.
- **Jumeirah** is the generic name given to the expanse of beach between Bur Dubai and Jebel Ali, although the Jumeirah suburb itself is only a quarter of this coastline. Beyond Jumeirah, new development at Dubai Marina is creating a second axis for the city. Inland, Dubailand is taking over the desert between the marina and Nad Al Sheba.
- Sheikh Zayed Road has a series of **numbered interchanges**: Interchange 1 is the closest to Bur Dubai and the city centre and Interchange 5 accesses Dubai Marina. It is about 45km (25 miles) from the airport along Sheikh Zayed Road to the Marina.

Buses

- Very few people other than construction workers getting to and from work take public buses. The government is hoping to encourage more use of public transport by erecting 400 air-conditioned bus shelters.

Taxis

- There are 5,000 **registered taxis** (with distinctive liveries) in Dubai. Avoid unofficial taxis (private cars without meters) as these are not insured for passengers; they are increasingly rare. For details about taxi companies and the latest fare increases: www.dubaitransport.gov.ae
- Taxi drivers will always use their meters but some are not averse to taking the long way to your destination. **Fares** are 1.5Dh per kilometre (0.5 miles) plus a 3Dh surcharge, unless you take an aiport taxi.
- Ensure that the driver knows where he is going; some taxi drivers have not been in the country for long.
- You can **hire a taxi for a 12-hour day** for 600Dh. Some private but licensed drivers can be rented for long journeys at a negotiable rate.
- The standard of driving of many taxi drivers is frighteningly poor. Don't be reluctant to ask your driver to slow down or pay attention.
- It is usual to **tip the driver** by rounding up the fare to the nearest 5Dh.

Abra

- *Abras* are the water taxis that criss-cross the Creek day and night.
- There are official *abra* **stations** strung along each side of the Creek, generally identified by a metal sign and a large crowd of people.
- *Abra* **fares** are 1Dh per journey. It's a bargain. Rather than sit in a traffic jam waiting to cross the Creek by bridge, it can be quicker to take a taxi to an *abra* station, cross the Creek by boat and pick up another taxi on the other side.

Metro

- The much-mooted Dubai Metro is finally underway after approval in 2005. It will supplement Dubai's rail system and the first stage is due to open in 2008 with completion of the project by 2012.

Driving

If at all possible, **avoid driving in Dubai** unless you are a confident and experienced motorist. Many of the driving practices are challenging and may include changing lane without warning, regardless of whether there is a car occupying the space, speeding, tailgating, braking late and driving without care or attention.

- **Do not lose your temper** with another driver. Any form of gesticulation is guaranteed to escalate the situation. Use the car horn instead.
- When **renting a car,** choose the largest within your price range. A four-wheel-drive vehicle will also allow you to visit areas that are inaccessible to two-wheel-drive cars, such as the rock pools at Hatta (➤ 145).
- All the major international car rental companies have desks at Dubai International Airport. Most also have offices in the city where you can collect the car at a later date.
- To rent a car you will need your driver's licence, passport and a credit card. Citizens of most European countries and the US do not require an international driving licence.
- Companies will only rent cars to drivers aged over 21 (or 25 for larger-capacity vehicles).
- Take out fully comprehensive insurance. This will cover you for driving throughout the UAE but to drive into Oman you will need to buy an additional insurance policy for aound 350Dh per week. Not all car rental companies permit you to take a rented car into another country.
- Dubai has chronic traffic congestion. **Avoid** driving, or take a taxi, during **rush hours** (7:30–9:30 am and 4:30–7:30 pm). The major troublespots are the bridges across Dubai Creek, but the whole of Sheikh Zayed Road grinds to a halt twice a day.
- Dubai has an appalling road-safety record, with an average of 18 deaths recorded every month. The police have launched a crackdown and can fine people for speeding and other infringements such as slowing to look at an accident. The website, www.dubaipolice.gov.ae, lists offences.
- Drivers and passengers are legally required to **wear seatbelts.**
- **Drive on the right in Dubai.** The **speed limit** is between 60kph/37mph and 120kph/74mph.
- **Breakdown services** cover Dubai: try the AAA (Arabian Automobile Association, www.aaauae.com) or IATC Recovery (International Automobile Touring Club; www.iatcuae.com).
- If you are involved in a traffic accident, you must stay at the scene with the vehicle and call the police (tel: 999). If it is only a very minor bump you should move the car out of the way of other cars, otherwise stay put.
- The police have a **zero tolerance policy on drink driving**. Do not drive if you have had any alcoholic drink; a jail term is the usual punishment.
- Pay-and-display car parks and parking meters are increasingly common in Bur Dubai and Deira. Charges are low, but always have a supply of coins to hand. Penalty tickets for parking illegally are 100–200Dh. Parking at shopping malls and other attractions is usually free.
- Fuel is inexpensive, costing about 6–7Dh per 4.5 litres (1 gallon). Fill up before venturing on a long journey.

Walking

Dubai is not a pedestrian-friendly city. Sights are not often within walking distance of each other and the climate means that walking anywhere for much of the year is extremely uncomfortable. If you do walk outside from March to November, wear a sunhat to ward off sunstroke and take a bottle of water to drink. However, in Bur Dubai and Deira it is possible walk around the old parts of the city (➤ 148–150).

Accommodation

Dubai is one of the few places in the world worth visiting simply to stay in the hotels. Many are attractions in their own right. The choice of hotels in the city is geared to the top end of the market, with a high proportion of luxury properties where standards are incredibly high. Prices increase year-on-year but this has not deterred visitors. In December 2005 the average beach hotel occupancy was 96 per cent. This is despite a 43 per cent rise in average daily room rates between September 2004 and September 2005. This means that you will need to book in advance for the peak period over Christmas and when the Dubai Shopping Festival takes place.

- **Off-season prices** (May–Oct) are creeping up to almost the same level as high-season rates. Many more hotels have just one year-round rate, but it is still worth looking for special offers, such as one free night, for accommodation during the summer.
- Fears that Dubai has too many high-end hotels don't appear to be affecting the market: many more luxury hotels are being built.
- **Hotel rooms** in the top hotels, which is most of them, are extremely **well-furnished**. High-tech facilities, such as wireless internet and flatscreen televisions, are commonplace.
- Water from the tap is safe to drink, but many hotels will provide complimentary bottles of drinking water.
- All hotels will have a website where you can make a reservation. Discounts may be offered if you ask, depending on occupancy levels.
- Holidays booked through a travel agent will typically include accommodation in the middle to upper range hotels.
- **Business travellers** tend to use the hotels on Sheikh Zayed Road, but all these hotels also have extensive leisure facilities.
- The **least expensive hotels** are found in Bur Dubai and Deira. Very cheap hotels are often in insalubrious parts of the city and are not recommended.
- The **most sought-after resort hotels** are those on the beach. However, international chains such as Sheraton and Le Meridien, may often permit guests at a city hotel to use the beach facilities of a sister property.
- Dubai's **luxury hotels are the centre of the city's social and entertainment scene** for the simple reason that only their bars, nightclubs and restaurants are licensed to serve alcohol.
- If **travelling independently** expect to spend upwards of 600Dh per night for an acceptable room. Cheaper hotels can cost 200–300Dh but it is worth spending more if possible. The most expensive hotels rooms can cost more than 10,000Dh per night.
- A **tip** of a few dirhams is appreciated by **hotel staff for room service,** baggage carrying and similar services.
- Dubai's Department of Tourism and Commerce Marketing assesses and grades all the hotelsl in the city. Additionally they operate an online hotel booking service (www.dubaitourism.ae) covering Deira, Bur Dubai, Jumeirah and Hatta.
- **Hotel apartments** might be a less expensive alternative to a hotel room for families. Found mainly in the old areas of the city, such as Deira and Bur Dubai, they typically offer a suite of rooms including a kitchen and living area, allowing for self-catering.
- There is a **youth hostel** in Deira, but other budget options such as guest houses, motels and bed-and-breakfast don't exist in the city.

Food and Drink

Dubai has world-class restaurants serving every conceivable cuisine from around the world. Most of the best restaurants are in the luxury hotels but there are several interesting venues outside the hotels that serve Arabic food (▶ 17 for more on Arabic and Emirati cuisine).

- **Hotel guests get priority at popular restaurants.** If you're not staying at the hotel, reserve in advance at its restaurant.
- Note that Dubai's restaurant scene is especially fast-moving; restaurants often close for a makeover and new establishments open frequently. Dubai's diners are always on the hunt for the next big thing which can mean that some restaurants are unjustly empty while the flavour of the month is booked solid.
- **Alcohol** is only served in hotel restaurants and bars. Wine lists are often initially impressive but the emphasis is often on big-name producers rather than smaller, less well-known wineries.
- During Ramadan (▶ 21) most restaurants do not serve alcohol. You may still drink alcohol in your hotel room.
- Competition is fierce between all the hotel restaurants and many hold special promotions that can turn a good meal into a bargain. Look for offers in hotel newsletters and local listings magazines and newspapers or on hotel websites.
- Bars often have a **"happy hour"** when prices are reduced considerably.
- For **eating out on a budget** go to the streets of Deira and Bur Dubai where there are numerous cafes, stalls and restaurants offering tasty Arab and Indian cuisine.
- **Dress codes are relatively relaxed** in Dubai's restaurants with only a handful of places requesting that customers wear jackets. But don't turn up at indoor restaurants in beachwear.
- Most hotel restaurants will stop serving food at a relatively late hour – typically last orders are at 11:30 pm.
- Most restaurants will include a 10–15 per cent service charge on your bill. Check before adding a tip.
- You don't have to eat in hotels all the time. Bur Dubai (▶ 55–78) is a good hunting ground to track down a huge range of inexpensive, independent restaurants, particularly if you're a fan of Indian food.
- Since Thursday and Friday is the equivalent of the weekend in Dubai, many hotel restaurants and pubs offer a buffet brunch on Friday, typically starting from noon. All-inclusive prices (typically 150–350Dh) sometimes include unlimited drinks.
- A **10 per cent Municipality tax** is usually included in the menu's prices but check the small print before ordering.
- **Water** is sold in all restaurants and bars but note the significant discrepancy between the prices of local brands of bottled water and imported brands and specify which you would prefer when ordering.

Five of the Best Brunches
Legends Steakhouse at the Dubai Creek Golf Club – for the views (▶ 50)
Spendido at the Ritz-Carlton – for the food (▶ 130)
Double Decker at the Al Murooj Rotana – for the price (▶ 99)
Mina A'Salam at Mina A'Salam – for the excess (▶ 127)
Spectrum On One at the Fairmont – for the champagne (▶ 101)

Shopping

For many people, Dubai's malls are the primary reason to visit the city. They're undoubtedly on a jaw-dropping scale and the range of shops inside the best can't be equalled anywhere else in the world. However, the days of finding a bargain in Dubai, outside the biannual sales, are gone. Prices have crept up to international levels. There's only one commodity that is significantly cheaper in Dubai – gold.

- There are almost 50 malls in Dubai and ever more opulent ones are being built. Currently, the largest is Mall of the Emirates with 400 shops and 65 restaurants, but it will almost certainly be superseded soon.
- The **larger malls** will have entertainment and childcare facilities for shoppers, as well as numerous restaurants and cafés (unlicensed). Information points provide maps.
- **Opening times** are typically Saturday to Thursday 10–10 with late opening at 2 pm or 3 pm on Friday. If you don't like crowds, avoid shopping on a Thursday. Friday nights can also be hectic.
- **Credit cards** are widely accepted, especially in mall-based shops. Thomas Cook opened a **currency exchange** office in Ibn Battuta mall in 2005 and it also has offices on Sheikh Zayed Road and in Bur Dubai, Deira, the Dubai World Trade Centre and in the airport where travellers' cheques can be changed at better rates than in the hotels (tel: 800 4145; www.alrostamaniexchange.com).
- It's not just international fashion designers who have outlets in Dubai. Marks & Spencer, Debenhams, IKEA, Carrefour and Harvey Nichols have large stores in the city.
- The closest you'll get to a traditionally **Arabic retail experience** is in the souks. The gold and spice souks in Deira are on the tourist trail but good deals can be struck there. Gold is one of the last bargains left in Dubai; prices are determined by weight of the item, rather than design.
- **Haggling** is expected in the old city's souks. The trader's first price can usually be halved but remember that the idea is to have fun, so keep the bargaining lighthearted.
- Cheap, if not counterfeit, goods can be found in several neighbourhoods in old Dubai. Karama, in Bur Dubai, is a large open-air market where anything and everything can be found, usually at an agreeably low price. Al Fahidi Street, also in Bur Dubai is the centre of the electronics trade.
- With the success of the annual Shopping Festival (➤ 20), when lavish prizes such as sports cars are given away daily, a summer shopping festival has been started: Dubai Summer Surprises. Retail prices are usually discounted during the festivals, but the raffles and competitions pull just as many crowds.
- **Returning goods** to shops is less clearcut than in other places. Shops may not offer a refund even for faulty goods, although exchanging goods is easier. Always keep the receipt and check the refunds and exchanges policy before you buy.
- Dubai Duty Free at Dubai ariport is one of the largest duty-free areas in the world with 65,000 different products on sale. You can shop here before you depart.
- ➤ 22–23 for more information on the city's best malls.

Entertainment

There are plenty of myths about what you can and cannot do in Dubai.
Generally the emirate is a very relaxed place, keen to make Western
tourists feel at home. However, the United Arab Emirates is a Muslim
country and that means certain restrictions apply.

- **Arabic is the official language** of the United Arab Emirates but **English
  is very widely spoken**. Most leading hotels have some multi-lingual staff.
- **Gambling is illegal**; to get around this you can predict the winner of a
  horse race at Nad Al Sheba and if correct win a prize.
- Films, songs, television, magazines, newspapers and other media are
  censored. Nudity, sex scenes and religious content are usually excised
  from films shown on television and in the cinema.
- Dubai's only **internet service** provider is Etisalat. It censors the content available to surfers. There are lots of cafés where you can use
  the internet, sometimes for free in branches of the Coffee Bean &
  Tea Leaf.
- The two **local papers** are the *Gulf News* and *Khaleej Times*. Both are
  self-censoring. There are numerous listings magazines, available from
  hotel lobbies, shopping malls, newsagents and book shops. Two other
  English-speaking newspapers are *Gulf Today* and *Emirates News*.
- Bars and nightclubs have to close promptly at 3 am. Generally, only
  bars, restaurants and nightclubs in hotels can serve alcohol. It is diffi-
  cult, but not impossible, to buy alcohol outside a bar or restaurant.
  Two off-licenses are permitted to sell wine, beer and spirits: African and
  Eastern (A&E) and Maritime and Mercantile International (MMI). They
  have branches in Bur Dubai, Deira, Karama, Mall of the Emirates and
  Ibn Battuta mall but prospective customers have to apply for a 150Dh
  licence and for holidaymakers it is not worth the effort.
- In many places Tuesday night is ladies night in Dubai (other establishments have similar nights on Mondays and Wednesdays). Women can
  often get free drinks all night in bars and clubs. The weekend differs in
  Dubai depending on who you work for, but Thursday night is guaranteed
  to be followed by a day off, so this is when most people go out.
- People dine late, drink later and arrive at a nightclub no earlier than
  1 am in Dubai. And there is no shortage of taxis to whisk revellers back
  home afterwards.
- There are three or four **superclubs** in Dubai at any one time and several
  small to medium venues. Bars number in the 50s. Entry is typically free
  unless a major live music act or DJ has been booked.
- **Live music** can be heard in several auditoriums around Dubai, although
  the heat prevents many outdoor shows in the summer. Dance and theatre are at an embryonic stage, with just one playhouse in the city at
  Madinat Jumeirah, hosting theatre, comedy and other performing arts.
  But this is set to change with the development of Dubailand
  (➤ 123–124).
- Cinemas, perhaps because they can be air-conditioned, are popular for a
  night out. There are multiplexes all over the city, and two IMAX screens.
  Films are generally the latest Hollywood fare, with a Bollywood production every now and then.

Deira

Getting Your Bearings 34 – 35
In a Day 36 – 37
Don't Miss 38 – 44
At Your Leisure 45 – 46
Where to... 47 – 54

Getting Your Bearings

Deira is a wedge of intensively developed, often congested and always bustling city protruding towards the mouth of Dubai Creek. The Creek forms one side of Deira. The other side is a mishmash of business and residential buildings stretching along the corniche to Al Mamzar Beach Park and the border with the emirate of Sharjah.

★ Don't Miss

1 Palm Deira ➤ 38
2 The Souks ➤ 39
3 Dubai Creek ➤ 42

At Your Leisure

4 Heritage House ➤ 45
5 Al-Ahmadiya School ➤ 46
6 Al Mamzar Beach
Park ➤ 46

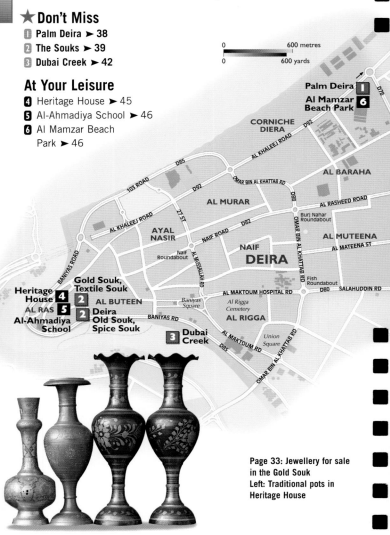

Page 33: Jewellery for sale in the Gold Souk
Left: Traditional pots in Heritage House

Behind this is urban Dubai at its most hectic. The area is bisected by the main road to Sharjah. This corner of Dubai is the city's oldest and its most frenetic. It can be exhilarating or frustrating in equal measure but there are plenty of sights that will amaze. The main area of interest for visitors is the triangle from the Maktoum Bridge to the corniche. The dhow wharfage is where the traditional ships are unloaded; some of their goods are later sold in Deira's souks.

Continuing down the Creek, a string of five-star hotels occupy prime waterfront positions.

Deira's souks are a delight for the senses – spices, fruits and fish and the warm beauty of gold. The Heritage House and the Al-Ahmadiya School offer an insight into how Emiratis lived in the years before four-wheel-drive cars and satellite television. Out to sea, an example of how far Dubai has come in 50 years is taking shape: a colossal Palm Island is being built offshore from Al Hamriya Port. By 2009 the man-made island will be larger than Paris.

ABU BAKER AL SIDDIQUE RD

Above: Local men buying silks
in the Textile Souk
Above right: Intricate
woodcarving in Heritage House
Left: A local trader
transporting his goods

Start at the Dubai Golf and Yacht Club, then enter old Dubai: take an *abra* trip, visit Heritgage House and the souks, and end your day with a dhow dinner cruise.

Deira in a Day

9:30 am

Start the day at the **Dubai Creek Golf and Yacht Club** (➤ 54). The yacht club is on the near side of the Park Hyatt hotel, the golf club on the far side. Breakfast on the terrace of the Boardwalk restaurant (➤ 49) at the yacht club as the sunlight bounces off the water and *abras* cross the waterway.

10:30 am

Golfers won't be able to resist a round on the club's championship level, par-71 course before lunch. Alternatively, it is cost effective for a small group (maximum six people) to charter one of the Yacht Club's boats for a tour of the Creek. A 3-hour boat trip will take you out into the Arabian Gulf as far as the Burj Al Arab hotel and back via the World offshore development.

1:30 pm

Return to shore for lunch. Vivaldi (➤ 50), an Italian restaurant at the Sheraton Dubai Creek, a short way down the Creek towards central Deira, is good for a light lunch. Sit under the awning on the terrace if the midday weather is cool enough.

3:30 pm

Take a taxi to **4 Heritage House** (➤ 45) on the other side of Deira. Of the heritage projects in the city, it provides perhaps the best description of traditional household life in the emirate, before the oil money started flowing in.

5:00 pm

You can walk from Heritage House to the **2 Gold Souk** (➤ 39–40) for some late-afternoon window shopping if you turn right out of the house and head into the heart of Deira. It's cool enough to be outside now, and the crossroads in the middle of the Gold Souk will be filling up with workers, sightseers and shoppers. This is one of the best places in the world to buy gold. Take time to explore the narrow alleys running off the souk's primary lanes – it is down these that you will find many of the more unusual shops. Make your way towards the **Spice Souk** by heading into the Al Buteen neighbourhood and turning left to reach the Creek. Then take a taxi up the Creek (or walk) to the Intercontinental Hotel for 7:45 pm.

8:00 pm

You can't miss the **Al Mansour Dhow** (➤ 49) – the boat is outlined in lights. It departs every evening for a sedate cruise up and down the Creek, to the accompaniment of Arabic music and a buffet. The **3 Creek** (➤ 42–44) is much more beautiful at night with the sparkling skyline of Sheikh Zayed Road in the distance and working dhows departing for North African ports.

Palm Deira

Of the three Palm Islands that are under construction off Dubai's shore, the latest and largest will be attached to Deira's seafront corniche. It was announced in October 2004 and will be completed by 2009, adding 400km (248 miles) to Dubai's coast. Its proximity to the old city of Dubai will make Palm Deira a major addition to Deira's visitor attractions.

The crescent protecting the Palm from the open sea will be the world's largest breakwater at a length of 21km (13 miles), while the 8.5km (5-mile) wide island will extend 14km (8.5 miles) into the Gulf and use one billion cubic metres of rock and sand for its foundations, which delve to 22m (72 feet) below sea level. Along the 41 fronds, 8,000 houses will be built, with attendant marinas, malls, sports facilities, hotels and restaurants. Private and public beaches will line the fronds, with between 150m (163 yards) and 400m (436 yards) of sea between each frond. The entire Palm, with an area of 80sq km (30 square miles) will be larger than Manhattan and comparable to Greater London.

Above: Once complete, Palm Deira will be larger than Manhattan

While Deira's corniche itself doesn't have the visual interest of a Creekside stroll, it's where many Dubai locals promenade on weekend evenings. The Shindagha fish market, in a car park close to the Hyatt Regency hotel, is open daily from 7 am to 11 pm. A museum in the marketplace explains Dubai's seafaring heritage and illustrates some of the 300 species of fish caught in the surrounding seas.

✚ 171 E4
✉ Deira corniche

2 The Souks

For shoppers, the street markets of Deira are a treasure trove of jewellery, clothing and exotic spices. The souks are one of the few places in Dubai where it is still possible to find a bargain – especially if you are buying gold. But they also explain Dubai's origins as an international trading post.

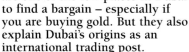

Dubai's souks are a hive of activity

Deep in the heart of Deira's old town, the **Gold Souk** is a lattice of streets lined with shops selling gold jewellery. Unless you work in Fort Knox you probably won't see as much gold in one place ever again – a fact that brings people from all over the world to shop here. Gold, according to local experts, is the one commodity that remains significantly cheaper in Dubai than anywhere else, which is why the Gold Souk's boundaries are marked by arches proclaiming "Dubai: City of Gold". Most of the gold is of the bright, pure 24-carat variety. It is said that if all the gold in the world was refined to 24-carat purity it would fit in a cube of

5.4sq m (60 square feet) – if so, much of it must be for sale in these streets. If you don't like the orangey-yellow 24-carat gold you can also find 18-, 21- and 22-carat pieces. If none of the bracelets, necklaces, earrings, rings or brooches appeal, craftspeople can create a piece of jewellery to your design. Some of the best souvenirs are small items such as gold tie clips or money clips. Gold traders don't need to lower their prices so don't expect much of a discount, except during January's Shopping Festival.

Off the main artery of the Gold Souk a few shops sell interesting antique silver items from Oman, which are highly sought. Beside the Gold Souk there is a smaller **Textile Souk** where you can find anything from Sinbad-style sandals, saris, and pashminas to shishas and other souvenirs. The Textile Souk is where haggling pays dividends. All along the souk's streets traders will attempt to catch your attention with

Below: Bargain hunters will be spoilt for choice in the Gold Souk

legitimate and not-so-legitimate deals: hustlers don't get any more intrusive than a muttered "Excuse me, sir, fake watches?". But showing any interest in the price of some jewellery or clothing is the signal for a persistent sales pitch.

Adjacent to the Old Souk *abra* station, on Old Baladiya Road, the **Spice Souk** occupies an alley alongside the perimeter road in the Al Ras neighbourhood. You can see why souks flourished in the narrow lanes of Deira: to one side dhows crept up the Creek and unloaded their cargoes on the wharf adjacent to the souks. Ships carrying spices and other commodities would stop at Dubai on their way from India and some of the goods would be traded on the waterfront. Goods are not limited to spices; there are sacks of frankincense, camomile tea, rose petals, dried chillis and lemons. Conveniently, there is a second alley behind the Spice Souk where you can buy

How to Haggle in Five Easy Steps

• Don't show interest in the item you want at first. Ask about something else, decline it. Then, as an afterthought, ask about the item you're really after.

• The salesman will offer a price. Look surprised. Cut the price by half or more. Ask if he'll accept that. He'll decline.

• If possible, say you'll take two for a price that's less than price asked for one. Otherwise, increase your bid by 10 per cent or so and say that is as much as you can pay for it.

• Stay polite but stick to your price. The chances are that the salesman will come down to your price because he will still make a profit.

• The final tactic is a last resort, but usually works. Say you're going to see what other shops are offering and will come back if his is the best price.

Above: Rugs and throws for sale

inexpensive kitchen utensils, including Indian *karahi* pans and tureens. The best buys in the Spice Souk are vanilla pods and saffron. The saffron is sold in varying levels of quality from the cheapest (the yellow ends of the crocus flower dipped in red dye, used only for colouring food) to the finest (the naturally red tips of the stamens, best for colour and flavour). Expect to pay up to 20Dh for 10g (0.3 ounces) of the best saffron, or about 15Dh for 10g (0.3 ounces) of whole flowers. To reach the Spice Souk turn left at Al Buteen mosque on 12th Street and keep walking.

Below: Local traders go about their daily business

➕ 170 B3
🕐 Daily 9–1, 4–10

3 Dubai Creek

The story of the Creek is the story of how Dubai developed from a desert trading post to the modern city it is today. Both sides of Dubai still exist on the Creek – you can see Dubai's past and its future on a short stroll along the shore.

In the middle of the 19th century the Maktoum family relocated from Abu Dhabi to a small village beside an inlet: Dubai. They settled on both sides of the Creek, which was to become central to their fortunes. Dubai slowly prospered and development stretched inland along both sides of the Creek – this is why Dubai's first five-star hotel is on the bank of the Creek and why Dubai's airport, built in 1960, is further up the shore. In 1820 Dubai's ruler, Mohammed bin Hazza, struck a deal with the British, whose navy had been hunting pirates along the Arabian coastline. In return for compliance the British Navy would look after Dubai's interests at sea, leaving Dubai free to capitalise on trade and commerce. The pearl-fishing industry, based in the Creek, brought money to the port and Dubai became known as a place that welcomed non-Arab immigrants – on the Bur Dubai side of the Creek it was Iranian traders who built Bastakiya (► 64–65). People from India and Arabia came to Dubai for business and the souks in Deira boomed, although at that time pearls were the only export.

Above: Dhows on Dubai Creek

However, it wasn't until Abu Dhabi struck oil that the city took off. In 1959 Sheikh Rashid bin Saeed Al Maktoum initiated the dredging of the Creek. It cost him $850,000 but it was money well spent because he could now charge Abu Dhabi to use his deep-water port to import all the heavy industrial equipment needed to drill for oil. Dubai was already a free-trade port, with import and export tariffs reduced in the early 20th century, and other businesses took advantage of the favourable taxes. The net result? Dubai's economy rapidly expanded.

Other factors weighed in during the 1960s and 1970s – the discovery of Dubai's own source of oil in 1966 and the formation of the United Arab Emirates in 1971 – but without the Creek Dubai would be a very different place today.

You don't have to go far to see what life on the Creek was like decades ago. The dhow wharfage between the Maktoum Bridge and the Sheraton Dubai Creek hotel is where dhows moor for the night, where they are repaired and where they

Right: Crossing the Creek in an *abra* is a great way to see the juxtaposition of old and new architecture

refuel for the next leg of their voyage. A dinner cruise on one of the tourist dhows by the Intercontinental hotel will come up as far as the wharfage and you'll be able to see sailors preparing for the night as you tuck into your buffet. And from the Intercontinental down to the mouth of the inlet, Deira's Creekside is lined with boats unloading anything from vegetables to televisions – despite the property deals taking place in skyscrapers elsewhere, this is very much a working port.

The further you go from the mouth of the Creek, the less developed the shore becomes, until you pass under Maktoum Bridge and the Creek widens. On the Deira side the Dubai Creek Golf and Yacht Club has a new marina with space for 300 yachts. Creekside Park on the opposite bank is Dubai's best park. Pass both these green spaces and you will go under Garhoud Bridge. Now the Creek curves round to the right and broadens out into the Ras Al Khor lagoon, haven of flamingoes and other migratory birds. This is where the Creek ends, in a wildlife sanctuary increasingly enveloped by the urban sprawl that the Creek itself initiated.

An *abra* crossing is an essential Dubai experience. These narrow boats motor back and forth across the Creek from station to station and from them you can see both the high-rise glass towers of modern Dubai and the wind towers and minarets of the old city. About 20 million passenger journeys are made by *abra* every year and it is the quickest and most enjoyable way to cross the Creek. The three alternative methods of crossing the Creek are under it in the Shindagha pedestrian tunnel and over it on the Maktoum or Garhoud bridges, both of which are gridlocked at rush hour. So, there's no excuse for not taking to the water and exploring the Creek by boat.

All stocked up for the journey across the Persian Gulf

Goods bound for the souks are unloaded from dhows and other vessels along the Creek

At Your Leisure

4 Heritage House

The Heritage House is one of the most fully realised and coherent restorations of a traditional house in Dubai. It was built in 1890 by Mattar bin Saeed bin Muzaaina and restored by the Dubai Municipality in 1994. Room by room, the exhibition explains everyday life in a typical Emirati family home between 1890 and the 1950s. The *majlis* or living room is the heart of an Emirati house. It's the room for receiving visitors, and since hospitable Arab families would welcome friends and strangers alike, the *majlis* is usually separate from the home's living quarters.

Women also would have their own *majlis* – a display in the Heritage House shows the household's women sewing, making Arabic coffee and applying henna. Men are not permitted into the women's *majlis*. Like the main *majlis*, the floor of the women's *majlis* is covered by Persian carpets. The main living room, the Al Makhzan is where families meet, eat and talk

together. Newly married couples, however, had the privacy of the bride room, Al Hijla. Each of these displays in the Heritage House explains what every item in the room was used for and the museum ranks as the most informative in Dubai. To find it, take the road running parallel to and behind Al Khor Road, close to Deira's corniche.

✚ 170 B4
✉ 28 Sikka Street ☎ 226 0286
🕐 Sat–Thu 8–7:30 pm, Fri 2:30–7:30;
Sat–Thu 9–5, Fri 2–5 during Ramadan
🎫 Free

Traditional Emirati family life is brought to life in the restored Heritage House

5 Al-Ahmadiya School

You'll find the Al-Ahmadiya School down the alley beside the Heritage House. The school was built in 1912 for the children of Dubai's ruling classes, with an upper floor added in 1920. In 1922, extra space was made for students when Sheikh Abdul Rahman bin Hafidahh and teachers from Zubair School in Iraq began teaching Islamic law, the Koran and the sayings of Prophet Mohammed; students would sit on mats surrounding their teachers. By 1963 the number of students had outgrown its premises, thanks to the introduction of English and science to the curriculum, and the school was relocated. The Al-Ahmadiya building was later restored using traditional materials of gypsum, coral, shell, stone and sandalwood.

✚ 170 B4
✉ Next to the Heritage House (➤ 45)
☎ 393 7151
⏰ Sat–Thu 8–7:30, Fri 2:30–7:30; Sat–Thu 9–4:30, Fri 2–4:30 during Ramadan 🎟 Free

6 Al Mamzar Beach Park

In a very urbanised area, the 90ha (222-acre) Al Mamzar Beach Park is a pleasant open space offering four beaches and several green swathes of land, chalets, picnic areas and childrens' playgrounds. The

Right: Islamic law and the sayings of the Prophet Mohammed were among the subjects taught at Al-Ahmadiya

construction of the Deira Palm (➤ 38) will undoubtedly impinge on the park's popularity, but watching the construction activity may also interest some people. Both of the swimming pools have lifeguards and changing facilities and there are also changing rooms at the beaches. For visitors staying in Deira, Al Mamzar is a better option for relaxing outdoors than braving the traffic to cross the Creek for Creekside Park (➤ 68) or Zabeel Park (➤ 88–89). You'll find Al Mamzar beyond Al Hamriya Port; take a taxi.

✚ 171 off F3
✉ Near Al Hamriya Port
⏰ Daily 8 am–11 pm, Wed women only
🎟 Expensive

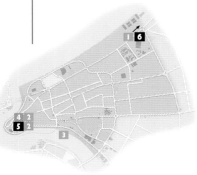

Where to... Stay

Prices
Expect to pay per double room, per night
$ 150Dh–600Dh $$ 600Dh–1,500Dh $$$ 1,500Dh–10,000+Dh

Coral Deira $$
Coral International is a home-grown Emirati hotel group, which makes this small, five-star hotel rather unusual in Dubai. The facilities are on a par with the big hotels and the ambience is warm and welcoming. Rooms are comfortable and facilities include saunas, a rooftop swimming pool and gym. As a Muslim-run hotel, alcohol is not available, although this shouldn't detract too much from the buffet at Al Nafoorah. Guests are entitled to free transport and access to the beach at the sister resort in Sharjah.

➕ 171 D1 ⊠ Al Muraqqabat Street
☎ 224 8587;
www.coral-international.com

Al Bustan Rotana $$
Although popular with business travellers for its proximity to the airport, the grand Al Bustan provides enough entertainment to appeal to leisure travellers too. There is an above-average collection of restaurants, the only nightclub on this side of the Creek (▲ 52) and health and fitness facilities. Rooms lean more towards the business fraternity, with a slightly anodyne styling and facilities such as high-speed internet, but you'll see plenty of holiday makers basking around the pool.

➕ Off map ⊠ Casablanca Road, Garhoud ☎ 282 0000;
www.rotana.com

Dubai Youth Hostel $
On the Sharjah side of the airport, Dubai's only youth hostel doesn't enjoy an especially auspicious location but makes up for the inconvenience by offering clean rooms at excellent rates if you're a member of the Youth Hostels Association (YHA).

There is an old section of the hostel where dorm rooms are a cost-effective choice for budget travellers, while a new wing has large, clean family bedrooms with a television and shower. General facilities include a gym, swimming pool and tennis courts.

If you want to see the sights of Deira, Bur Dubai and venture into Sharjah, the Dubai Youth Hostel is great value and much better than a similarly priced hotel. However, as soon as start taking taxis into Jumeirah you might find you're spending more than you save.

➕ 170 A4
⊠ 39 Al Nahda Road,
Al Qusais ☎ 298 8161

Hilton Dubai Creek $$$
A chic city-centre hotel, the Hilton Dubai Creek is a modernist's dream, designed by renowned architect Carlos Ott. A lobby cased in glass and chrome leads up to the first-floor restaurant Verre (▲ 50). The bedrooms are just as exciting, with dramatic black and white bath-rooms and with just 154 rooms, service is personal. Facilities include pools, a gym and a child-minding service.

➕ 170 C2 ⊠ Baniyas Road
☎ 227 1111; www.hilton.com

Hyatt Regency $$–$$$
This hotel dates from 1980, when it was one of the first international hotels in Deira. The Hyatt is in a prime position for shopping trips to the Gold Souk. Other advantages include several good restaurants, including the Italian eatery Focaccia (▲ 49) and the city's only revolving restaurant. Each of the 414 rooms and suites has satellite television and internet access.

Business guests outnumber holiday visitors, but don't let that put you off because recreational options such as an ice-skating rink in the hotel's Galleria mall and a mini-golf course make it welcoming for families. There are excellent views, but remember that this is a very built-up district and the closest beach is at Al Mamzar Beach Park.

🚹 171 D4 ⊠ The Corniche ☎ 209 1234; www.dubai.regencyhyatt.com

Intercontinental $$

The Intercontinental was Dubai's first five-star hotel and celebrated its 30th anniversary in 2005. The rooms are showing their age, but that's hardly surprising when they've hosted 630 film stars, 1,500 musicians and 1,230 ambassadors in their time. Dubai's hotels have moved on and the Intercontinental's relatively small bathrooms no longer match up to the competition. However, the hotel does benefit from an excellent position on the edge of the Creek and close prox-

imity to Deira's sites of interest and its restaurants are good. For this reason it seems to attract more leisure travellers than other Deira hotels. Facilities include a rooftop pool and a gym.

🚹 170 C2 ⊠ Baniyas Road ☎ 222 7171; www.dubai.intercontinental.com

JW Marriott $$

The Marriott, close to the Hamarain shopping centre, is slightly isolated by two main roads from the creekside attractions of Deira, but it is convenient for business travellers. However, those on holiday can take advantage of the daily shuttle bus service to the beach. Other benefits include a range of restaurants, a health club and pool. The 351 rooms and suites are furnished to high standard.

🚹 171 D1 ⊠ Abu Baker Al Siddique Road ☎ 262 4444; www.marriott.com

Park Hyatt Dubai $$$

An elegant haven, the Middle East's first Park Hyatt, opened in 2005

and has been a hit with the style-conscious. It's certainly one of the more arresting hotels in the city, with its modernist Moroccan theme of whitewashed walls, blue domes and secluded courtyards. Rooms are equally impressive; the innovation is to have a bathroom, with stand-alone bath and separate wet room open to the bedrooom. Décor is minimalist but luxurious. Some ground-floor rooms have their own garden, while upper-level balconies look out over the Creek. The Park Hyatt is the only dedicated leisure hotel on this side of the Creek, it's also one of the best in the city.

🚹 172 C2 ⊠ Dubai Creek Golf and Yacht Club ☎ 602 1234; www.dubai.park.hyatt.com

Sheraton Dubai Creek $$$

The imposing Sheraton Dubai Creek was renovated in 2002 to bring the hotel up to date.
Although the designers have followed the blueprint for Dubai's luxury hotels by swathing every-

thing in marble, this is a handsome place, with a good range of restaurants offering uninterrupted views of the Creek. Most rooms also have views of the Creek, as well as top-notch business services, a hi-fi and video player (tapes can be borrowed from the guest lounge). A free shuttle bus connects the Sheraton Dubai Creek with it's Jumeirah sibling, where guests can use the beach. The bus also drops guests off at the Deira City Centre mall (► 51).

🚹 170 C2 ⊠ Baniyas Road ☎ 228 1111; www.sheraton.com/dubai

Sheraton Deira $$

The Sheraton Deira is a less expensive alternative to the Dubai Creek hotel. It's in the heart of Deira and consequently is a little noisier and a little less convenient for seeing the sights beyond Deira, but it is popular with businessmen and visitors from Asia.

🚹 171 E2 ⊠ Al Matina Street ☎ 268 8888; www.sheraton.com/deira

Where to...
Eat and Drink

Prices
Expect to pay for a three-course meal for one, excluding drinks and service
$ under 60Dh $$ 600h–100Dh $$$ over 100Dh

Blue Elephant $$

Blue Elephant Thai restaurants are popular all over the world for fine Thai food at good prices and the Dubai branch, inside this large hotel, does an excellent job of maintaining that reputation. The décor is elaborate, with a waterfall and dark wood furnishings. Cross a bridge over a carp-filled pool to get to your table. Starters include delicious Thai fish cakes with cucumber sweet-and-sour sauce. For mains the menu features most Thai favourites, including a well-judged green curry. Although somewhat out of the way, near the airport, if you're in the area the Blue Elephant merits a visit.

➕ Off map ⊠ Al Bustan Rotana Hotel, Casablanca Road, Garhoud ☎ 282 0000; www.blueelephant.com 🕐 Daily noon–3 pm, 7–11:30 pm

The Boardwalk $–$$

The Boardwalk serves breakfast, lunch and dinner in an idyllic setting on the Creek. While the food is hit and miss, the location alone draws casually dressed locals and visitors. In the winter sit outside on the wood decking to watch cabin cruisers and *abras* chug past with the ship-shaped yacht club, complete with mast and port-holes, overlooking you. The evening is the time when the Boardwalk comes alive. The menu is typical multinational pub food, which can be disappointing. Starters such as buffalo chicken-wings are a safe option, and go for the simplest main courses. To make up for the mediocre food, there's a good range of beers and cocktails, plus, of course, the views.

➕ 172 C2 ⊠ Dubai Creek Yacht Club ☎ 295 6000 🕐 Daily 8 am–midnight

Century Village $$

Century Village is a large alfresco restaurant complex behind the Aviation Club and tennis stadium in Garhoud.

There are about a dozen venues to choose from, all offering outdoor seating and a variety of cuisines; rather than list them individually, we recommend you visit the Village and see what catches your eye. Many restaurants have evening promotions. De Gama (tel: 282 3636) reopened in 2006 after a revamp but still serves a curious mix of Portuguese food, with the odd Mexican dish thrown in. The baked fish is a good bet. La Vigna (tel: 282 0030) is a luxurious Italian restaurant.

➕ 172 C1 ⊠ Near the tennis stadium, Garhoud

Focaccia $$

Focaccia is a mock-rustic restaurant in the venerable Hyatt Regency hotel serving some of the city's best Italian food. As befits the Italian farmhouse theme, the dishes are not flashy but substantial, tasty and good value. A good place for a lively meal out.

➕ 171 D4 ⊠ Hyatt Regency Hotel, The Corniche ☎ 317 2222 🕐 Daily lunch, 7–11:30, Thu 7:30–midnight

Al Mansour Dhow $$$

Dinner cruises on dhows are an entertaining way of seeing the

Creek at night, when the city on either side is lit up. The large Al Mansour dhow, operated by the Intercontinental hotel, is the best of the lot, with an buffet below decks and superb vantage points from the top deck. The food takes second place to the views from the twinkling dhow.

The tour of the Creek takes about two hours and travels up to the dhow wharfs and down to the mouth of the Creek. Arabic music is piped around the boat to add to the ambience. The dhow is licensed and serves wine. Expect to pay 300–400Dh per person.

🚭 170 C2 ⊠ Intercontinental hotel, Baniyas Road ☎ 205 7333 ⏲ Daily 8 pm departure opposite the hotel

Legends Steakhouse $$$

Steaks are the name of the game at this sophisticated steakhouse overlooking the golf course and the Creek. The dress code is smart, but it shouldn't be a problem to turn up straight from the fairway. Starters

include pan-fried foie gras or a silky lobster bisque. If that hasn't pushed your cholesterol levels too high, the steaks come in two sizes and are sourced from the US and New Zealand.

🚭 172 C2 ⊠ Dubai Creek Golf Club ☎ 295 6000 ⏲ Daily 7–11 pm

Shabestan $$–$$$

This excellent Iranian restaurant, serves comfortingly aromatic breads, kebabs, chicken dishes and other Persian classics. Slow-cooked lamb with rice, dill and broad beans is a favourite with regulars. Live music adds to the experience. The interior is a lavish approximation of a sultan's castle with art, antiques and traditional Arabian archways.

🚭 170 C2 ⊠ Intercontinental hotel, Baniyas Road ☎ 205 7333 ⏲ Daily 12:30–3:15, 7:30–11:15

Traiteur $$$

The closest food preparation gets to theatre in Dubai is at Traiteur, the haute-cuisine restaurant at the Park

Hyatt. The two-tiered venue is a lofty, attention-grabbing room overlooking the Creek. The focus of the room, however, is the large open kitchen where nine chefs prepare all the modern European-style dishes.

It's a riveting scene as the chefs work in what seems like a technicolour light show that never misses a beat. The food is superb and the wine list is extensive. A sommelier extracts the bottle from what is not so much a wine cellar as a wine pillar in an adjoining room.

🚭 172 C2 ⊠ Park Hyatt Dubai ☎ 602 1234; www.dubai.park.hyatt.com ⏲ Daily 12:30–3:30, 7–midnight

Verre $$$

Verre marked the arrival of Dubai as one of the world's great dining cities: it was Gordon Ramsay's first overseas venture and he's confident that Dubai's restaurant scene will become the match of New York or London. For now, however, Verre, on the first floor of the Hilton, is

one of the most desirable dinner spots in town.

The interior designer has played safe with an understated layout of glass panels and moody light. The menu, compiled by Ramsay protégé Jason Whitelock, is a snapshot of contemporary European cooking, with dishes such as caramelised pork belly with celeriac puree and seared scallops. The exquisite food is good value; the wine list will dent your finances.

🚭 170 C2 ⊠ Hilton Dubai Creek ☎ 227 1111 ⏲ Sun–Fri 7–midnight

Vivaldi $$–$$$

For all-day dining in a prime creekside location, the simple pasta dishes at this chic Italian restaurant hit the spot. An elevated terrace is shaded by an awning but the views are equally good from inside the glass-walled dining room.

🚭 170 C2 ⊠ Sheraton Dubai Creek, Baniyas Road ☎ 228 1111 ⏲ Daily 6:30 am–1.30 am

Where to...
Shop

Deira City Centre

Deira City Centre, Dubai's long-standing favourite mall, is standing up well to competiton across the Creek. A new extension, Bin Hendi, has added the sort of marble-coated flashiness that you find in Wafi City. Before you reach Bin Hendi, an 11-screen cinema may tempt you inside with the latest Hollywood releases. At the opposite end of the mall – and it is a long walk – the children's area, Magic Planet, will delight younger members of the family. In between lies a very diverse collection of shops. On the largest scale, Carrefour dominates the centre of the ground floor while a Debenhams department store, stocking the entire homeware range, is located on the second floor. Unlike most malls, shops of a particular type are grouped together at Deira City Centre, so you'll find electronics shops on the ground floor near the information desk and the Arabian Treasures mini-mall on the second floor in the west court. This is where Kashmiri shawls, Persian rugs and Arabian antiques are sold. The remainder of the outlets is a well-balanced mix of mainstream brands and designer boutiques. Shops on the ground floor include Mothercare, Woolworths, Next, United Colors of Benetton, Zara, Diesel, The Body Shop, Nine West and the Watch House. The MAC branch is Dubai's largest and has an enormous selection of make-up. On the second floor you'll find Banana Republic, Gap, Karen Millen, Topshop, Old Navy and Adidas among many others. One attraction of Dubai's malls is that they seem to attract leading retailers from across the world so you get high street shops from the US, Britain, Italy and Japan. Fashionistas should follow the signs to Bin Hendi, the new two-storey addition to the mall. As well as brands like Hugo Boss and G-Star, some of the names may be unfamiliar: Braccialini stocks quirky handbags, Ungaro Fever has bright women's fashions while Phat Farm sells a hip-hop label in a shop decorated with zebra prints, a chandelier and ornate mirrors. You can examine the spectacular diamonds at Graff from the comfort of a leather armchair in wood-panelled splendour. The Noodle House in Bin Hendi is good for a bite to eat, serving a range of noodle dishes, soups and appetisers at trestle tables.

Travel light and use the left luggage office on the second floor near Debenhams where you can leave shopping bags rather than carry them all day. At weekends it can be hard to find a parking space; it is better to take a taxi here.

➕ 170 off C1 ⊠ At the junction of Al Garhoud Bridge Road ☎ 295 1010; www.deiracitycentre.com ⊙ Sat–Tue 10–10, Wed–Fri 10–midnight

Al Futtaim Centre

This shopping complex, half way down this wide thoroughfare, is home to a giant Toys R Us and Dubai's first Marks & Spencer department store. Toys R Us stocks everything from bikes and DVDs to dolls and clothes. The Marks & Spencer store has the same range of items as the British shops, including the food hall.

➕ 171 D1 ⊠ Al Muraqqabat Road ☎ 222 5859 ⊙ Sat–Thu 10–10, Fri 4–10

Al Ghurair City

Al Ghurair is on a parallel street to the Al Futtaim Centre. It is Dubai's oldest mall (20 years and counting) but a revamp in 2003 updated it. Locals visit Al Ghurair as a less-hectic alternative to Deira City Centre and because there are some useful shops, including a Spinneys supermarket. Other malls may have more appeal to holidaymakers.

➕ 170 C2 ⊠ Al Rigga Road ☎ 222 5222

Where to...
Be Entertained

IKEA at Festival City

The largest IKEA store in the UAE opened in this new development in November 2005. Festival City, currently under construction and due for completion by 2015, is a colossal "city-within-a-city" on the edge of the Creek beyond the Garhoud airport road. It will have hotels, malls, leisure centres and workplaces; one of the first attractions to open was the IKEA department store. It provides a vast amount of space in the centre of Festival City in which to shop for typically good-value household items at Swedish-owned store. By 2007 the IKEA outlet will be surrounded by 450 shops and 12,000 parking spaces. The aim is to revitalise downtown Dubai, but thankfully a new bridge is being built across the Creek at Ras Al Khor Wildlife Sanctuary to improve access to the site.

🚹 Off map ⊠ Dubai Festival City
🕿 203 7555; www.ikeadubai.com
🕒 Sat–Fri 10–10

The Souks

Deira's souks should be on the to-do list of every visitor to Dubai, if only because they're a vibrant reminder of what Dubai was like before the air-conditioned malls arrived. Goods would be unloaded from dhows at creekside and sold in the adjoining web of lanes and alleys. Today the Spice Souk is a fragrant but crowded lane of small shops, each with sacks of spices and exotic foods outside. It's as much fun to guess what the sacks contain as it is to haggle over a pinch of saffron. Further away from the Creek, in the centre of Deira's souks, is the Gold Souk. To an extent this has become a sanitised stop on the tourist circuit, but the jaw-dropping effect of more gold than you'll see in lifetime remains. There's a small Textile Souk beside the Gold Souk where you can buy sandals, clothes and other souvenirs.

🚹 170 B3 🕒 Sat–Thu 10–10,
Fri 4–10

BARS

The Irish Village

Once you've overcome your surprise at finding a corner of Dublin in Dubai, enjoy a pint of Guinness at the outdoor tables, which are crowded with a mix of expats in the winter months. The interior is a smoky environment, but outside you can appreciate the illusion created by the pub's designers from the fake Irish shopfronts to the Irish telephone box. The Irish Village is next to a much larger complex of bars and restaurants called Century Village (▶ 49–50).

🚹 172 C1 ⊠ Dubai tennis stadium, 31st Street 🕿 282 4750 🕒 Fri–Tue 11–1:15 am, Wed–Thu 11–2:15

Oxygen

Underneath the glitzy Al Bustan Rotana lurks this mid-sized nightclub, the only venue on the Deira side of the Creek. The music policy is varied, with famous DJs appearing intermittently with house and R&B on the playlist most nights. Oxygen could be a enjoyable end to a night spent at the nearby Irish Village complex. Monday is ladies night, with drinks for 2Dh.

🚹 Off map ⊠ Al Bustan Rotana hotel, Garhoud 🕿 282 0000;
www.rotana.com 🕒 Daily 7pm–3 am

QD's

Winter is the perfect time to sit outside at this smart creekside bar and watch the sun go down over

Dubai's skyline across the Creek. On the outdoor terrace the Creek bubbles by at your feet, while waiters serve bar snacks such as potato wedges or chargrilled satays. The cocktail list is worth plundering and you can also smoke shisha (flavoured tabacco).
🚇 172 C2 ✉ Dubai Creek Yacht Club ☎ 295 000 🕙 Daily 6–2

The Terrace
Stolichnaya, Absolut, Smirnoff, Ketel One, Wyborowa, Grey Goose and Belvedere: these are just a few of the vodkas served at this classy creekside bar at the Park Hyatt hotel (▶ 48). Food can be ordered until midnight and is a notch up from typical bar snacks such as burgers with cheese (Emmental, Cheddar or Provolone) and red cabbage (60Dh). Sit outside in a cushioned area to watch the sunset.
🚇 172 C2 ✉ Park Hyatt Dubai ☎ 317 2222; www.dubai.park.hyatt.com 🕙 Daily noon–1 am

SPAS

Amara
Amara's unique selling point is that there are no communal areas. You have your treatment room to yourself and you also get changed in it. Each room has a private garden with a refreshing rain shower. The spa also boasts a 25m (82-foot) swimming pool and couples rooms if you want to enjoy your treatment with a partner. Take the opportunity to explore the hotel's amazing Moroccan-themed courtyards – the luxurious interior is just as good-looking. The spa, which opened in 2005, is proving popular with golf widows and supermodels so it must be doing something right.
🚇 172 C2 ✉ Park Hyatt Dubai ☎ 602 1234; www.dubai.park.hyatt.com 🕙 Daily 9am–10 pm

Paris Gallery Day Spa
The Paris Gallery Day Spa may not have the exclusive milieu of Amara,

located as it is in Deira City Centre, but it's a great place to pop into after a hard day flexing the credit card. Hair, make-up, facials and pedicures revamp you from top-to-toe. This is a women-only spa.
🚇 170 off C1 ✉ Deira City Centre ☎ 294 4000; www.uae-parisgallery.com 🕙 Daily 10–10

CINEMA

Cinestar
A total of 11 screens tempt shoppers into this deceptively large cinema, located on the second floor of the mall before you enter the new Bin Hendi extension. Movies are the usual Hollywood fare.
🚇 170 off C1 ✉ Deira City Centre ☎ 294 9000; www.deiracitycentre.com

ACTIVITIES

Aerogulf Services
Get a birds-eye view of Dubai on a helicopter tour of the city. It's not the cheapest way of seeing the city, but you get an unparalleled overview of how it has developed around the Creek and then along Sheikh Zayed Road. The helicopters can carry four passengers.Prices range from 780–1470Dh depending on the number of passengers.
🚇 Off map ✉ Dubai International Services; Garhoud Road ☎ 220 0331; www.aerogulfservices.com

Aviation Club
This tennis club has eight courts (with fake grass) and offers lessons with professional coaches. The Aviation Club hosts several major tennis tournaments in Dubai and has a 5,000-seater stadium. One-on-one lessons from 130Dh
🚇 172 C1 ✉ The Tennis Stadium, Garhoud ☎ 282 4540; www.cftennis.com

Balloon Adventures Dubai
Touring Dubai in a hot-air balloon is a leisurely alternative to a helicopter (see above). Balloon

Adventures' two large craft can each carry 40 people and they can be booked for groups or individuals (750Dh per person). Flights take off in time for the sunrise.

171 D2 Near Claridge Hotel, Deira 273 8585; www.ballooning.ae Daily Oct–May only

Dubai Creek Golf and Yacht Club

Bordering the Creek between the Maktoum and Garhoud bridges, the Dubai Creek Golf and Yacht Club is more than just a stunning piece of architecture (▶ 12). The Yacht Club has a large marina where visitors without their own boat can charter one of the Club's four motor cruisers. The 9.5m (32-foot) *Sneakaway* is a specialist tournament-rigged game-fishing vessel on which up to six people can sail into the Gulf to fish for tuna, kingfish, barracuda and sailfish. Prices include tackle, bait, fuel, soft drinks and the crew's undivided attention.

The Princess V42 Sports Boat is better suited to cruising the Creek and the Gulf but can also be rented for game-fishing expeditions. A six to eight-hour cruise will take you all the way down to the Jumeirah Palm Island and the new Marina development, past the Burj Al Arab and around the offshore construction sites.

The Dubai Golf Club itself, on the other side of the Park Hyatt hotel, has an outgoing nine holes designed Thomas Bjorn. The par-71 championship course is open to non-members who have brought their handicap certificate. PGA professionals can introduce first-timers to the nuances of golf, while experienced golfers can practise on the floodlit driving range. Golf: visitors Thursday–Saturday 525Dh, Sunday–Wednesday 425Dh for 18 holes (peak season rates). Fishing: 7–6; 4 hours 2,550Dh, 8 hours 3,550Dh. Cruising; 7–6; minimum 2-hour cruise 1,955Dh or 13,900Dh for full day.

172 C2 Creekside, between Maktoum and Garhoud bridges 295 6000; www.dubaigolf.com

Emirates Motorsports Federation

The EMSF organises a large number of motorsports events in the Emirates throughout the year, from desert rallies to classic car shows. Motorsport fans can check the events calendar online to find out what is going on when.

171 C1 Near Aviation Club, Garhoud 282 7111; www.emsf.ae

Magic Planet

The futuristically-styled funfair at the top and on the right flank of Deira City Centre is so colourful that it is positively psychedelic. There isn't a sharp edge in the place and the overall effect is a little like being trapped in a lava lamp.

However, for all the surface style, Magic Planet delivers. It has an superb range of rides and games including two car racing simulators and the Robo Coaster; a ride controlled by a giant robotic arm. Younger patrons can play on the Flying Tigers and on Jumping Star while older children can be strapped into the wildest ride, Equinox. On the right of the escalators going up to Magic Planet are six pool tables and a match-size snooker table. On the left a 9m-high (30-foot) climbing wall provides a challenge to adults and children. Cosmic Bowling is an appropriate name for the 12-lane, neon-lit bowling alley, split over three levels. Carousels, Ferris wheels, pirate ships and bumper cars all whizz around, adding to the whirlwind of activity. Magic Planet has several fast-food outlets, including a branch of the Johnny Rockets burger bar and TGI Fridays.

170 off C1 Deira City Centre mall 295 1010; www.deiracitycentre.com
Fri–Wed 10–midnight, Thu 10–1am
Day passes from 500h, rides 8–250h individually

Bur Dubai

Getting Your Bearings 56 – 57
In a Day 58 – 59
Don't Miss 60 – 68
At Your Leisure 69 – 71
Where to... 72 – 78

Getting Your Bearings

On the opposite side of the Creek from Deira, Bur Dubai is the other half of Dubai's old city centre. The quarter initially developed around the port and at the mouth of the Creek, which is why there are several heritage sites clustered here: Sheikh Saeed Al Maktoum House, the Heritage and Diving Village, Bastikya and Dubai Museum in Al Fahidi Fort. Bastakiya, in particular, offers a convincing, if sanitised, depiction of old Dubai. It is a whole neighbourhood dating back to the traders of the 1900s but populated now by Arabic restaurants and galleries. These sites alone, all within walking distance of each other, will occupy you for a day, but there is much more to Bur Dubai than just a history lesson.

Above: There's something for everyone at Creekside Park. Page 55: Goods for sale at the Antique Souk

Development spread inland, along the Creek, until it reached Garhoud Bridge. Beyond Garhoud even the desert is now being colonised by projects such as International City and Academic City.

Between the Creek's two bridges is one of the city centre's most important green spaces, Creekside Park. It has 2.5km (1.5 miles) of shoreline and gardens, eating areas and children's play areas. There are several key attractions around Creekside Park, including Children's City, Wonderland, the Al Boom Tourist Complex, the Grand Cineplex and Wafi City mall. They are within walking distance of each other but the main roads here mean that is probably easier to take a taxi between them. Again, this little area of Bur Dubai makes for an enjoyable day out.

Creekside Park and the heritage sites of old Bur Dubai are at opposite ends of the area. In the between is a no man's land of busy, often choked roads and commercial buildings. At the heart of this area is Karama, a residential district famed for its bargain-shopping opportunities. If you want a 10Dh pair of fake Chanel sunglasses, you'll find them here. The restaurants in Karama are also worth exploring when you've had your fill of hotel buffets – they're inexpensive but vibrant.

The second major mall in Bur Dubai borders Karama but the contrast couldn't be greater. BurJuman Centre is as glamourous as Karama is down-to-earth. The four-storey mall has been extended in recent years and the new section is the home of designers such as Lacroix, Gaultier, Dior and Alexander McQueen.

★ Don't Miss

1 **Sheikh Saeed Al Maktoum House** ➤ 60
2 **Dubai Museum** ➤ 62
3 **Bastakiya** ➤ 64
4 **BurJuman Centre** ➤ 66
5 **Creekside Park** ➤ 68

At Your Leisure

6 Heritage and Diving Village ➤ 69
7 Children's City ➤ 69
8 Wonderland ➤ 70
9 Al Boom Tourist Village ➤ 71
10 Ras Al Khor Wildlife Sanctuary ➤ 71

This relaxing day starts with a visit to Majlis Gallery, then its off to Creekside Park. Next visit Wafi City mall for some shopping and then take in a movie.

Bur Dubai in a Day

9:30 am

Start with breakfast in the Basta Art Café beside the **3 Bastakiya** (► 64-65) heritage quarter. Bit by bit, the Dubai Municipality is turning this small area of creekside Bur Dubai into an accurate impression of pre-skyscraper Dubai. This is the day's dose of culture so have a look around the **Majlis Gallery** (► 78) next door before walking through Bastakiya to the Creek. You can ask the Basta Art Café to make up some sandwiches if you like the idea of a picnic in the Creekside Park.

11:00 am

Take an *abra* to **5 Creekside Park** (► 68). You'll need to hire a water taxi for the journey (for no more than 50–60Dh) but it's A much more pleasant way to travel than the four-wheeled variety. As you travel upstream Deira is on the left bank of the Creek, it's high-rises petering out as you pass the dhow wharfs and then the sail-like silhouette of the Dubai Creek Golf Club will come into view.

12:30 pm

After exploring Creekside Park, have lunch in one of the cafés in the park. If you've brought some food, find a picnic spot under the trees or at one of the purpose-built tables. After lunch, don't forget to take a ride on the park's cable car.

2:30 pm

Exit the park at one of six gates and hail a taxi for the short trip to **Wafi City** mall (➤ 76), Dubai's designer wonderland. Children can play in the third-floor Encounter Zone while adults explore the mall's 300 shops.

5:00 pm

Get an early meal at Planet Hollywood next to Wafi City. For adults without children, the Pyramids complex at Wafi City has a range of restaurants and cafés.

6:30 pm

Take the free shuttle bus from Wafi City to the **Grand Cineplex** (➤ 78). The latest blockbusters are shown on the 12 screens here so you should be able to find a film to keep everyone happy.

9:00 pm

If it is too early to take a taxi back to your hotel and you've got the energy to continue the night, head to Seville's (➤ 75) at Wafi City and let your hair down at this Spanish restaurant with a resident flamenco guitarist. There's a fine tapas menu and an enticing drinks list.

❶ Sheikh Saeed Al Maktoum House

The house of former ruler Sheikh Saeed Al Maktoum has been restored and turned into a museum documenting Dubai's transition from desert state to skyscraper city.

Rather than a re-creation of traditional Emirati life, which can be found on the other side of the Creek in Deira's Heritage House (► 45), this museum takes a more conventional approach. Duck under the low doorways to find a model of old Dubai and galleries of black-and-white photographs of Dubai in the 1960s and 1970s. At this time, the land surrounding the house was largely sand and date palm trees.

A guide can explain that the Maktoum family's roots were in a Bedouin tribe from the desert near Abu Dhabi. They

Sheikh Saeed Al Maktoum's former residence is one of the oldest buildings in Dubai

Above: A night-time view of the museum

moved to Al Ain but realising that sea trade would be good for business and that Abu Dhabi didn't have anything like Dubai's Creek, the Maktoums moved in on Dubai and occupied the area, sparking two centuries of arguments among cousins. This state of unrest continued until the 1950s, when Abu Dhabi hit oil. However, they were unable to import the heavy drilling equipment without coming to an agreement with the Dubai branch of the family: the Maktoums could keep Dubai if they let Abu Dhabi use it for importing the oil-

industry equipment. Until the 1950s the Emiratis had only an oral history – nothing was written down. Indeed, Dubai didn't have electricity until the 1960s; today the tribal leaders are the CEOs of international companies.

The house was constructed from coral covered in lime and sand plaster in 1896 and is one of Dubai's oldest buildings. It was restored in 1986. The museum also contains coins, maps and documents covering matters such as the pardoning of prisoners and local property agreements.

Above: Exhibits reveal how the city emerged from the sand dunes

✚ 170 B4
✉ Al Shindagha ☎ 393 7139
🕐 Sat–Thu 8 am–8:30 pm, Fri 3:30–9:30; Sat–Thu 9–5, Fri 2–5 during Ramadan ⬛ Expensive

2 Dubai Museum

Believe it or not, Dubai dates back 5,000 years. Find out how life has changed since then in the excellent galleries of Dubai Museum's underground extension. If you go to only one museum in Dubai, make it this one.

Enter the 18th century Al Fahidi Fort, through a door guarded by cannons. The fort was built to protect the traders and seafarers living at the mouth of Dubai's Creek from invasion. The museum illustrates the history of this 5,000-year old city from its trading and seafaring origins, through the pearl diving period, conflict, the oil boom and finally the current construction fever.

The open-air courtyard has some large displays, such as an *abra*, the boats still used to cross the Creek. To the right, inside the fort's walls, there's an exhibition of armour and weaponry. There's little information on the exhibits, so you aren't told, for example, that the Khanjar dagger, with its curved bone handle, is an Omani weapon. On the facing-wall are more modern weapons, including locally made guns and bullet belts, which share

space with musical instruments – the standout exhibit is a "tambura" (a large harp).

Re-entering the courtyard, cross to the opposite corner for the new galleries below ground. You'll pass a European bronze cannon, last used in the 19th century. The new galleries have sections on archaeology, traditional housing, the souk in 1950, the mosque, the desert, a marine gallery and astronomy. The 1970s was when the blueprint for modern Dubai was drawn up. The decade change began in 1971 when the United Arab Emirates was formed and closed with the construction of Jebel Ali Port (the world's largest dry dock) and Free Zone, Sheikh Rashid bin Saeed Al Maktoum's first big risk, and the erection of Dubai's first skyscraper, the World Trade Centre (➤ 86).

Models depict the lives of merchants, boat builders, potters and jewellers. The Architecture room shows how wind towers (still seen in restored buildings in Old Dubai) were used to cool houses. Narrow lanes also provided shade, as did zigzag entrances to buildings; anything to stop direct sunlight.

An exhibition on the Bedouin explains why water was a constant obsession. In summer Bedouins pitched their tents around 1km (0.5 miles) from water; in winter, when their animals would drink once every four days, tents were pitched 23–48km (20–30 miles) from wells. An interesting section covers desert ecology and how plants and animals survive average temperatures of 40°C (104°F) in summer and just 120mm (4.5 inches) of rain annually.

Interesting galleries describe Arab business and recreation. Camels are the most important animals in the region, providing transportation, food, milk, fuel (from their dung) and trading currency. They can travel without water for two weeks, smell water from 2km (1 mile) and walk for 18 hours at a time. If they're the workhorses of the region, falcons are the treasured pets: used to hunt rabbits, bustards and other birds. Fast-flying falcons are called "Al Shaheen", while endurance fliers are called "Al Hur Kamal".

The most fascinating tableau is that of the pearl diver. Pearl divers worked in the region for 1,000 years and by the turn of the 20th century there were about 300 pearl diving dhows. Divers would sail to the pearl beds ("Al Hiraat") and make incredibly deep dives with only a turtleshell noseclip, a rope basket, a 5kg (11-pound) stone to pull them down and a rope looped around their foreheads to guide them back to the surface.

The final gallery on Archaeology has displays of pre-Christian objects found near Dubai: bronze daggers, delicate arrow heads and fish hooks, shell belt buckles and buttons. The next stop is the museum's gift shop before you exit on to Al Fahidi Street. The tour will take no more than two hours.

🞧 170 B3 ✉ Al Fahidi Street ☎ 353 1862
🕐 Sat–Thu 8 am–10 pm, Fri 8–11, 4–10; 9–midnight during Ramadan 🎟 Expensive

Left: Dubai Musuem is housed within an 18th-century fort.
Above and right: Exhibits within the museum

3 Bastakiya

Bastakiya is a collection of buildings on the shore of the Creek dating back to the 1900s, when Iranian traders settled here. They've been restored to re-create a small section of traditional Dubai, currently comprising about 50 buildings. The best way to experience it is to explore the quarter on a winter evening when the smell of Arabic food wafts from restaurants and dhows in the distance ply the Creek as they have done for hundreds of years.

All the buildings in Bastakiya used the same construction method of coral walls covered with a sand plaster. The buildings feature an ancient form of air-conditioning, *barjeel*, which uses a system of wind towers to funnel breezes down into the houses. Now these buildings are art galleries (▶ 78), museums, shops and restaurants – all subtly integrated into the historic surroundings. The Sheikh Mohammed Centre for Cultural Understanding in Bastakiya (tel: 353 6666, www.cultures.ae) explains Emirati life in detail and can help organise a guide if required.

Bastakiya is also an early example of the forward thinking of Dubai's rulers: they granted Iranian traders tax concessions and easy immigration, much as today's government encourages immigration. It is now one of the oldest heritage sites in Dubai and you can pass through it if you take a creekside stroll or visit some of the attractions nearby, such as the Dubai Museum (▶ 62–63). The whole neighbourhood is largely car-free, which offers some respite from Bur Dubai's bustle. This is also a good point from which to take boats to explore other areas of the Creek.

🔢 170 B3

Iranian traders once lived and worked in Bastakiya

BASTAKIYA: INSIDE INFO

Top Tip Calligraphy House in Bastakiya celebrates the Islamic art form of calligraphy. Traditionally the technique is handed down from father to son (although more women are taking it up) and it is used to adorn the mosques and holy books of Islam. There are two elements to a work of calligraphy: the letters themselves and the decoration of the piece, often by another artist.

4 BurJuman Centre

Entering BurJuman is a little like entering an Escher drawing. The farther you venture in, the bigger it gets and the more angular the design becomes. Successive expansions mean that BurJuman currently has 300 outlets in 72,000sq m (800,000 square feet). The emphasis at this mall is on high fashion. Out of the 95 shops selling womenswear, however, the most notable is Saks 5th Avenue, the second-largest branch outside the USA. The store takes up two levels of BurJuman, the lower level housing the cosmetics counters, the men's area and the café. The second level of Saks is where you'll find the designer labels and jewellery.

BurJuman's shops are a good mix of exclusive names – Dior, Lacroix, Dolce & Gabbana, Hermes and Tiffany & Co. – with more affordable retailers, including Gap and Zara. Shoppers hunting for a more laidback look can try Diesel, Levi's or Quiksilver. Once you're shopped out, there are 15 fast-food outlets, 17 cafés (including Starbucks and Dome) and nine restaurants to choose from. Take the escalator up to the top floor where several cafés and restaurants surround a rooftop garden: the T Junction sells refreshing flavoured and standard teas in a funky yellow bar. A huge TV screen dominates one end of the top floor, which benefits from natural light coming through the sculpted glass roof.

A tourist information booth on level one of the North Village (tel: 352 0003) can help you plan the rest of your day.

➕ 170 A2
☎ Trade Centre Road
📠 352 0222; www.burjuman.com
🕐 Sat–Thu 10–10, Fri 2–10, some stores open later on Fri

Above and below: Whether you're browsing or buying there are plenty of items to tempt you

Left: With 300 stores, BurJuman Centre is a shopper's paradise

5 Creekside Park

Creekside is the best park in Dubai. Why? It has something for everyone. Active types can explore the 2.5km (1.5 mile) shore line on rented bicycles. Gardeners will be interested in the themed gardens containing 280 species. Sightseers will marvel at the sensational views. And families will love the open space and activities.

At 222ha (90 acres) Creekside is a very large park; you should allocate at least half a day to do it justice. The best idea is to wander from one end to the other, following the signposted paths that pique your interest. Along the way you may find the Rings of Friendship sculpture, a gift from Dubai's American community. Pagodas and landscaped gardens are sequestered among the park's slopes; the desert garden features indigenous desert-dwelling plants while the

date palmgrove is interspersed with traditional Arabic watchtowers. On weekends many families come to Creekside park to cook barbecues in the special pits and laze about in the sun (note that you should not strip down to swimwear in the park – the beach is the only place where that is appropriate). Some bring fishing tackle to try their luck from the piers, while others take the mini-train around the park's perimeter.

However the main attraction of Creekside Park is its cable car system, which runs along a stretch of shoreline 30m (98 feet) above the ground. From a distance you can see the rounded pods slowly making their way through the air, but from the cable cars you have fantastic views of the Dubai Creek Golf Club (▶ 54), an elegant, modern building on the opposite side of the creek intended to resemble the sails of a dhow. The new Park Hyatt hotel next to the Golf Club is also quite a sight. The cable cars opened in 2000, when they were the first cable cars in the United Arab Emirates. There are several gates accessing the park, each with a car park. If there are no taxis waiting you may have to walk to the main road to hail one.

🚹 172 C2 ✉ Riyadh Road
🕐 Fri–Tue 8 am–11 pm, Wed–Thu 8 am–11:30 pm
🖐 Activity prices vary

The park's cable car system is just one of it's attractions

At Your Leisure

THE DIVING VILLAGE

6 Heritage and Diving Village

At the very tip of the creekside prom-enade, by the Sheikh Saeed Al Maktoum House, this cultural centre endeavours to show how Emiratis lived in the past. When the place is staffed, people are employed to demonstrate how goods were made and pearls harvested. However, there seem to be long periods when the Heritage and Diving Village is not in full operation. More restoration work is going on around the courtyard and perhaps this will spark the place into life. If you haven't made it into the Dubai

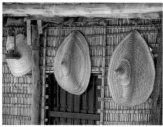

Dubai's historical pearl diving industry is the focus of this musuem

Museum, the Diving Village does a good job to explain how pearl divers made their perilous living.

🚹 170 B4 ⊠ Nr Al Shindagha Tunnel
☎ 393 7151 🕐 Sat–thu 8–10, Fri 8–11, 4–10; Sat–Thu 9 pm–midnight during Ramadan

7 Children's City

Fresh, funky and bright – Children's City doesn't look like a place of education. But that's the idea behind this brilliant theme park for children. The building

itself, a collection of blue, yellow and red asymetric shapes, looks like it is has been constructed from Lego and was inspired by a children's game. Inside the space is divided into well-conceived zones themed on the human body, physical science, international culture, nature, computing and space exploration. It's not as dry as it sounds – all the displays are interactive in some way and involve some aspect of play. The auditorium can accommodate 300 people for shows, while the planetarium will be the highlight for many visitors. The project, which cost 77 million Dh, has gained international recognition from the UNESCO World Museum Council – it certainly merits an hour or two's investigation.

➕ 172 B2 ✉ Creekside Park
☎ 334 0808; www.childrencity.ae
🕐 Sat–Thu 10–10, Fri 4–10; 8 pm–1 am during Ramadan 👛 Expensive

8 Wonderland

Wonderland encompasses a water park, Splashland, with slides and rides, and a theme park. There's a pay-as-you-go system with rides such as the roller coaster on the right side of the park costing 10Dh a time and others, such as the pirate ship for younger children, a mere 5Dh each. However, Wonderland suffers in comparison with Wild Wadi, the water park in Jumeirah (➤ 116), and Children's City and looks increasingly decrepit. Call before visiting because the opening times vary.

Above and left: Children's City makes learning fun

■ 172 B1 ✉ Garhoud Bridge
☎ 324 1222; www.wonderlanduae.com
🕐 Water park: daily 10 am–11 pm;
Theme park: daily 5–11
💷 Expensive

9 Al Boom Tourist Village

A somewhat multifarious complex using the same car park as Wonderland (➤ 70), Al Boom's main business is sending guests out for dinner cruises on one of their dhows. They're the largest dhow operator on the Creek with boats ranging in capacity from 20–300. However, unless you're staying in the vicinity of Al Boom it makes more sense to take a dhow from the Deira side in the city centre.

■ 172 B1 ✉ Garhoud Bridge
☎ 324 3000

10 Ras Al Khor Wildlife Sanctuary

Few wildlife sanctuaries can have a skyline such as Dubai's as a backdrop. Although urbanisation is creeping up to and around Ras

Al Khor, this large, watery wildlife reserve remains the country's largest bird sanctuary and a paradise for birdspotters. That's not surprising when you learn that on a winter's day up to 15,000 birds will congregate around the lagoon.

The easiest birds to spot are the Greater Flamingos. This migrant colony, up to 1,500 strong, arrives for the winter and the hope is that one day they will be induced to nest at Ras Al Khor for the first time. Observant visitors should also look out for the Western Reef Heron, the Spotted Eagle, the Lesser Sand Plover and two varieties of Sandpiper: the Broad-billed and the Terek.

Ras Al Khor was designated a wildlife sanctuary in 1993 in order to protect the flamingoes, which had been hunted in the 1980s. Today, there are three hides at Ras Al Khor, two off Oud Metha Road and a third off Ras Al Khor Road – coming from Dubai you'll need to double back on yourself to get on the right side of the road to pull off. The hides are equipped with binoculars and a telescope but serious birders will want to bring their own equipment. A sun hat is also advisable. The best time to visit is in winter, when the weather is favourable and the migratory birds have arrived.

■ 172 off B1 ✉ Ras Al Khor Road, accessed from Bukadra Interchange on Dubai-Al Ain Road ☎ 206 4240 💷 Free. Large groups by appointment

Above: Flamingos are just some of birds that migrate to Dubai

Where to... Stay

Prices
Expect to pay per double room, per night
$ 150Dh–600Dh $$ 600Dh–1,500Dh $$$ 1,500Dh–10,000+Dh

Four Points by Sheraton $$
You can't beat the location of this mid-range hotel; Bastakiya heritage district and the Burjuman Centre are within walking distance and other sights on the same side of the Creek are readily accessible. With just 125 rooms, the Four Points attracts equal numbers of business and leisure travellers. There are two bars and three restaurants, one of them an excellent Indian restaurant (▶72).

Other facilities include an outdoor heated swimming pool, a gym and covered parking.

✚ 170 A3 ✉ Khalid Bin Walid Street
☎ 397 7444; www.sheraton.com

Golden Sands Hotel Apartments $$
The many supermarkets make self-catering a viable proposition in Dubai. Golden Sands is a convenient option in Bur Dubai. You can have a one- or two-room studio, with a kitchenette, air-conditioning and housekeeping. Furnishings are functional but rooms all are fitted with a television, telephone and cooking facilities. A free shuttle bus carries guests to Jumeirah and there is an on-site swimming pool. Long-term stays are also possible.

✚ 169 F3 ✉ Bank Street
☎ 355 5553;
www.goldensandsdubai.com

Grand Hyatt Dubai $$$
Only an aerial view of the colossal Grand Hyatt (674 rooms and 13 restaurants in 15ha/37 acres) reveals that the shape of the hotel spells "Dubai" in Arabic. Such details aside, the Grand Hyatt is so large that it's a world within a world: with a different restaurant to try each night. Guests can use the hotel's own running track, three swimming pools, four tennis courts and a gym to stay trim.

Despite the impersonality of such a large establishment, staff are well-drilled. The Grand Hyatt is the only city-centre resort hotel (most are by the beach, although a Park Hyatt opened in 2005 on the other side of the Creek) and business facilities are separate from leisure areas so guests don't cramp each other's style. Rooms are large and all have the expected high-tech features for a business or leisure stay.

✚ 172 A1 ✉ Oud Metha Road
☎ 317 1234;
www.dubai.grand.hyatt.com

Jumeirah Rotana $$–$$$
Stuck in no-man's land between the ancient alleys of Bur Dubai and th beaches, the Rotana isn't actually on Jumeirah's sought-after shoreline at all but is near many attractions. It is popular with both business and holiday visitors. Facilities include internet access and a shuttle bus to the beach and Mercato mall. Rooms are comfortable although not particularly stylish.

✚ 168 C4 ✉ Al Dhiyafa Street,
Satwa ☎ 345 5888; www.rotana.com

Mövenpick Hotel $$–$$$
Swiss quality and Arab opulence come together in the Mövenpick hotel between Wafi City and Lamcy Plaza malls. The 232 rooms might be a bit characterless, but the specially imported beds are comfortable and the suites each get a Jacuzzi bath.

The location isn't convenient for beach goers and the views are hardly postcard quality, but it is outside the hurly-burly of central

Bur Dubai and close to several attractions and the airport. Facilities are aimed at business travellers, with wireless internet in all rooms, but leisure travellers will be pleased by the outstanding rooftop fitness area comprising a pool and jogging track. The spa facilities include a steam room and sauna, while notable restaurants at the hotel include the Lebanese restaurant Fakhreldine and Jimmy Dix (▶ 77).

🏠 172 B3 ☒ 19th Street, Oud Metha
☎ 336 6000;
www.moevenpick-burdubai.com

President Hotel $

Dubai is the wrong place to visit for budget accommodation – the selection is disappointing and particularly unappealing during the heat of summer.

The President Hotel is a typical example: underlit and understaffed but making an effort nevertheless. The price is the main attraction because the location, near Karama,

isn't quiet or picturesque, and it is quite a way to the beach.

🏠 169 E2 ☒ Trade Centre Road,
Karama ☎ 334 6565

XVA $$

The XVA art gallery is hiding a secret: eight guest rooms, individually decorated with art and antiques. This is one of the more unusual places to stay in Dubai, and all the better for it. The neighbourhood includes the Basta Art Café and the creekside Bastakiya heritage quarter.

Indeed, the XVA is in a restored traditional building with a wind tower and adobe walls. Don't expect a pool or internet access; instead there's a rooftop terrace on which to watch the sunset. The reasonable rates mean that the XVA's rooms fill up quickly and you'll need to book as far in advance as possible.

🏠 170 B3
☒ Al Musalla-Al Fahid roundabout,
Bastakiya
☎ 353 5383

Prices

Expect to pay for a three-course meal for one, excluding drinks and service
$ under 60h $$ 600h–1000h $$$ over 1000h

Antique Bazaar $$

The Antique Bazaar, on the second floor of the Four Points hotel, is one of Dubai's best Indian restaurants and attracts a devoted Asian clientele. The experience is as much about the furnishings – heavy teak tables and chairs, Indian antiques and reproductions – and the live music, as the excellent food. Indian beers can accompany specialities largely from northern India. The music isn't intrusive, but there are more intimate restaurants.

🏠 170 A3 ☒ Four Points by
Sheraton ☎ 397 7444 🕒 Daily 7:30
pm–2 am, Sat–Thu 12:30–3 pm

Basta Art Café $

Basta Art Café is an essential pitstop on any tour of old Bur Dubai. You'll find it between Dubai Museum and Bastakiya on Al Fahidi Street. It's in a traditional building with a pretty interior courtyard shaded by umbrellas and trees.

The food is excellent for the price and snacks such as the Souk Salad of couscous, chicken, cashew and lettuce or the Greek village salad of tomatoes, cucumber, olives, feta and red onion seem perfectly matched to the surroundings. You can also buy sandwiches – the chicken and mango is very tasty –

or have a big breakfast. A juice bar serves tangy blends such as lime and lychee.

Despite its proximity to central Bur Dubai, the tranquil Basta Art Café seems immune to the traffic and bustle outside. As the name hints, the café is decorated with the work of local artists and many of their pieces are for sale.

⊞ 170 B3 ⊠ Al Musalla-Al Fahid roundabout, Bastakiya ☎ 353 5071 ☺ Daily 10-10

Bastakiah Nights $$–$$$

When the sun goes down this excellent Arabic restaurant comes into its own. Warm lights welcome you into the traditionally furnished house and you can choose to sit in the main ground-floor room or on a rooftop seating area – the best choice for winter evenings.

The menu is a blend of Arabic cuisines, although the Lebanese dishes are best. Starters such as tabbouleh or home-made yoghurt are followed by mains such as mari-

nated chicken or lamb. The set meal at 128Dh is a great choice if you have trouble choosing or if you have a substantial appetite.

⊞ 170 B3 ⊠ Bastakiya ☎ 353 7772 ☺ Daily noon–midnight

Dome $

This café, one of an international chain, does an admirable job of refuelling weary shoppers with coffee, cakes and snacks. It's outside, on a roadside corner of the BurJuman Centre but also attracts locals who come to pass the time of day. Décor is mock-French and the waiters play their part in black-and-white uniforms and dinky berets.

⊞ 170 A2 ⊠ Burjuman Centre ☎ 355 6004 ☺ Daily 7:30 am–1:30 am

Gazebo $

One of the best Indian restaurants in Dubai can be found in Karama. Gazebo has both great food and excellent service. Tandoori-cooked meats are a speciality, as are

biriyanis, all freshly prepared for a largely Indian clientele by a skilful chef. You should be able to eat here for less than 60Dh per head, which is a bargain. Note that Gazebo does not serve alcohol.

⊞ 169 E2 ⊠ Trade Centre Road, opposite Spinney's, Karama ☎ 397 9930 ☺ Daily noon–3, 7–11:45

Kanzaman $$

For wonderful views up the Creek, follow the promenade down to the mouth of the river where you'll find a number of Arabic restaurants attracting tourists with shisha pipes, traditional Arabic dishes and fine views of the action on Dubai's crucial waterway. Come at night when the dhows are lit up with lights and families are strolling along the waterfront.

Kanzaman's menu is the standard combination of Lebanese and Arabic favourites but the real reason to dine here is the view, so

ensure you get a table outside and enjoy the atmosphere.

⊞ 170 B4 ⊠ Heritage and Diving Village ☎ 393 9913 ☺ Daily 10 am–11:30 pm

Lemongrass $

Like Gazebo (see opposite), Lemongrass has made a virtue out of being an independent restaurant. Service is sharp and the food compares well with that of the city's much more expensive hotel-based Thai restaurants.

All the Thai staples are on the menu, along with some local twists. But the lack of an alcohol licence means that you can't wash down a green curry with beer.

⊞ 172 A3 ⊠ Lamcy Plaza, Oud Metha ☎ 334 2325 ☺ Daily noon–3, 7–11

Local House Restaurant $$

Curious about what camel tastes like? Find out at this traditional Arabic restaurant next door to the

Basta Art Café (▶ 73). Local House opened in 2006 and will serve more substantial dishes than Basta Art Café. Although there are snacks and salads on the menu – the Bastakiya salad of mango, lettuce, avocado, chicken, chilli, olives and feta costs 38Dh – they're fair value next door. However, the main dishes are competitively priced at 45Dh, and you can have chicken instead of camel.

✛ 170 B3
⊠ Al Musalla-Al Fahid roundabout, Bastakiya
☎ 353 2288; www.localhouse.net
⏲ Sat–Thu 10–10, Fri 1:30–10:30

Planet Hollywood $$

Kids will prefer the primary colours and exuberance of this branch of the popular American chain to the studied nonchalance and high-concept design of the other eateries inside Wafi City all.

There are no surprises on the menu – burgers figure large – but the children's menu will prove

popular. During the lively Friday brunch children can also get involved in games and activities such face painting. You'll find Planet Hollywood signposted outside the mall – look for the giant globe.

✛ 172 A2
⊠ Wafi City Mall
☎ 324 4777;
www.planethollywood-dubai.com
⏲ Daily noon–midnight; open from 11.30 am for Friday brunch

Seville's $$

For entertainment with your tapas, look no further than Seville's. The Spanish-themed restaurant-bar employs a flamenco guitarist to serenade diners in the restaurant and on the rooftop garden terrace. The menu features well-prepared classics. On winter evenings, as the cocktails flow, the atmosphere can become positively Balearic.

✛ 172 A2
⊠ Wafi City
☎ 324 7300
⏲ Daily 12–3, 7–1 am

Where to... Shop

BurJuman Centre

BurJuman is so sure of itself that it's not content with a printing a pull-out pamphlet, it also publishes a full-size glossy magazine. The mall majors in high fashion but there are also stores selling jewellery, home furnishings, childrenswear, cosmetics, electronics, books, DVDs and music.

The headliner is Saks 5th Avenue, but the American store is ably supported by, among others: Banana Republic, Calvin Klein, Donna Karan, Guess, Kenzo, Cavilli, Laura Ashley, Loewe, Monsoon, Ralph Lauren, Paul Smith, Whisles, Valentino and Versace, to name a few.

For families with young children the BurJuman provides a mother

and baby room and, on the top floor, the Fun City entertainment area. BurJuman is justifiably popular and is one of Dubai's top five malls.

✛ 170 A2 ⊠ Trade Centre Road
☎ 352 0222; www.burjuman.com
⏲ Sat–Thu 10–10, Fri 4–10

Karama

The neighbourhood of Karama is just beyond BurJuman on Sheikh Khalifa bin Zayed Road, but it is a different world. Rather than pay 6,000Dh for a designer watch, you'll pay 60Dh. The Karama Shopping Complex is the place to come for inexpensive (counterfeit) designer brands and unusual souvenirs. The sales pitches are not overly intrusive but show some interest and you will be badgered until you buy.

Lamcy Plaza

This offers bargain hunters better pickings than may be found in the nearby Wafi City shopping complex. The five-storey mall is popular with locals because it offers everyday items at rock-bottom prices and there is a play centre for children. Don't expect too many designer names at Lamcy; the emphasis is on practicality, with a pharmacy, dry cleaners, post office, money exchange and even a driving school.

✛ 172 A3 ⊠ **Adjacent to Sheikh Rashid road–Umm Hurair Road interchange** ☎ 335 9999; **www.lamcyplaza.com** ⊙ **Daily 9 am–10 pm**

Wafi City

Exclusivity and variety are the watchwords of Wafi City. The mall is rather more compact than other contenders for the title of Dubai's best mall so it is not such a chore seeing every shop. But what it lacks in scale, it more than makes up for in opulence; the interior has layers of glitz and it can feel like you're in a luxury hotel lobby rather than a shopping mall. And, with names

such as Versace, Chanel and Nicole Farhi, Wafi City has the shops to match. Wafi City is Dubai's most designer-led emporium; it's also the home of Marks & Spencer, with a large store on the first floor.

Shops to look out for on the ground floor include Gianfranco Ferre, Chanel, Aigner and Nicole Farhi for women, while men get Calvin Klein, Pierre Cardin, Strellson and Cerruti, among others. Wafi City's jewellers also attract Dubai's shoppers: the sparkling window displays of Graff, Swarovski and Tiffany & Co. are enough to mesmerise the most parsimonious passerby. But amid the diamonds and designer names, Wafi City has a handful of shops that are a little bit special. Comtesse has a sales floor devoted to Meissen pottery, some of the finest porcelain in the world while Scarabee (tel: 324 8066, open Sat–Thu 10–10, Fri 4–10), also on the ground floor, sells a range of sterling silver ornaments.(tel: 324 0527; Sat–Thu

10–10, Fri 4–10). On the first floor Wafi Gourmet (tel: 324 4433; Retail Fri–Wed 9–noon, Thu 9-1; Restaurant Fri–Wed 10–noon, Thu 10–1; www.wafi.com) is a food shop and restaurant owned by Sheikh Manah, cousin of Dubai's ruler, Sheikh Mohammed. The delicatessan specialises in Lebanese and Arabic cuisine, selling olives, dried fruits, spices and herbs, rose water, sweets such as almond, cashew, seeds, pistachio, nougat combinations, petit fours, baklava and Arabic coffee. On the restaurant's menu you'll find Lebanese salads and *meze*, grilled fish and meat (kebabs and swarma) and Arabic sweets. They do takeout.

Two clothes shops, both on the ground floor, stand out from the crowd. The boutique of Italian designer and shop owner Mariella Burani (tel: 324 5245; Sat–Thu 10–10, Fri 4–10) shows off her colourful, one-off pieces. And children's clothing shop Oilily (tel: 324 2335, Sat–Thu 10–10, Fri 4–10;

www.oilily-world.com) offers an introduction to bohemian chic for the under-12s with its collections of ultra-fashionable and limited-edition childrenswear – think patterned knits, timeless prints and hand-embroidered bags.

Take the elevator to the second floor for the Encounter Zone, which is divided into two areas, one for the under-9s and the other for older children. In the youngsters Encounter Zone there is a soft play area with a Crater Challenge for the more active children. Their older brothers and sisters can try the Crystal Maze, a flight simulator followed by a parachute simulator and a 3-D movie screen.

For more entertainment options, there's a free shuttle bus from Wafi City to the Grand Cineplex (▶ 78). A soon to open extension will add an underground souk, 90 more shops, a Raffles hotel and a new department store.

✛ 172 A2 ☎ 324 4555; **www.waficity.com**

Where to...
Be Entertained

BARS AND CLUBS

Ginseng

Ginseng is an independent, licensed, nightspot that includes a bar, lounge and restaurant. The restaurant serves Thai specialities, but many people come for the quaffable champagne cocktails – on Tuesdays it's two drinks for the price of one. The interior is elegant, and the clientele also arrives dressed to impress.

🏠 172 A2 ⊠ Planet Hollywood complex, Wafi City, Umm Hurair ☎ 324 8200; www.ginsengdubai.com ⏰ Fri–Wed 7 pm–2 am; Thu 7–3 am

Jimmy Dix

An unpretentious, rumbustious place to party, its reputation for back-to-basics drinking and dancing means that it is not the venue for the more discerning clubber. But you can certainly have fun in this (loosely) speakeasy-style bar.

🏠 172 B3 ⊠ Mövenpick Hotel, Oud Metha ☎ 336 8800 ⏰ Daily 7 pm–3

MIX

MIX is notable for two reasons. First, with three floors, a live music room and a lounge area, it is one of Dubai's largest nightclubs. Second, there is no cover charge for entry. With a capacity of 800 people, a less-than-full night can be a bit of an anticlimax. But, MIX books international DJ stars, and on these nights you'll have to queue.

🏠 172 A1 ⊠ Grand Hyatt Hotel ☎ 317 1234 ⏰ Sun–Fri 6–3 am

Vintage

Cheese, wine and an endearing lack of snobbery: this cosy wine bar ticks all the boxes. Wine-lovers will spend hours browsing a wine list that covers most of the world's wine regions – but unlike the rarefied atmosphere of other bars, Vintage is about having a laugh. The proof? Weekend fondue nights.

🏠 172 A2 ⊠ Pyramids, Wafi City ☎ 324 4100 ⏰ Fri–Wed 6–1:30 am; Thu 4–2 am

SPAS

Cleopatra's Spa

Yes, the theme at this spa is ancient Egypt, although the hammam-like wet room mixes Mediterranean influences. The spa is in the members-only Pharaoh's Club and you get access to the lush environs of the club's swimming pool.

🏠 172 A2 ⊠ Wafi City ☎ 324 7700; www.waficity ⏰ Women: Sat–Thu 9–8, Fri 10–8. Men (separate door): Mon–Sat 10–10, Sun 10–7

The Grand Spa

Despite the size of the surrounding hotel, the Grand is private and relaxing with candlelit rooms, plunge pools, sauna, steam room and Jacuzzi. The therapists are renowned for their facials. Use of the Grand Hyatt's extensive fitness facilities is also permitted with some of the packages.

🏠 172 A1 ⊠ Grand Hyatt Hotel ☎ 345 6770; www.dubai.grand.hyatt.com

House of Chi and House of Healing

Tai chi, yoga, shiatsu, reiki and pilates: they're all offered by this alternative health centre. Guests can also try reflexology or traditional Chinese medicine at the House of Healing. The massages cover a variety of oriental styles or you could try on of the martial arts classes instead.

🏠 170 A3 ⊠ 6th Floor, Al Musalla Towers, Khalid Bin Walid Street ☎ 397 4446; www.hofchi.com

Grand Cineplex

Choose from 12 screens and the latest blockbusters at this enormous cinema complex. It's close to Wafi City mall and Creekside Park so you make a day of it.

☐ 172 A1 ☒ Umm Hurair, near Grand Hyatt Hotel ☏ 324 2000; www.grandcinemas.com

Majlis Gallery

Perhaps the best-known gallery in Dubai, the Majlis Gallery can accommodate the work of several artists in its exhibition rooms. The artists are as likely to be local as international and their areas of interest aren't confined to paintings; exhibitions have covered furniture, sculpture and fabric printing. Take time to look around the area as well – there's plenty of interest in this heritage quarter.

☐ 170 B3 ☒ Al Musalla-Al Fahid roundabout, Bastakiya ☏ 353 6233
◷ Sat–Thu 9:30–8

XVA

This restored wind tower has an art gallery, café and a handful of sought-after guestrooms (▶ 73). The artists featured are a varied bunch. You're likely to encounter an exhibition on Dubai's "vertical world" as a sculpture show. It's near the Majlis Gallery (left).

☐ 170 B3 ☒ Al Musalla-Al Fahid roundabout, Bastakiya ☏ 353 5383
◷ Sat–Thu 9 am–10 pm, Fri 9–6

Al Boom Tourist Village

Nine dhows set off from Al Boom every evening. The price includes onboard dining but the slightly out-of-the-way location means you will also have to pay for a taxi to and from your hotel.

A late-night cruise departs at 10:30 pm until midnight. There are two land-based restaurants at Al Boom; Al Areesh serves international cuisine while Al Dahleez serves some Emirati dishes.

☐ 172 B1 ☒ Umm Hurair, next to Garhoud Bridge ☏ 324 3000;
www.alboom.ae ◷ Late-night cruise expensive

Bluesail Dubai

Bluesail can organise anything nautical from 1-hour trips up the Creek to week-long charters. They have two speedboats, two 12m (42-foot) yachts and three motor cruisers and they can provide crews and skippers too. The speedboat is an exciting way to see the Creek and you can have a go at driving.

☐ 170 B2 ☒ Al Seef Road, opposite British Embassy ☏ 397 9730;
www.bluesailyachts.com
◷ Expensive

Dubai Watersports Association

Just beyond the dhow building yard the DWSA can provide short wake-board or waterskiing lessons in the Creek. Non-members are welcome but have to pay a small entry fee.

☐ 172 B1 ☒ Al Jaddaf ☏ 324
1031; www.dwsa.net ◷ Expensive

Pursuit Games

Let off steam with a group of like-minded friends, a paintball gun and a bagful of paintball pellet. This is the only paintballing operator in Dubai and it has been successful since it opened in 1996. They have a good safety record and up-to-date kit.

☐ 172 B1 ☒ Wonderland, near Creekside Park ☏ 050 651 4583;
www.paintballdubai.com
◷ Expensive

Al Nasr Leisureland

Leisureland is an ageing complex (it was built in 1979) with an eight-lane bowling alley, ice-skating rink and tennis and squash courts. All equipment can be rented but it is wise to book lanes or courts.

☐ 172 A3 ☒ Umm Hurair Road, Oud Metha, in the vicinity of the American Hospital ☏ 337 1234; www.alnasrll.com
◷ Daily 9 am–11 pm
◷ Expensive

East Jumeirah

Getting Your Bearings 80 – 81
In a Day 82 – 83
Don't Miss 84 – 94
At Your Leisure 95 – 97
Where to... 98 – 104

Getting Your Bearings

Jumeirah is the suburb where Dubai's first expat workers set up home in the 1980s and stretches from Jumeirah Mosque, the only mosque in the United Arab Emirates open to non-Muslims, down to the third interchange on Sheikh Zayed Road, just before the Burj Al Arab hotel. The area also extends inland beyond Sheikh Zayed Road, which runs parallel to the coast, to the Maktoum family's favourite place to relax: Nad Al Sheba racecourse. The Godolphin Gallery in Nad Al Sheba chronicles the family's passion for equestrianism. If you continue inland from Nad Al Sheba you'll soon enter an unpopulated desert, although the huge Dubailand development (➤ 123) will soon change that.

Jumeirah itself is a very wealthy district; there are few high-rise blocks along the seafront, instead detached villas are the most usual residential accommodation, commanding some of the highest rents in Dubai. This is the stamping ground of the Jumeirah Janes – the name locals give to the wives of Dubai's well-to-do businessmen. Accordingly, there are plenty of spas, shops and cafés along Beach Road, the main thoroughfare between the seafront and Sheikh Zayed Road. Beach Road itself was widened in 2006, meaning that there is less space for pedestrians; you won't enjoy walking along it and it can be tricky to find a pedestrian crossing. You'll need to take a taxi between attactions as they are spread out.

This section of Jumeirah also includes the most exciting end of Sheikh Zayed Road, with spectacular architecture on both sides of the 12-lane artery. The most notable project here is Burj Dubai, destined to be the world's tallest building. A wave of development will surround the Burj, turning desert into commercial and residential property. If you continue past the Burj Dubai to Interchange 2 you'll reach Safa Park, one of Dubai's most engaging parks. Turn right here, towards the Gulf and you'll end up in Jumeirah Beach Park, another pay-to-enter green space in the midst of affluent suburbia. The beach from the city centre down to the Burj Al Arab hotel has a mixture of public and private access. The luxury hotels, such as the Jumeirah Beach Club Resort next to the Beach Park, will maintain their own stretch of sand. The general public either pays to enter a park or hotel beach (➤ 143–144) or settles on a public beach.

Arabian Gulf

Harbour

D94

JUMEIRAH ROAD (BEACH RD)

AL UROUBA ST 311

AL WASL RD

Jumeirah Beach Park
10

JUMEIRAH (2)

D94

35 ST

5 **Majlis Ghorfat Um Al Sheef**

AL ATHAR ST

D92

Safa Park
11

AL HADIQA ST

Left: The iconic Emirates Towers
Page 79: The Emirates Towers at night

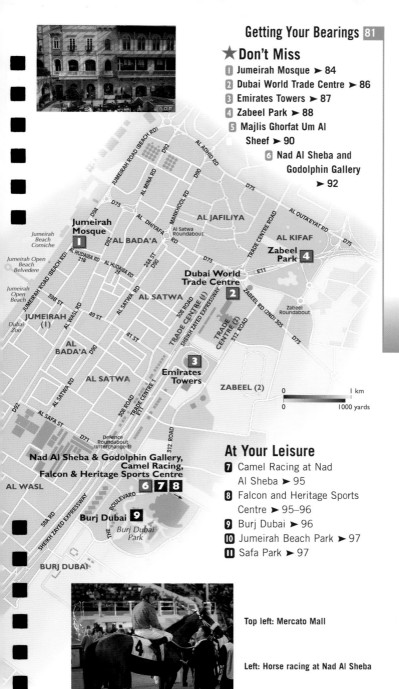

★ **Don't Miss**

1 Jumeirah Mosque ➤ 84
2 Dubai World Trade Centre ➤ 86
3 Emirates Towers ➤ 87
4 Zabeel Park ➤ 88
5 Majlis Ghorfat Um Al Sheef ➤ 90
6 Nad Al Sheba and Godolphin Gallery ➤ 92

At Your Leisure

7 Camel Racing at Nad Al Sheba ➤ 95
8 Falcon and Heritage Sports Centre ➤ 95–96
9 Burj Dubai ➤ 96
10 Jumeirah Beach Park ➤ 97
11 Safa Park ➤ 97

Top left: Mercato Mall

Left: Horse racing at Nad Al Sheba

The day begins at the lovely Jumeirah Mosque, followed by a look at the nearby beach. Explore Dubai's heritage in the afternoon, then hit a bar or restaurant at night.

East Jumeirah in a Day

10:00 am

Start the day at the **☐ Jumeirah Mosque** (➤ 84–85). If it is a Tuesday, Thursday or Sunday you will be able to look around inside, otherwise you will have to content yourself with admiring the exterior's minarets. Note that the mosque is oriented towards Mecca and the crescent on top indicates that it is a place of worship.

11:00 am

Cross the road to dip your toes in the sea at what is known as Russian Beach and properly called **Jumeirah Open Beach**; a free stretch of sand where the sunbathers are now more international than the nickname suggests. A promenade behind the beach attracts mothers with pushchairs and young men on their lunch breaks. Return to Jumeirah Mosque by crossing Beach Road again, then turn right.

12:00 pm

Before you reach Magrudy's bookshop and the start of a string of shopping centres, the Lime Tree Café (➤ 100) will tempt you in for lunch with freshly made sandwiches and salads and cakes. The Lime Tree is a Jumeirah institution and you can watch the expats while you eat.

2:00 pm

After lunch explore the shopping options. The standout mall on Beach Road is **Mercato** (➤ 102). No, you aren't hallucinating: the extraordinary blend of mock-Tuscan and Venetian architecture really is intended to

bring the sights of the Mediterranean to a Dubai shopping mall. Alternatively, if it's a heritage hit you're after, tell the taxi driver to continue past Mercato, towards the Jumeirah Beach Hotel, until you see an HSBC bank on the left. On this side street, the **5 Majlis Ghorfat Um Al Sheef** (► 90) is where Dubai's rulers brainstormed the future of the city.

3:00 pm

Don't stay too long at Mercato or the Majlis: you want to catch a bit of sunshine at **11 Safa Park** (► 97) before beating the rush hour to Sheikh Zayed Road.

6:00 pm

Arrive back at Sheik Zayed Road and head to the **3 Emirates Towers** (► 57) to watch the sunset from the 51st-floor Vu's bar (► 103).

8:30 pm

Most of the hotels in the vicinity have at least one superb restaurant. Spectrum on One (► 101) in the Fairmont across the road is deservedly popular and Hoi An (► 100) in the Shangri-La a short way down the road makes for an extra-special evening. Or stay at the Emirates Towers and try the excellent modern European cooking at Vu's.

◻ Jumeirah Mosque

Jumeirah Mosque is one of the largest and prettiest mosques in Dubai, and is the only mosque in the United Arab Emirates open to non-Muslims. Visiting it is a chance to learn more about Islam, as well as to admire the building.

From some angles, Jumeirah Mosque's elegant minarets (towers) stand with a backdrop of some of the world's most advanced architecture. But the mosque has also moved with the times; a loudspeaker calls Muslims to prayer rather than a man at the top of a minaret. And, with 700 mosques in Dubai, one of the highest concentrations in any world city, you won't miss the muezzin's call. It is government policy for a mosque to be within walking distance for everyone.

Joining the hour-long morning tour with a guide from the Sheikh Mohammed Centre for Cultural Understanding is not just a chance to admire the interior pastel-coloured patterns and designs of the mosque, but an opportunity to understand a culture that may be unfamiliar to many visitors to Dubai. Find out anything you've ever wanted to know about Islam but were afraid to ask – questions are encouraged and you won't offend. But it's not a platform for proselytising or preaching and the whole encounter is gently informative.

The mosque was built in 1975 in the Fatimy style, a copy of a larger mosque in Cairo, Egypt. From the outside, aspects of a mosque's form belie its function: the crescent indicates that it is a place of worship and the lines of the dome are intended to draw the eye up towards God. The minarets allow the call to prayer to travel as far as possible. A separate wing, behind the wooden doors to the left, is the women's prayer section – women don't worship with men in United Arab Emirates.

The façade of the mosque has some filigree stonework, intended to add depth and warmth to the exterior. The interior shows Turkish and Egyptian influences – the decoration is deliberately low-key. The mosque can hold 1,200 people, which, in the global scale, makes it a small- to medium-sized. Inside, there's a square arrangement of pillars, a central, painted dome, the *qubba*, and the *mihrab*, the pulpit from where the imam, or leader, faces Mecca (with his back to the other worshippers). The orientation of the mosque and the worshippers is determined by the relative position of Mecca, in Saudi Arabia, and, more specifically, the black stone cube at Mecca called Ka'bah.

Shoes are removed before entering the mosque. This is because Muslims pray and prostrate themselves on the floor of mosques, rather than sitting on chairs or benches. So the removal of shoes is a sign of respect for other worshippers who press their foreheads to the floor. There is no physical distance between worshippers because everyone is equal: the king prays alongside the taxi driver.

Male and female visitors should dress conservatively, covering arms and legs. Women should also cover their heads with a headscarf.

If you miss seeing Jumeirah Mosque in person, you'll find it on the 500Dh bank note.

➕ 168 B4 ✉ Beach Road
☎ 353 6666
❓ Tours for non-Muslims at 10 am on Tue, Thu and Sun with a guide from the Sheikh Mohammed Centre for Cultural Understanding, a short way down Beach Road

Left and right: Visitors to Jumeirah Mosque can gain a valuable insight into the Muslim faith

2 Dubai World Trade Centre

The Dubai World Trade Centre has a single, but significant, claim to fame. This honeycombed, 149m (489-foot) structure was Dubai's first skyscraper when it was completed in 1979. From this date ever more elaborate skyscrapers marched down Sheikh Zayed Road culminating now in the Marina development.

It might look dated, but the Dubai World Trade Centre tower was the precursor to modern Dubai. It still performs a valuable function, housing a reasonably priced hotel (➤ Novotel page 99) and the consulates of Australia, Italy, Japan, China, Switzerland, Turkey and the US in its 39 storeys. The Arabic Language Centre, also based here, offers courses in Arabic to beginners and more practised Arabists. To see how far Dubai has come in 25 years, pull out a 100 dirham note and hold the image of the Dubai World Trade Centre on it up against the newest skyscraper in Dubai's skyline, and the world's tallest building: the Burj Dubai (➤ 96).

➕ 168 C2
✉ Trade Centre Roundabout
☎ 332 1000; www.dwtc.com

Dubai World Trade Centre – the first of its kind

3 Emirates Towers

The two Emirates Towers are the stars of Dubai's architectural hall of fame. Standing at the gateway of Sheikh Zayed Road, they draw the eye with a remarkable charisma and a science-fiction other-worldliness.

Alongside the Dubai World Trade Centre, the contrast couldn't be greater: the city's first skyscraper retains a certain 1970s charm, but the Emirates Towers are currently Dubai's most compelling creation. Yes, the Burj Al Arab hotel impresses, and the Burj Dubai takes your breath away, but the towers involve viewers. Their relationship changes degree-by-degree as your viewpoint moves; from one angle they're embracing, then they're turning away from each other. Their piercing apexes symbolise Dubai's drive to succeed. Designed by the Norr Group, the taller of the towers was completed in November 1999 at an official height of 354.6m (1,163 feet). Its shorter partner (at 305m/ 1,000 feet and 56 storeys) was completed five months late on 15 April, 2000. It is the second tallest hotel-only structure in the world (coming in behind the Burj Al Arab, ► 112), dedicated to the Emirates Towers Hotel. The two towers are connected by a 810sq m (9,000 square feet) underground mall, The Boulevard, which has a good selection of shops but doesn't compare with the BurJuman nearby. A visit to Vu's bar (► 103) on the 51st floor is essential; the view down a shimmering Sheikh Zayed Road at night makes the prices almost palatable. Alternatively, the Zen garden at the foot of the Emirates Towers is the perfect place to meditate on Dubai, the home of the modern skyscraper.

➕ 168 B2
✉ Sheilh Zayed Road
☎ 330 0000; www.jumeirahemiratestowers.com

Striking a pose, the Emirates Towers have a captivating presence

4 Zabeel Park

Take a break from shopping and sightseeing in the city centre with a stroll around this high-tech park. Landscaped gardens are combined with ultra-modern attractions.

It may be in an inauspicious location, straddling a busy intersection at the start of Sheikh Zayed Road, but Zabeel Park is notable for several reasons. It's the first technology-themed park in the Middle East and features Dubai's first suspension bridge, an attractive, curved design crossing Sheikh Zayed Road. The project cost 200 million Dh and opened in December 2005, providing a green respite from downtown Dubai for residents, shoppers and sightseers. Much of the money has been spent on the landscaping the 47ha (5,456-acre) park and the results are superb, with an abundance of date palms and shrubs in a sculpted topography with very few straight lines.

Entry is at the largest area of the park on the north side of Sheikh Zayed Road, best accessed by taxi, although there is plenty of parking space. In this section of Zabeel Park, the Stargate dome houses an IMAX screen and the egg-shaped

Zabeel Park is an oasis in a concrete jungle

2,000-capacity Megabowl amphitheatre will be used to host live music shows. Children will enjoy the Space Maze, based on the planetary system, to one side of the Stargate dome. As with Creekside Park (▶ 68) there are barbecue areas, with picnic tables and benches, for visitors to cook their own food, or you can eat at several food courts around the park.

Although there's an entry fee, most attractions are free once you are inside the park, such as the jogging track circling the largest area of parkland. Cross the bridge, suspended from a 52m (171-foot) spar and 16 steel cables, to reach the southern section of the park, which is dominated by a boating lake, complete with a geyser fountain, which erupts to a height of 20m (66 feet) every 20 minutes, a cascade and an island with its own gazebo. Pedal, rowing or battery-powered boats can be rented. On this side of the park, children can burn off some energy on the Assault Course or join in a game of cricket on the mini-cricket pitch. A mini-golf course is a more sedate option – rent clubs from the ticket office.

Adding to the futuristic feel, visitors can rent a two-wheeled Segway to get around the park (100Dh per hour). A sense of balance is required; stand on the platform and lean forwards to get the device moving. For those who decline such gimmicks, a road train chugs around the park. While a lot of effort has gone into developing Zabeel Park, and it is a welcome patch of greenery in the heart of high-rise Dubai, Creekside Park is a better venue for a special day out. However, if you're in the city centre already, it's an excellent spot to explore for two or three hours.

➕ 169 D1　✉ Zabeel　🕐 Daily 8–11　💰 Expensive

5 Majlis Ghorfat Um Al Sheef

It may look unprepossessing, but this heritage site illustrates how locals lived as recently as the 1950s and 1960s. In the space of two decades, Emiratis made the transition from wind towers to air-conditioning units, from collecting rainwater to desalination plants.

Most houses had a *majlis,* a meeting place and room for receiving guests. However, the Majlis Ghorfat Um Al Sheef is a more significant site than most, which is why it has been restored. It was here, in the late 1950s, that discussions took place about Dubai's future direction, discussions that may have touched on how Dubai was to replace oil revenue with business and tourism.

The complex was constructed in 1955 and was used by the late Sheikh Rashid bin Saeed Al-Maktoum as a summer resort. At that time the area was populated by date palms and fishermen living in beach-side shacks. Today the Majlis is surrounded by suburban villas and it can seem rather underwhelming, but it shows how people lived a generation ago.

The courtyard has a traditional irrigation system (an irrigated garden is called a *falaj),* which shows how water ran down a series of stepped channels. There is also a pond, a garden and a traditional palm shelter, now used to protect a soft-drink dispenser.

The Majlis is a two-storey structure, with an open-sided verandah *(rewaaq)* at ground level and upstairs a *majlis,* complete with cushions, rugs and tea-making facilities. The walls are made from coral and gypsum, while the doors and window frames are fashioned from solid teak. In traditional Arab architecture form follows function and a wind tower guides cooling breezes into the room.

➕ 166 off A4
✉ Signposted from the corner of Beach Road and 17th Street, by the HSBC bank ☎ 394 6343
🕐 Sat–Thu 9 am–midnight, Fri 3:30 pm–8:30 pm
💷 Inexpensive

The Majlis illustrates how Emiratis lived only a generation ago

6 Nad Al Sheba and Godolphin Gallery

Almutawakel, Street Cry and Dubai Millennium: all are winners of the richest prize in world horse racing, the $6 million Dubai World Cup, held annually in March at Nad Al Sheba. And all were owned and trained by Godolphin, the Maktoum family's private racing stable.

It's difficult to overstate the love the Maktoums have for horses and horse racing and the Nad Al Sheba racecourse and the neighbouring Godolphin Gallery testify to this obsession. Race Night at Nad Al Sheba – the season runs from October to April – should be an essential part of any winter-time visit to Dubai. General admission and parking is free (except for the Dubai World Cup race) and the start time is 7 pm. Visitors have to dress smartly and buy a day membership to enter the clubhouse, but the view of the floodlit course is just as good from outside. The track itself features a 2,000m turf course inside a dirt course (2,200m/2,398 yards), running

Below: The evening races at Nad Al Sheba are thrilling events

Above: The Godolphin Gallery is named after a famous 18th-century horse

Below right: A statue on the steps of the gallery

past the roll-shaped grandstand. The illegality of gambling in the United Arab Emirates has been circumvented by the giving away of prizes for correct predictions of race results.

All Dubai society turns up for the World Cup event and if you can find a space among the 50,000 spectators it is a great opportunity for watching people as well as horses. Even those who have little interest in horse racing may be won over by the Godolphin Gallery, a cleverly conceived celebration of horses, racing and winning, incorporating a trophy gallery, cinema, touch-screen presentations and detailed histories of the Maktoum's most successful horses.

The Gallery opened on Dubai World Cup Day in 1999 and, like the stables, is named after a horse: the Godolphin Arabian (► 11). The square exhibition space is organised chronologically into smaller galleries, starting from the left of the entrance. In the centre there is a cinema playing a rather poetically produced film about the training of the Sheikh's horses in both Dubai and England, where Godolphin has stables near Newmarket.

Special horses have their own showcases in the galleries, with pride of place going to Dubai Millennium (► 11). Wherever you look there are trophies; in October 2005 Highlander became Godolphin's 1,000th winner. Frankie Dettori alone, Godolphin's retained jockey, has won 467 races out of 1,449. But the largest trophy in international horse racing, the 5.2kg (185 ounce) Dubai World Cup, is also displayed at the gallery in a room of its own. Whether you're a horse racing fan or not, a circuit of the Gallery is rewarding and you might take away some of the Maktoums' passion for the animals.

Nad Al Sheba Stable Tour

It's worth arriving early for Nad Al Sheba's stable tour, which includes a full cooked breakfast. The highlight, however, is watching the early morning gallops (September–March) when Sheikh Mohammed's prize thoroughbreds are put through their paces.

On a misty morning, before the sun turns day's heat up, it's a beautiful sight; remember that you're watching several million dirhams-worth of animal, each of which is treated with tender loving care by the liveried stablehands. The tour also includes a walk through the Millennium grandstand and a visit to the Godolphin Gallery.

Nail-biting action at Nad Al Sheba

🞢 167 off E1

Nad Al Sheba Race Night
✉ Nad Al Sheba is 5km south of central Dubai and is best accessed from the Al Ain-Dubai road. It is signposted from Interchange 1 and Interchange 2 on Sheikh Zayed Road
☎ 332 2277; www.dubairacingclub.com
🕓 Race nights at Nad Al Sheba begin at 7 pm

Godolphin Gallery
☎ 336 3031; www.godolphin.com
🕓 Mon–Sun 9–5

Stable Tour
☎ 336 3666; www.nadalshebaclub.com
🕓 Mon–Wed, Sat 7 am, Sep–Jun 🞤 Expensive

NAD AL SHEBA: INSIDE INFO

Top tips If you missed seeing the camels racing (▶ opposite, you can cross the road and see them in the camel farms where they are bred and fed. The sandy tracks across the road will be obvious, or you can follow a group of camels as they return from racing.

After you have visited Nad Al Sheba, spend the rest of the day visiting the sights on the same side of Sheikh Zayed Road – the Falcon and Heritage Sports Centre (▶ 95–96) and the Burj Dubai (▶ 96–97).

At Your Leisure

7 Camel Racing at Nad Al Sheba

Horses aren't the only animals to get pulses racing at Nad Al Sheba. Camel racing has long been a favourite entertainment of Emiratis and the camel-racing track at Nad Al Sheba is a hive of activity in the mornings. The season runs from November to April and races take place on Thursdays and Fridays from 7 am; the action is over by 8:30 am. During the remainder of the day you can see camels being trained at the racetrack, with small groups of camels being led across the Al Ain road to their stables in the desert. A racing camel is smaller and faster than an ordinary camel and can cost several million dirhams. In the past, they would be piloted by small, child jockeys, usually recruited from India or Pakistan, but this practice has been outlawed and all jockeys are supposed to be aged over 15, weigh more than 35kg (77lb) and be a resident of the United Arab Emirates. Radio-controlled robot alternatives to human jockeys have been successfully trialled in recent years – you will see what looks like a monkey-sized device with a rotating whip strapped to the camel's back. An operator follows the camel during the race and controls the robot with a joystick.

Beside the dusty race-course, the Nad Al Sheba camel market sells every camel-related accessory imaginable, including attractive, multi-purpose blankets.

➕ 167 off E1
✉ Nad Al Sheba is 5km (3 miles) south of central Dubai and is best accessed from the Al Ain-Dubai road. It is signposted from Interchange 1 and Interchange 2 on Sheikh Zayed Road
🕐 Thu–Fri 7–8:30 am
✋ Free

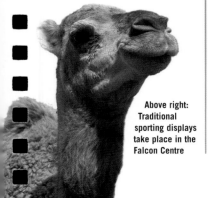

Above right: Traditional sporting displays take place in the Falcon Centre

8 Falcon and Heritage Sports Centre

As you exit the Nad Al Sheba camel racing area, turn right for the new Falcon and Heritage Sports Centre. This new building, designed to

EAST JUMEIRAH: INSIDE INFO

The builders were so determined to guarantee that their tower would be the world's tallest building that at one point they considered hydraulically raising a spire should a rival top it. But when completed the tower looks assured of assuming the mantle of the world's tallest man-made structure. And it won't be a short-lived wonder either, even if it is beaten to the title some day: it has been designed to last for 100 years.

If you're inspired to see more of the UAE's bird species in the wild after visiting the falconry centre, many operators offer birdwatching tours (► 156).

mimic traditional Arabic architecture, on a magnified scale, houses shops and a tented exhibition space dedicated to falcony and other traditional sports of the Arab elite; flying displays take place outside. Falconry has a dedicated following in Dubai and some birds cost up to 150,000Dh.

🕀 167 off E1
✉ Next to Nad Al Sheba camel racing track ☎ 338 0201
🕐 Opening times vary
💷 Inexpensive

9 Burj Dubai

At the time of writing, the Burj Dubai (Dubai Tower) was growing floor by floor, day by day. When it is complete it will be the tallest man-made structure in the world,

although no one is yet quite sure just when the builders will stop pouring the concrete: somewhere between 700 and 900m (2,296 and 2,952 feet) is the best guess. One thing is certain: the Burj Dubai will the most astounding building in Dubai and perhaps in the world. Architect Adrian Smith of Skidmore, Owings and Merrill found inspiration for the Y-shaped base of the tower in a desert flower's petals. The triple-lobed shape also helps resist the region's strong winds, while an outer layer of reflective glazing and steel and aluminium panels will withstand the ferocious Dubai summer heat. Some details are known about what will be inside the tower. A Giorgio

Burj Dubai slowly takes shape

Armani hotel will occupy several of the lower floors. Above the hotel will be private apartments – many of which sold within 8 hours. An observation deck will be on the 124th floor. The tower will be surrounded by a lake and shopping, entertainment and residential developments to rival Dubai Marina.

The developers point out that when Burj Dubai is finished it will be the first time that the Middle East has had the world's tallest structure since the 1300s, when Britain's Lincoln Cathedral took the honour

Ⅱ Safa Park

The emphasis in Safa Park is on fun, with bumper cars, trampolines, an obstacle course and a small Ferris wheel. Conventional activities are also possible – volleyball, football, basketball and tennis – and you can rent bicycles to get around the large park. Several play areas for children mean Safa Park is very popular with families and weekends can get busy.

✚ 166 A3
✉ Al Wasl Road 🕐 Daily 8 am–11 pm, Tue women only ☎ 349 2111
💲 Expensive

from Egypt's Great Pyramid of Giza, which had held the title for 38 centuries.

✚ 167 D2
✉ Near Interchange 1, Sheikh Zayed Road ☎ www.burjdubai.com

⑩ Jumeirah Beach Park

The 5Dh fee to enter is definitely worth it. The park gets very busy on Friday with locals enjoying the beach, playing games in the gardens or cooking at the barbecues. Food and drink is also sold from kiosks. Lifeguards patrol from early morning to sunset; swimming is not permitted after this time.

✚ 166 B5
✉ Beach Road, Jumeirah
☎ 349 2555
🕐 Daily 8 am–11 pm
💲 Expensive

Enjoy a picnic or barbecue at Jumeirah Beach Park

Where to... Stay

Prices
Expect to pay per double room, per night
$ 150Dh–600Dh $$ 600Dh–1,500Dh $$$ 1,500Dh–10,000+Dh

Crowne Plaza Dubai $$$

Most of the hotels on this stretch of Sheikh Zayed Road are geared towards business travellers, but the Crowne Plaza makes a play for leisure travellers with competitive pricing and a down-to-earth selection of bars, restaurants and nightclubs.

➕ 168 B2
🗺 Sheikh Zayed Road
☎ 331 1111; www.ichotels.com

Dubai Marine Beach Resort and Spa $$

This is the closest beach resort to Dubai's commercial heart and it is slightly less expensive than the resorts further down the coast.

There are 195 comfortable rooms, from singles to suites, in 33 villas spread around an attractive beach complex.

Guests can chose from 12 bars and restaurants, including hot bar Sho Cho (▶ 103), Tex-Mex restaurant The Alamo and the riotous Cuban-style Malecon, where the main attraction is the Latino dancing and live music. With a spa, health club, three swimming pools and its own stretch of sand, the Dubai Marine Beach Resort might be showing its age, but it offers good value for money.

➕ 168 B4
🗺 Beach Road, Jumeirah
☎ 346 1111; www.dxbmarine.com

Dusit Dubai $$–$$$

The two-legged Dusit is another spectacular building. It's supposed to represent a pair of hands pressed together in a Thai greeting.

The Asia theme is continued by sarong-wearing staff and the interior design. It is less expensive than the Shangri-La (▶ 99) or Fairmont (below) and the 321 rooms are perfectly comfortable. Facilities include an open-air pool on the 36th floor, a small gym and several restaurants.

➕ 167 E2
🗺 Sheikh Zayed Road
☎ 343 3333; www.dusit.com

The Fairmont $$$

Often ranked as Dubai's leading business hotel, the 34-storey Fairmont has a lot to offer holiday visitors including some of the area's most desirable restaurant tables among them at the Exchange Grill (▶ 100) and Spectrum On One (▶ 101), two pool decks and a spa. Nightlife, in Cin Cin and the Tangerine (▶ 103), is also some of

the best in the city. Styling in the bedrooms is tasteful and contemporary, while business guests can use state-of-the-art facilities, including wireless internet in all public areas.

The Fairmont doesn't suffer from the uniformity of other international chains and, despite the size of the hotel, the service is excellent.

➕ 168 B2
🗺 Sheikh Zayed Road
☎ 332 5555; www.fairmont.com

Ibis $$

For economical accommodation, the Ibis is hard to beat. On the surface it seems like a no-frills option – the rooms are clean, functional and comfortable but not very spacious, and the buffet breakfast costs extra.

But there are some pleasing points, among them the Philippe Starck furniture and some stylish bars and restaurants, such as Cubo, that make the hotel excellent value.

➕ 168 C2
🗺 Dubai World Trade Centre
☎ 332 4444;
www.ibishotel.com

Jumeirah Beach Club Resort and Spa $$$
Perhaps the most low-key Jumeirah property, this bijou resort has just 50 suites and the guests can share two pools (with underwater music), three squash courts, seven tennis courts, two volleyball courts, a water sports centre and a spa (➤ 104). An exclusive experience.

166 B4 ✉ Beach Road, Jumeirah ☎ 344 5333; www.jumeirahbeachclub.com

Al Murooj Rotana Hotel $$$
An ornate pink confection on the desert side of Sheikh Zayed Road, the Al Murooj has a ringside view of the Burj Dubai. Don't be put off by the impersonal, glass-fronted lobby; the 253 rooms and suites have contemporary styling with all the facilities a mixed-use hotel should provide. The 10 restaurants include Latino House (➤ 100) and two poolside venues.

167 E2 ✉ Al Saffa Street ☎ 321 1111; www.rotana.com

Novotel $$
The Novotel is for visitors who intend to get out of their hotel and see the city. Business travellers will be satisfied with the facilities, but leisure travellers will find that the pool is on the small side.

168 C2 ✉ Dubai World Trade Centre ☎ 332 0000; www.novotel.com

Shangri-La $$$
Of all Dubai's luxury hotels, the 41-floor Shangri-La is one of the most stylish. The tone is set by the vertiginous, avant-garde lobby and is carried through to the sumptuous bedrooms. Press a button and your room's curtains open to reveal one of the best views of Sheikh Zayed Road.

Another perk is priority booking at the hotel's buzzing restaurants Anwaj (right) and Hoi-An (➤ 100). Facilities also include a rooftop pool with bar and sunbeds, plus a gym and spa.

167 E2 ✉ Sheikh Zayed Road ☎ 343 8888; www.shangri-la.com

Where to... Eat and Drink

Prices
Expect to pay for a three-course meal for one, excluding drinks and service
$ under $60Dh **$$** 60Dh–100Dh **$$$** over 100Dh

Amwaj $$$
This restaurant is one of the top seafood destinations in Dubai with inventive dishes flowing from an open kitchen. Amwaj boasts some of Dubai's most sought-after dining tables, so expect prices to match. The delicious desserts, such as panna cotta with dragon fruit, will sweeten the blow of the bill. Brunch on Friday, however, offers lavish buffets for a relatively reasonable price.

167 E2 ✉ Shangri-La, Sheikh Zayed Road ☎ 405 2703 ⌚ Sun–Fri 12–3, 7–midnight

Double Decker Pub $
Double Decker is the Al Murooj Rotana's (➤ 99) cheap-and-cheerful, London-themed pub. It is a two-tiered venue with dining downstairs and drinking upstairs.

Brunches, served from noon to 5 pm, are particularly good value. Food is no-frills British fare, so don't expect culinary flights of fancy but it's a good choice for a more substantial lunch or a quick dinner before drinks.

167 E2 ✉ Al Murooj Rotana, Al Saffa Street ☎ 321 1111 ⌚ Noon–3 am

The Exchange Grill $$$

The Exchange was revamped in 2005: while the dining room can still seem austere, the unbeatable steaks and an outstanding wine list will create a warm glow. The speciality remains the high-quality beef, cooked expertly in any number of ways, but there are options for vegetarians. This is one of the Fairmont's more refined venues – for a livelier night out, head down to Spectrum On One.

✚ 168 B2 ☒ Fairmont Hotel, Sheikh Zayed Road ☎ 332 5555
☉ Daily 7 pm–1 am

Hoi-An $$$

In a convincing mock-Saigon-style dining room with ceiling fans and green window shutters, silk-clad waitresses serve delicious Vietnamese dishes. Starters include Saigon street-vendor soup, a clear broth with translucent noodles, chicken and black mushrooms, and Dungeness crab baked in green bamboo. For the main course, chargrilled lemon grass chicken – skewered chicken fillets on bamboo with chargrilled courgette (zucchini) and sticky rice – is a tasty, lemony choice. Hoi-An is the sort of fine-dining restaurant that can serve a choice of 10 teas, including Gu Zhang Dao Jian, a green tea plucked only 10 days every year.

✚ 167 E2 ☒ Shangri-La, Sheikh Zayed Road ☎ 405 2703
☉ Daily 7 pm–1 am

The One Café $

Adjacent to the Jumeirah Mosque, The One is a lifestyle store selling soft furnishings, kitchen equipment and other household items. The opening of the festive Christmas displays is always a must-see event in Dubai. The shop's café, on the first floor, is a suitably trendy place to get a bite to eat and a drink from an inventive and appetising menu. Snacks range from salads and sandwiches to hot dishes and the standard is well above average. For refreshment, there are freshly squeezed fruit juices.

✚ 168 B4 ☒ Jumeirah Beach Road ☎ 345 6687; www.theoneme.com
☉ Sat–Thu 9-9, Fri 2-9

Latino House $$$

Latino House, which opened in 2006, is a steak house with a twist. All the dishes are inspired by South American countries, such as lobster and potato salad with strawberry dressing from Colombia as a starter and an Argentinian steak with crunchy vegetables and cassava for the main course.

For dessert, Venezuelan chef Issam Koteich has introduced Tres Leches, a traditional Venezuelan milk cake. Choose between sitting around the foot of a spiral staircase, or by a pool outside.

✚ 167 E2 ☒ Al Murooj Rotana , Al Saffa Street ☎ 321 1111
☉ Daily 7 pm–11:30

Lime Tree Café $

Although this Dubai favourite is stylishly decorated with lime-green walls and dark wood furniture, it's the exceptionally good food that accounts for the Lime Tree's popularity.

A Mediterranean slant sees focaccia sandwiches filled with roast vegetables and ricotta or chicken with pesto aioli. Paninis, wraps and a daily-changing selection of salads are also sold and you can count on some Arabic flavours such as couscous or halloumi cheese.

If you miss lunch just have a freshly squeezed fruit juice or a coffee and a generous slab of home-made cake on the terrace. There's no better place in Jumeirah for a snack. It gets very busy at weekends.

✚ 168 B4 ☒ Near Jumeirah Mosque, Beach Road ☎ 349 8498
☉ All day

Al Nafoorah $$

This is one of the city's best Lebanese restaurants. The food is

Where to... 101

prepared to an expert standard: you can expect excellent hot and cold meze. End dessert – usually involving dates, honey and Arabic sweets – with a smoke on a hookah pipe.

♦ 168 B2 ⊠ The Boulevard, Emirates Towers, Sheikh Zayed Road ☎ 319 8088 🕐 Daily 12:30–3, 8–11:30 (Fri lunch 1–3:30)

The Noodle House $

For fast food without the fries, The Noodle House chain is an excellent and healthy choice. There are branches in many of the major malls in Dubai; this one is in the Boulevard shopping mall beneath the Emirates Towers Hotel.

Seating is on a first-come, first served basis, at long, dark wood trestle tables. Interior décor uses a handsome, black-and-red Oriental theme, animated by an open kitchen and friendly staff. Ordering couldn't be easier. Simply tick the dishes you would like on the menu card at each table. The spiciness of each dish is noted with a chilli symbol, other symbols tell you whether a dish contains nuts or is vegetarian. Noodles, unsurprisingly, form the foundation of many dishes, but you can have them in a soup, such as prawn wonton soup with roast duck, or pan fried. Noodle Houses are the best fast-food option in the city, perfect for lunchtimes.

♦ 168 B2 ⊠ Boulevard Mall, Emirates Towers, Sheikh Zayed Road ☎ 330 0000; www.thenoodlehouse.com 🕐 Sat–Thu 10–10, Fri 4–10

Prasino's $$$

An elegant eatery on a beach-side terrace, Prasino's is a wonderful spot for a special meal. The food, from a short but well-balanced Mediterranean menu, readily stands up to the breathtaking views of the Gulf and is competitively priced. There's live jazz during the mellow Friday brunch service, when an extra 50Dh will buy all the sparkling wine you can drink.

♦ 166 B4 ⊠ Jumeirah Beach Club Resort, Beach Road, Jumeirah ☎ 344 5333 🕐 Daily 12:30–3, 7:30–11

Spectrum On One $$$

You should find something to tickle your palate at the Fairmont's busiest restaurant, accessed via a one-stop lift towards the back of the lobby. It's the more laidback of the hotel's dining rooms and attracts a lot of non-guests, meaning that there's a considerable buzz about the place.

The globetrotting cuisine covers the four corners of the world, from China, Thailand, India and Japan to Europe via Arabia. Seating areas are by region and there are eight open kitchens where you can watch chefs rolling sushi, stirring sauces or grilling meats.

Food quality is excellent; you can mix and match dishes, but the Thai curries are a reliable choice, while many of the European dishes, such as Norwegian salmon with melted leeks, sugar snap peas and a creamy horseradish sauce also exceed expectations. There are starters to share, such as Arabic meze. The restaurant opens specially for the unmissable Friday brunch, with unlimited champagne.

♦ 168 B2 ⊠ Fairmont Hotel, Sheikh Zayed Road ☎ 311 8000 🕐 Daily 7 pm –1 am

Wagamama $$

Several international chains have set up shop in the Crowne Plaza hotel, including TGI Friday's, but Wagamama, the Japanese noodle specialists, is the best bet.

Dishes from the universal menu are well-executed and service is good. Wagamama is suited to a quick, inexpensive meal and the trestle tables and benches are shared with other diners.

♦ 168 B2 ⊠ Sheikh Zayed Road ☎ 305 6060; www.wagamama.ae 🕐 Daily noon–midnight

Where to... Shop

The malls in this, the older end of Jumeirah, are a few years behind those at the other end of the city. They sprang up to meet demand from local residents rather than tourists, which means that you won't necessarily find the big designer brands, but some more interesting outlets in their place. The malls are also on a smaller scale so window shopping is less energy sapping than in the mega-malls.

In terms of design, most of the malls are refreshingly down-to-earth. The exception is Mercato. This mall is an extraordinary homage to classic Tuscan and Venetian architecture, with balconies, archways and plenty of marble behind a pink façade.

Palm Strip

The only open-air mall in Dubai has a Starbucks and a Japengo Café plus good-value clothes by Karen Millen and the Spanish retailers Mango. But it's not the place to shop in the height of summer.
🖪 168 B4 ⊠ Beach Road ☎ 346 1462 ⊕ Sat–Thu 10–10, Fri 5–10

The Village

Leave the children in the Peekaboo play area while you explore some of the city's more unusual boutiques, or unwind in the sensational SensAsia Urban Spa. The Village serves the local community so you will find shops that don't appear in the larger malls, such as florists, a post office and beachwear outlets. The interior design is also relaxing, with water features and shrubbery.
🖪 168 B4 ⊠ Beach Road ☎ 344 7714 ⊕ Sat–Thu 10–10, Fri 4–10

Jumeirah Plaza

There's an eclectic selection of shops at this pink-painted mall,

including a good second-hand bookshop, a Dome café and a Dubai police kiosk.
🖪 168 B4 ⊠ Beach Road, opposite Jumeirah Mosque ☎ 349 7111 ⊕ Sat–Thu 10–10, Fri 5–10

Town Centre Jumeirah

Beauty products are a speciality of the shops in this small mall, including a Nail Station and SOS Salon. Get a foot massage at Feet First before continuing shopping.
🖪 167 E4 ⊠ Beach Road, next to Mercato ☎ 344 0111; www.towncentrejumeirah ⊕ Sat–Thu 10–10, Fri 4–10

Magrudy's

Magrudy's is best known as a book-shop. It carries the greatest range of titles in Dubai and there are several branches around the city. The shelves here carry most subjects, from travel to art via cookery and biography. But there are other reasons to step inside the Magrudy's complex, including a pharmacy, a

health-food shop and Gerard's, a famed patisserie.
🖪 168 B4 ⊠ Beach Road, near Jumeirah Mosque ☎ 344 4193; www.magrudy.com

Mercato

More than 90 outlets have come to this brave new mall. They include Dubai's largest Virgin Megastore, a Spinney's supermarket and seven-screen cinema. Women's fashion is more Topshop, Mango and Next than designer, but men can shop at Hugo Boss and Cerruti. There's an Early Learning Centre for children. Teenagers get more choice with a Miss Sixty and Diesel. Household items are also represented by the funky KAS Australia branch and carpet shops. On the top floor there is a mother-and-baby room, while children can play in the Fun City area. When leaving, competition for the limited supply of taxis is fierce.
🖪 167 E4 ⊠ Beach Road ☎ 344 4161; www.mercatoshoppingmall.com ⊕ Sat–Thu 10–10, Fri 2–10

Where to...
Be Entertained

BARS

Boudoir

You'll need to be smartly dressed and preferably in a mixed group to get past the bouncers at this exclusive club. Once inside, the interior has a *fin-de-siècle* decadence, with candles, heavy damask fabrics and sumptuous sofas. This is one of the more fashionable places to party in Dubai, where you can enjoy starlit nights in the outdoor area accompanied by a slick soundtrack. Monday night is jazz night and ladies enjoy free champagne on Tuesday nights and cocktails on Wednesday.

⊞ 168 B4 ⊠ Dubai Marine Beach Resort & Spa, Beach Road ☎ 345 5995; www.myboudoir.com ⏰ Daily 7.30 pm–3 am

Cin Cin

Cin Cin opened in December 2005 and is now Dubai's top destination for oenophiles. Assistant Manager Jean-Philippe Joncas is continuously adding to the collection of 280 wines, from South African sauvignon blanc for 35Dh per glass to 40,000Dh for a bottle of 1982 Chateau Lafite Rothschild.

In Dubai it's the big names that sell, although Joncas is gradually introducing customers to more unusual New-World wines. Choose between tall, padded chairs or low-slung leather couches. The sommeliers are very knowledgeable and helpful.

⊞ 168 B2 ⊠ The Fairmont hotel ☎ 332 5555; www.fairmont.com ⏰ 6 pm–2 am

Harry Ghatto's

The best karaoke bar in Dubai starts late and you can continue crooning until 3 am. It's a compact place, behind the sushi restaurant Tokyo, but that, and the cocktails, just adds to the atmosphere.

⊞ 168 B2 ⊠ Boulevard, Emirates Towers Hotel ☎ 330 0000 ⏰ 8–3 am; karaoke from 10 pm

Sho-Cho

White leather furniture, large fish-tanks and subtle blue lighting gives the impression of being underwater in this trendy, minimalist Japanese restaurant and bar.

⊞ 168 B4 ⊠ Dubai Marine Beach Resort & Spa, Beach Road ☎ 346 1111; www.dxbmarine.com ⏰ 7–2:30 am

Tangerine

Revamped in 2006, Tangerine attracts the beautiful people at the end of the week.

It's a huge place, but the maze of rooms makes intimacy easy to come by. Don't forget the plastic as drinks are expensive.

⊞ 168 B2 ⊠ Sheikh Zayed Road ☎ 332 5555

Vu's

Take the high-speed lift to the 51st floor of the Emirates Tower Hotel for one of the headiest views in town: few places look as futuristic as Sheikh Zayed Road at night, although, for obvious reasons, you miss out on seeing the profile of the Emirates Towers. Console yourself with a pricey cocktail and watch the smart crowd arrive. Although the slanting window hampers the view a little, this is a must-visit bar.

⊞ 168 B2 ⊠ 51st Floor, Emirates Towers Hotel, Sheikh Zayed Road ☎ 330 0000 ⏰ Daily 5 pm–2 am

Zinc

Zinc is a well-established, popular nightclub aimed at people who want to let their hair down and party rather than strike a pose. The music policy is determinedly mainstream and there are regular appearances by the live house band. The interior has a slightly 1980s look about it, with lots of bare metal. Happy hour drinks are generous.

✠ 168 B2 ⊠ Crowne Plaza, Sheikh Zayed Road ☎ 331 1111; www.crowneplaza.com ⏰ 7 pm–3 am

SPAS

Satori

This small but relaxing and private spa, with a interior oriental garden, is reserved for members and resident guests. A wide range of treatments, including Balinese wraps, use Elemis products.

✠ 166 B4 ⊠ Jumeirah Beach Club Resort, Beach Road ☎ 310 2759; www.jumeirahbeachclub.com ⏰ Daily 9–9

SensAsia Urban Spa

One of a handful of spas not found in a luxury hotel, SensAsia Urban Spa is stylish and highly regarded

among Jumeirah locals who come for treatments such as facials and body polishes or head-to-toe massages. There's an Oriental theme, so expect Balinese massages, but there are also innovative treatments such as the Hi-Heeler for women who wear stiletto shoes.

✠ 168 B4 ⊠ The Village Mall, Beach Road, Jumeirah ☎ 349 8850; www.sensasiaspas.com ⏰ Sat–Thu 10–10, Fri noon–9

Willow Stream Spa

On the ninth floor of one of Dubai's finest hotels, the Willow Stream Spa offers a steam room, Jacuzzi and two pools. Treatments are based around a marine theme, while the overall design is Greco-Roman – expect marble pillars, mosaics and candles. All guests receive a pre-treatment consultation.

✠ 168 B2 ⊠ Fairmont Hotel, Sheikh Zayed Road ☎ 311 8800; www.fairmont.com ⏰ Daily 10–10 for spa treatments, 6 am–midnight for fitness activities

Kitepeople

At the far end of this stretch of Jumeirah's shore is Kite Beach. It has assumed the name due to the kitesurfers who once flocked to the free beach at weekends. With regular onshore breezes and warm water, kitesurfing is a popular sport in Dubai, but increasingly strict regulations mean that they are moving away from Jumeirah's main strip. Kitepeople sells and rents equipment, offers lessons to anyone wishing to try the sport and advises on the best kitesurfing spots. Their main outlet is the shop Picnico on Jumeirah's Beach Road, beside the Eppco petrol station.

✠ Off map ⊠ Adjacent to Interchange 3 on Sheikh Zayed Road ☎ 050 8438584; www.kitepeople.net

Dubai Offshore Sailing Club

The Dubai Offshore Sailing Club is a welcoming place offering private and group sailing lessons to non-

members. Lessons cost between 100–245Dh.

✠ 166 B4 ⊠ Beach Road, by Safa Park ☎ 394 1669; www.dosc.ae ⏰ 8:30–12:30

Green Art Gallery

The Green Art Gallery exhibits original contemporary art in a large villa. Themes vary, but Arab-influenced work is often to the fore. Fifty, mainly Arab, artists are represented here.

✠ 167 F4 ⊠ Villa 23, Street 51, behind Dubai Zoo ☎ 344 9888 www.gagallery.com ⏰ Exhibitions Oct–May

Grand Mercato Cinema

Located in the mock-Italian Mercato mall, the Grand has seven screens showing the latest releases.

✠ 167 E4 ⊠ Mercato mall, Beach Road, Jumeirah ☎ 349 8765; www.century-cinemas.com ⏰ Sat–Thu 10–10, Fri 2–10

West Jumeirah

Getting Your Bearings 106 – 109
In a Day 110 – 111
Don't Miss 112 – 124
At Your Leisure 125 – 126
Where to… 127 – 134

Getting Your Bearings

Dubai west of the Burj Al Arab is an ever-expanding area. Initially, development – hotels, malls and theme parks – crept down Sheikh Zayed Road, further and further from the old Dubai around the Creek. Today, there are construction sites from Interchange 3 onwards, reaching beyond the Palm Jumeirah, beyond the new Dubai Marina to Jebel Ali Port. But the most extraordinary work is going on inland: Dubailand is, quite simply, the world's largest construction site and it is taking over the empty desert behind this part of Jumeirah.

West Jumeirah is a convenient, catch-all name for this section; although the Palm Island is called Jumeirah, the real Jumeirah neighbourhood is back up the coast next to Bur Dubai. The districts at this end of Sheikh Zayed Road, from the Burj Al Arab and away from the Creek, are, in order: Umm Suqeim, Umm Al Sheif, Al Sufouh and Al Mina Al Seyahi, occupying Interchanges 3 to 6 on Sheikh Zayed Road.

MARSA DUBAI

Dubai Marina

5

E11

Jumeirah Lake Tower Complex

Since there were few existing residential buildings along the coast, developers have had a free hand to build right up to the shoreline. The first to arrive were five-star hotels such as the Ritz-Carlton. Now, a second layer of development is going up behind the beach-side buildings; the most intensive construction site is Dubai Marina, which is surrounding an inland waterway in Al Mina Al Seyahi. At the moment, this is the most modern part of Dubai. In time, it will be a second, alternative, axis to the city; there'll be no reason for residents to go into old Dubai at all.

East to west, the attractions of Jumeirah West have one thing in common; they're all modern. On the coast adjacent to Interchange 3 are two of the most distinctive hotels in Dubai: the wave-shaped Jumeirah Beach Resort and the iconic Burj Al Arab. Dubai's best and very popular theme park, Wild Wadi, is at the entrance to the Burj Al Arab. There are some truly entertaining innovations at Wild Wadi, such as Wipeout, an endlessly breaking wave, known as a flowrider, on which to practise surfing.

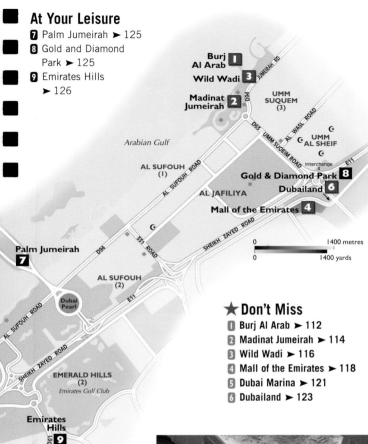

At Your Leisure

7 Palm Jumeirah ► 125
8 Gold and Diamond
Park ► 125
9 Emirates Hills
► 126

Burj **1**
Al Arab
Wild Wadi **3**

Madinat **2**
Jumeirah

UMM
SUQUEM
(3)

Arabian Gulf

UMM
AL SHEIF

AL SUFOUH
(1)

Interchange
4

Gold & Diamond Park **8**

AL JAFILIYA

Dubailand **6**

Mall of the Emirates **4**

0   1400 metres
0   1400 yards

Palm Jumeirah
7

AL SUFOUH
(2)

Dubai
Pearl

EMERALD HILLS
(2)
Emirates Golf Club

Emirates
Hills
9

★ Don't Miss

1 Burj Al Arab ► 112
2 Madinat Jumeirah ► 114
3 Wild Wadi ► 116
4 Mall of the Emirates ► 118
5 Dubai Marina ► 121
6 Dubailand ► 123

Next to the Burj Al
Arab, Madinat Jumeirah is
the most artificial display
of opulence in the city. It
is a sprawling complex
with two luxury hotels (Al
Qasr and Mina A'Salam)
and public areas including
a souk, restaurants and a
large nightclub. The inspiration for Madinat
Jumeirah seems to be a
combination of old-world

Above: Fun and Frolics at Wild Wadi

Left: Diners enjoy a relaxed lunch in the sunshine

Venice and new-world Palm Springs: the complex seems to float on water and guests are ferried from room to restaurant in *abras*, motoring silently along the wide waterways. Except, at Al Qasr and Mina A'Salam, they don't have restaurants, they have "experiences". Madinat Jumeirah is truly a fantasy world, providing everything for its citizens, including Dubai's only theatre and its largest nightclub.

The surreal world of Dubai enters another dimension at Mall of the Emirates, the vast shopping complex at Interchange 4, behind Madinat Jumeirah. If you're wondering what that silver tube protruding from its side is, here's a clue: it's the only place in the UAE where you'll need to wear a woolly hat and warm gloves. Yes, Dubai has the region's first indoor ski resort. This is not just an ordinary ski slope; there's

a "black" run and four other slopes, alpine-style restaurants, ice caverns, a snowboard skills park and chairlifts to the top. Dubai must surely be the only place in the world where you can go surfing in the morning (at Wild Wadi) and skiing in the afternoon.

The Mall of the Emirates is one of the world's largest shopping malls, with more than 400 shops, including Harvey Nichols, a luxury hotel and, of course, the ski resort.

At the next interchange on Sheikh Zayed Road, Dubai Marina is already wowing residents and visitors alike with its skyscrapers. The ongoing development already has luxury hotels, restaurants and work-residential areas such as Dubai Media City, Internet City and Knowledge Village. The development revolves around the Marina, where immaculate yachts and cruisers are moored.

Even the Marina pales in comparison to the planned Dubailand, accessed by an exit on Sheikh Zayed Road between Interchanges 4 and 5. When complete (by 2018), Dubailand will be twice the size of the world's next largest group of theme parks, the Disney resorts, and one hundred times the size of Monaco. The money being spent on the project is simply astronomical (➤ 123) and

Below:
Dubailand,
Global Village

part of this work in progress is already open. In time, the aim is that Dubai's barren desert will be transformed into the world's number one tourist destination.

An amazing day awaits. After a morning shopping at the huge Mall of the Emirates, head for ski slopes in the afternoon, followed by surfing at Wild Wadi.

West Jumeirah in a Day

9:00 am

Breakfast at your hotel. It'll be a long drive down to Jumeirah if you're staying in Deira or Bur Dubai so try to spend at least a couple of nights at a beach resort in this part of Dubai (➤ 127 for hotel listings).

10:00 am

Be first through the doors at the ❹ Mall of the Emirates (➤ 118–120), Dubai's largest mall with more than 400 shops. A free map will help you to find the shops you want to visit. Children will love the Magic Planet entertainment zone (➤ 132) which has games and rides.

1:00 pm

Lunch at the mall. An eating area on the first floor has numerous restaurants, including a Japengo Café, a TGI Fridays and cuisines from all over the world. You'll need the energy for your next task: skiing Dubai's first indoor ski slopes.

2:00 pm

Ski Dubai (➤ 119–120) on the first floor of Mall of the Emirates. is an extraordinary place, with real snow, restaurants and ski runs. You can book a two-hour session and if you're not sure of your skills, lessons are available. Woolly hats are provided.

4:30 pm

From skiing to surfing in one day: arrive at the **3 Wild Wadi** (➤ 116) theme park in time for the reduced-price sundowner sessions. Wild Wadi's slides, wave pools and themed play areas are set in a very well-made tropical landscape of rocks, waterfalls and palm groves.

7:00 pm

Drop the shopping bags off at your hotel and freshen up for an alfresco dinner at one of the restaurants on the waterfront at **5 Dubai Marina** (➤ 121–122) There are several to choose from, including Chandelier (➤ 129–130) by the entrance or Inferno (➤ 130) to the right. All around you, the second hub of Dubai is taking shape.

10:00 pm

Finish the night with a cocktail at the luxurious Buddha Bar (➤ 132) attached to the Grosvenor House hotel on the opposite side of the Marina. The bar, deriving from the Paris-based bar of the same name, is one of the top nightspots in Dubai.

1 Burj Al Arab

This futuristic marvel sums up Dubai's forward-looking, upwardly mobile attitude. It's the world's tallest hotel and probably the most luxurious too. Admire the view of The World (➤ 24) from the Skyview Bar over a cocktail; just don't forget the credit card.

It is fitting that Dubai's iconic building isn't a government edifice, a historic landmark or a place of religious worship; rather, it's a hotel. This was certainly the intention of architect Thomas Wills Wright and builders WS Atkins, who were briefed to create something that would signal Dubai's ambitions to the world. But there are also references to Dubai's seafaring past in the sail-like façade of the Burj Al Arab, which is a Teflon-coated, woven glass-fibre material. During the day its colour is a retina-buring white but at night it becomes the backdrop to a technicolour lightshow, which can be viewed from the hotels along Jumeirah beach.

The Burj Al Arab stands on its own man-made island 280m (305 yards) offshore, so it feels like the hotel itself is afloat. Getting past the security guards at the bridge's gatehouse requires a reservation at one of the hotel's restaurants (➤ 129; book in advance). You can enter the hotel just to have a drink at the Skyview Bar, or afternoon tea at Sahn Eddar but again you need to make a reservation. It's worth the effort, if only to see for yourself the over-the-top interior decoration. Credited to Kuan Chew of KCA International, the red, yellow and blue swirly carpets and gold and silver plating is enough to make your head spin. And it's true, if it looks like gold it probably is: 1,600sq m (1,904 square yards) of 24-carat gold leaf was used.

The hotel's other vital statistics are equally jaw-dropping: there are 1,500 members of staff for 202 suites, each of which has its own butler. A fleet of 10 white Rolls-Royces is at the disposal of guests, while a helicopter shuttle service from the airport costs 9,000Dh. Perhaps the highlight of a visit to the Burj Al Arab is the high-speed exterior lift, which whisks passengers to the top floor at an ear-popping 6m (19.5 feet) per second.

Although there have been rumours about subsidence, the foundations of the 321m 1,053-foot) building are 2.5m (8-foot) diameter piles, sunk 40m (131 feet) deep. Construction began in 1994 and the hotel opened in December 1999. It will be some time yet before the Burj Al Arab – beautiful from the outside, ugly from the inside – will be superseded as Dubai's icon.

➕ 165 E3
✉ Umm Suqeim
☎ 301 7777; www.burj-al-arab.com

Right: Luxury dining at Al Mahara restaurant

The impressive atrium
within Burj Al Arab

2 Madinat Jumeirah

Madinat Jumeirah is excess all areas: part-hotel, part-leisure complex, it takes theming to another level. The bulk of the resort is the Mina A'Salam Arabian-themed hotel, but public areas include Dubai's only theatre, a nightclub and a souk.

Madinat Jumeirah beach resort

No other resort matches the over-the-top design of Madinat Jumeirah. Everything here is fake, from the wind towers to the *abras* that ply the 3.7km (2.2 miles) of waterways, but that doesn't detract from the dizzying experience of exploring the resort. Unless you're staying at the Mina A'Salam, a boutique hotel with a mere 292 rooms, or in one of Al Qasr's suites (some costing 30,000Dh per night), you'll be restricted to the restaurants, the souk or one of the entertainment venues, such as Dubai's largest nightclub, Trilogy, or the city's only theatre, the 442-seat Madinat Theatre. There are 70 shops in the souk shopping area. It's not the most realistic interpretation of a souk, with wide walkways and a non-negotiable pricing policy, but you may find some well-made souvenirs here. The standard of the goods is very high and the most interesting shops are those selling arts, crafts, jewellery and antiques – for a price. The entrance to the theatre is in the souk. Outside, live-music events are staged in the 1000-seater amphitheatre, which backs onto a waterway. Trilogy nightclub is on a similarly super-sized scale, with

Below: Buy a souvenir or browse the arts and crafts shops in the souk area

MADINAT JUMEIRAH: INSIDE INFO

Top tips Short of staying at one of the two hotels in Madinat Jumeirah, the best way to get inside the complex for look around is to book a table at one of the 29 bars and restaurants.

For the best views of Madinat Jumeirah without setting foot inside, take the lift to the Skyview Bar at the Burj Al Arab hotel (➤ 112–113).

Don't miss Try to see the mock dhow marooned in the harbour. The *abras* you see ferrying guests around are powered by silent electric motors.

A bird's-eye view of the elaborate resort

three floors of dance music and a rooftop bar; the venue is the leading night out for Dubai's party set and many will warm up in one of the resort's excellent bars or restaurants. Madinat Jumeirah is certainly worth visiting once, for the spectacle, but unless you're staying at the Mina A'Salam or Al Qasr hotels you won't be seeing the whole complex.

🔢 165 D3
✉ Interchange 4, Sheikh Zayed Road
☎ 366 8888; www.madinatjumeirah.com

③ Wild Wadi

Wild Wadi, a 5ha (12-acre) theme park complex, occupies a prime position at the entrance of the Burj Al Arab island on Beach Road. This is an excellent day out, with 23 rides for adults and children, plus restaurants to help you keep your strength up for the thrilling rides.

The Burj Al Arab was never going to tolerate a second-rate water park on its doorstep and in Wild Wadi it has one of the world's best, with 23 rides for children and adults and some superlative landscaping. Attractions that you might have to queue for are the Jumeirah Sceirah (pronounce "scarer") ride, a 33m (108-foot) drop at 80kph (50mph) on the biggest waterslide outside North America; Whitewater Wadi, which connects to 11 water slides, and the Flood River Flyer, with 6 slides – for strong swimmers only.

There's a story behind the theme park: legend has it that Juha, a friend of Sinbad the Sailor, was sailing his dhow home, across the Arabian Sea, when a violent storm struck. Juha and his dhow fetched up in a tropical

There's plenty of water-based fun to be had at this world-class park

WILD WADI: INSIDE INFO

Top tips Pick up body boards and rent towels at a counter to the left of the Burj Al Arab entrance. The boards are free but towels cost 20Dh. Lockers are also available for 20Dh.
• The park has two entrances: The main entrance is by the Burj Al Arab causeway; the other is for Jumeriah resort guests.
• There is limited parking so take a taxi to the park.

Hidden gem Breakers Bay where you can surf in continuous waves.

lagoon where waterfalls cascaded from rocky outcrops and palm groves provided shade from the sun. Visitors can enjoy the family play area in Juha's Dhow, which has 100 games for the smallest children, or explore the Wadi Wash and Fossil Rock; every hour, thanks to sound-and-light technology, a storm breaks here, with thunder, lightning and even a flash flood. Whitewater rafting experiences are provided by the Flood River and Rushdown Ravine. If you're not scared of the dark, try running the Tunnel of Doom, an underground tunnel of twists and turns in total darkness.

However, the best reason to get wet at Wild Wadi is Breaker's Bay, where you can learn to surf in man-made waves of varying sizes, and in the smaller-scale WipeOut and Riptide Flowrider waves.

🔟 165 E3
✉ Burj Al Arab causeway
☎ 348 4444; www.wildwadi.com
🕐 Daily 11–6, Nov–Feb; daily 11–7 Mar–May and Sep–Oct; daily 11–9 Jun–Aug
💲 Expensive

4 Mall of the Emirates

Superlatives are barely enough to describe the Mall of the Emirates; it is, until Mall of Arabia is completed, the largest mall in Dubai, with 400 shops. But as well as sending shoppers to heaven, it can put children on a Magic Planet and slide skiers down the first indoor ski runs in Dubai.

You can't miss Mall of the Emirates; it's that palatial complex on the desert side of Sheikh Zayed Road with the silver, cigar-shaped extension sticking out of it (which houses Ski Dubai, see opposite).

You will need more than one day to explore all of the shopping mall itself. Built on three levels, over 585,000sq m (6.5 million square feet), it's a town within a city. There are several entry points and you should pick up a map at one and plan your route around the mall. The biggest outlets in the mall are the department stores Debenhams on the ground floor and

Exploration of this epic mall will take several trips

Shoppers in one of the 400 stores within the mall

floor and Harvey Nichols on the first floor. The Magic Planet children's zone (► 132) and the Peekaboo play area for younger children are on the first floor, close to Ski Dubai, while the Cinestar cinema complex is also on the first floor. Shops at the Mall of the Emirates cover every conceivable category; if you can think of it, you can probably buy it here. Men's and women's clothing represents the largest category, with a distinct zone in the Via Rodeo for the likes of Armani, Marc Jacobs and Yves St Laurent, but you can also buy home-ware at about 20 stores, electronics, carpets, toys, perfumes, jewellery, accessories, books and music.

At the time of writing, Mall of the Emirates was open but incomplete. By 2007 it will have Dubai's second theatre venue, the Dubai Community Arts Theatre, which will be a welcome addition to the cultural scene.

Ski Dubai

Even looking into Ski Dubai from the viewers' gallery, it becomes apparent exactly what a technological achievement this project is. Quad chairlifts relay skiers up to the top of the five slopes, including the world's first indoor black run. Other skiers get a bite to eat at the all-too-convincing St. Moritz Café at the foot of the hill, or the Avalanche Café half-way up. Everywhere is frosted with snow, created by what is, in simple terms, a giant air-conditioning system. Pure water is fed through the unit and when it is sprayed from the snow guns it turns to

Right: Enjoy an indoor winter wonderland at Ski Dubai

crystalline snow in the -8°C (18°F) temperatures of the snow-
making sessions. Up to 30 tons of snow is made daily, covering 22,500sq m (26,775 square yards) including a 3,000sq m
(3,570 square yards) Snow Park. Insulation keeps Ski Dubai
cool even in the summer months – the designers have
described it as the world's largest refrigerator. The 23 air-
conditioners maintain a chilly -1°C (30°F) temperature. Ski
Dubai's runs are up 85m (279 feet) high, 80m (87 yards) wide
and 400m (436 yards) long, so there's enough space for 1,500
people at any one time. Although the resort opened late in
December 2005, it has proved extremely popular with locals
and visitors and advance booking is recommended at weekends. The resort provides all equipment, clothing (except
gloves) and tuition if you don't meet the minimum skills
level. Lessons are in groups of up to 10 people or you can
have one-on-one lessons with an instructor for 300Dh an
hour. If you're not cut out for skiing, there's always the twin
bobsleigh track, or a purpose-built snowball thowing gallery
and a 90m (98 yards) long quarter pipe for snowboarders. In
a city of the outlandish, Ski Dubai manages to amaze.

**Visitors hit the
artifical slopes**

**An ice dragon
adds to the
magic of Ski
Dubai**

🕂 165 D1

Mall of the Emirates
✉ Interchange 4, Sheikh Zayed
Road ☎ 409 9000;
www.malloftheemirates.com
🕔 Sat–Tue 10–10, Wed–Fri
10–midnight
Ski Dubai
☎ 409 4000; www.skidxb.com
🕔 Sat–Tue 10 am–11 pm (last
ticket 9:30 pm), Wed–Fri
10–midnight (last ticket 10:30 pm)

5 Dubai Marina

The centrepiece of a second axis to the city, Dubai Marina is a dramatic development, combining leisure and residential facilities. You can try out some excellent restaurants and cafés as you watch a city rise up before your eyes.

Skyscrapers with restaurants, luxury apartments and businesses line the waterfront of Dubai Marina

The new Dubai Marina is located around the waterway that runs inland around the luxury hotels of Al Sufouh. It's a man-made harbour, and the developers have placed plenty of vantage points all around the perimeter so you can see what is going on – although it's rare that you see any of the yacht owners actually sail their boats. The best way to appreciate the marina is to go down on a winter evening and take a stroll along the waterfront, watching the diners on the restaurant terraces and the dazzling lights of the skyscrapers surrounding the marina. Property prices are very high here, with apartments costing more than 1 million Dh even though many haven't even been finished yet. Another much-mooted development is Hydropolis, the world's first underwater hotel, which will have an educational centre. At the time of writing plans had hit a technical hitch, but Dubai has a reputation for ironing out such wrinkles.

The Marina is a super spot for water sports fans to look around. The Dubai International Marine Club organises races for almost every category of sea-going craft, including the Gulf's premier powerboat racing series, dhow racing, and races for jet skis, keelboats, dinghies and anything else that floats. There are car parks at the entrance of the Marina, just off the busy Interchange 5 of Sheikh Zayed Road and a taxi rank awaits. The boardwalk to the left and the right of the entrance is where many of the mostly unlicensed restaurants are located. On weekends families come here and while the children play in the ornamental fountains, dad smokes a shisha pipe in a café. While the Marina has curiosity value alone – how often do you see a forest of almost 100 skyscrapers being built? – remember that it is surrounded by a construction site. Residents have to clean their cars of dust once a day.

Street cafés offer good vantage points for people watching

🚹 164 B2
✉ Interchange 5, Sheikh Zayed Road   ☎ No telephone;
www.dubai-marina.com
Dubai International Marine Club
☎ 399 5777; www.dimc-uae.com

Dhow racing in Dubai Marina

⑥ Dubailand

Billed as the ultimate entertainment, leisure and tourism destination, Dubailand epitomizes the emirate's now famous tradition for innovative and ambitious development projects. Although far from completion, the figures for this exciting and bold multi-themed complex are already captivating but visitors can get a taste of what's to come by visiting Autodrome and Kartdrome, the first attractions to be opened.

Six vast, themed worlds comprise Dubailand, the personal project of Sheikh Mohammed. At they time for writing they were Attractions and Experiences World, Retail and Entertainment World, Leisure and Vacation World, Eco-Tourism World, Sports and Outdoor World and Downtown. Within each world there will be several separate theme parks and attractions.

The concrete realities of the project defy belief. Since announcing the project in October 2003, the Dubai government has committed 3 billion Dh to creating the infrastructure of the site, which covers 270 million sq m (3 billion square feet) of land. And that's just building the roads and installing a water and power supply. It is hoped that seven of these projects will be open in 2008, with completion of the entire Dubailand anticipated a decade later in 2018. By this time, developers are planning for annual visitor numbers of 15 million, with a further 300,000 people employed at Dubailand's attractions or in its 55 hotels. An estimate for the final, total cost of Dubailand is 65 billion Dh (or $18 billion).

Above: Autodrome is the first of Dubailand's attractions to be opened

An ariel view of the Autodrome track

The Autodrome and Kartdrome

You can already enjoy the first of Dubailand's attractions: a racing car circuit, the Autodrome, and Kartdrome, a circuit for go-karts. The Autodrome was designed to be able to host Formula 1 events and is on a giant scale. The spectators' stand is on the right side of the entry road, while Kartdrome is on the left shortly afterwards. The Autodrome already hosts several motorsports events during the year, including Le Mans-style 24-hour races. However the main attraction of the Autodrome is that aspiring Schumachers can sign up for lessons from the resident instructors and then drive a high-powered car around the circuit. The garages contain Audi A3s with 200bhp, Audi Quattro A4s with 250bhp and Subaru Impreza WRX STIs with 315bhp. A range of "Driving Experiences" are sold at the Autodrome.

On the opposite side of the entrance road, Kartdrome offers similar thrills in a smaller package. There are high-powered karts available to rent and a 1.2km (0.7-miles) circuit on which to put them through their paces. There are two types of Honda-powered kart, a Kid Kart with 5bhp and a full-size Kart with 13.5bhp; children have to be older than seven years to drive. The track has been constructed to a very high standard and includes a bridge, a tunnel and floodlights for use at night. This is a professional operation and you'll feel like a professional driver with one of the 24 pit garages devoted to your kart and a race-ready timing and scoring system. Safety equipment, including full-face helmets, is provided. For grown-up boys it's an exciting day out, if there are enough drivers on the circuit. Certain time slots, called Arrive and Drive, are allocated for public use and cost 100Dh per 15 minute session.

🚑 165 off D1

Kartdrome "Arrive and Drive"
🕐 Sun–Mon 4–9:15, Tue–Wed 11–9:15, Thu 5:30–9:45, Fri 6–9:45, Sat 4:30–9:45
Autodrome and Kartdrome
☎ 367 8700; www.dubaiautodrome.com
www.dubailand.ae

Go-kart racing for kids and big kids alike make Kartdrome a thrilling day out

At Your Leisure

7 Palm Jumeirah

Although it is not, strictly speaking, in Jumeirah, Palm Jumeirah benefits from the association with Dubai's swanky beach suburb. It was the first Palm Island to make it off the drawing board and into the Arabian Gulf. This, the smallest of the Palm Islands, is well on its way to completion, although purchasers of some of the island's villas have complained about endless construction delays.

There are 17 fronds to Jumeirah's Palm and a central trunk where the Trump Hotel, resembling nothing so much as a hatching chrysalis, will be sited. Another hotel, the Lighthouse, will shine a beam of light across the Palm Island at night; it's scheduled to be completed in 2008. As the first Palm Island to open, Palm Jumeirah will attract visitors anxious to see what the fuss is about. As for whether buying property on the island was a good investment, 30 Premiership footballers can't be wrong. Can they?

➕ 165 A3

8 Gold and Diamond Park

Competition in this purpose-built complex is fierce so traders are open to negotiation, although buyers won't be able to haggle as much as they might in the Gold Souk (➤ 40). There are over 30 shops all selling a similar selection of 18-carat gold jewellery with diamonds and other precious stones. At Moments (tel: 374 0834, www.momentsjewelry.com), for example, prices range

from 500Dh for a pair of earrings to 500,000Dh for a set of diamond earrings, necklace, bracelet and rings. Prices here are a useful benchmark for the cost of jewellery at the Gold Souk. You can also ask for a free tour of the Park's jewellery-making factory and watch craftsmen at work.

➕ 165 E1
✉ Sheikh Zayed Road
☎ www.goldanddiamond-park.com
🕐 Sat–Thu 10–10, Fri 4–10

9 Emirates Hills

The distinctive Bedouin tents on the desert side of Sheikh Zayed Road herald the Emirates Golf Club. The other give away is the luxuriant lawns of the fairways against the dusty construction sites of this end of town. Each year the Emirates Golf Club hosts the Dubai Desert Classic, one of the richest golf competitions in the world. Top-ranked golfers make the journey to the emirate to compete on a course that is, in the words of Tiger Woods, "in wonderful condition".

Then, the world number one was rumoured to have been paid $2 million to attend the event. There are two courses, the Majlis and the Wadi course, at the Emirates Golf Club, both par-72. A floodlit driving range and putting green allows after-hours practice of your tee-off and finishing technique. Green fees cost 625Dh for 18 holes. The Majlis was the first grass golf course in the Middle East and opened in 1988; the inaugural year of the Desert Classic was 1989. However, the Emirates Hills area is more than just a golf course. It is also an up-and-coming new residential zone with mid-market villas selling for about 2.5 million Dh.

➕ 164 C1
Emirates Golf Club
☎ 380 2222; www.dubaigolf.com

World-class golfers have played at the Emirates Golf Club

Where to... Stay

Prices

Expect to pay per double room, per night
$ 150Dh–600Dh $$ 600Dh–1,500Dh $$$ 1,500Dh–10,000-Dh

Grosvenor House West Marina Beach $$$

Grosvenor House is the first hotel to be completed in the burgeoning Marina development and the car park, packed with Bentleys, Porsches and Range Rovers, gives some idea of the crowd this impressive hotel attracts to its restaurants. The hotel is a tapering 45-storey tower on the waterfront. The interior layout is a little confusing with separate lifts for the 217 rooms and the 205 apartments, but once you've made it to your room you won't want to leave. Furnishings are the epitome of good taste and the facilites are state of the art, with a widescreen television and high-speed internet. The Retreat Health Spa offers top-to-toe treatments and guests may also use the facilities and beach access of sister hotel Le Royal Meridien Beach Resort across the road. Grosvenor House has a strong line-up of restaurants and bars with the most sought-after seats at the Buddha Bar. Make time to try the modern Indian cuisine from chef Vineet Bhatia in Indego.
⊞ 164 C3 ⊠ Dubai Marina
☎ 399 8888;
www.starwoodhotels.com

Habtoor Grand Resort and Spa $$$

Housed in a rather brutalist pair of towers, the Habtoor has a prime seafront position. It's a large hotel with 442 rooms. Most suites have a sea view and the facilities include high-speed internet. There are 14 restaurants and bars including the The Underground, a British-style pub. The Elixir offers holistic East-meets-West treatments.

Le Meridien Mina Seyahi Beach Resort and Marina $$$

The Mina Seyahi has a couple of strings to its bow that its rivals can't match. It owns one of the largest stretches of private beach and it has its own 238-berth marina. Don't despair if you haven't arrived by yacht; guests have free use of all non-motorised water sports, including windsurfing and kayaking. Other water sports include game fishing, wakeboarding and water skiing. The hotel has just 211 rooms, meaning that guests get a personal service. It is also very family friendly with a kids' club.
⊞ 164 C3 ⊠ Al Sufouh Road
☎ 399 5000; www.habtoorhotels.com

Stand-out restaurants and bars include Barasti bar and Bussola (▶ 129).
⊞ 164 C3 ⊠ Al Sufouh Road
☎ 399 3333; www.lemeridien-minaseyahi.com

Mina A'Salam $$$

Although described as a boutique hotel, this newly completed behemoth has 292 rooms, each with a sea view and a balcony. It has an Arabic theme, but the effect is almost suffocatingly grand. However, there's no denying that the location and setting are perfect. Be pampered at the award-winning Six Senses spa or laze about on the private beach. One of the perks is that you can explore Madinat Jumeirah beyond the public areas by taking an electric boat around the man-made waterways. There are eight restaurants and bars and the Friday brunch sessions are reputed to be the most lavish in the city.
⊞ 165 D3 ⊠ Madinat Jumeirah
☎ 366 8888; www.jumeirah.com

Oasis Beach Hotel $$

Sandwiched between the Sheraton and Hilton beach resorts, the Oasis Beach Hotel is the least expensive resort in the area, but it's rooms and facilities, especially the beach area, stand up to it's more luxurious neighbours. The 252 rooms have a subtle oriental theme and are kitted out with Molton Brown products and satellite television but only the Club and Executive rooms get internet access. Rooms with a seaview (as opposed to a view of a giant construction site) cost 700Dh more but also have a large balcony. There are six bars and restaurants to choose from, including Oregano, a colourful Mediterranean-themed restaurant, and Charlie Parrot, a bar hosting live entertainment and theme nights. Other facilities include a wellness centre and some well-organised water sports and activities. Children have their own pool (the adults' pool has a swim-up bar) and a play area. The Oasis is hugely popular with package holidaymakers and competition for rooms during peak periods is fierce.

+ 164 B3 ✉ Al Sufouh Road
☎ 399 4444;
www.jebelali-international.com

One&Only Royal Mirage $$$

The exclusive One&Only has three different accommodation areas, the suites of the Residence and the Palace and the Arabian Court. Even the basic deluxe rooms are a feast for the senses with palatial furnishings. Families are very welcome at the sophisticated resort, with a complimentary programme looking after children with games and activities while teenagers can learn to sail, but the Royal Mirage is better suited to honeymooners.

+ 164 C3 ✉ Al Sufouh Road
☎ 399 9999;
www.oneandonlyresorts.com

The Ritz-Carlton $$$

The six-floor hotel is being overshadowed by a 40-storey residential development behind it. However, all 138 rooms face forward towards the Gulf and none overlook the building work. The Ritz-Carlton is a resort hotel and is family friendly, with kids' play areas in the landscaped gardens, a supervised kids' room (ages 4–12 years) and a children's outdoor pool with slides. Facilities include several restaurants, including an Arabic-style outdoor eating area with low tables and cushions and Splendido, an Italian venue offering antipasti, fish and meat.

+ 164 B3 ✉ Al Sufouh Road
☎ 399 4000; www.ritzcarlton.com

Le Royal Meridien Beach Resort and Spa $$$

Le Royal Meridien is Le Meridien's most luxurious hotel in Dubai. It has 500 sea-facing rooms, each with a private balcony, while guests in the new extension enjoy the attention of a personal butler. The basic rooms are the best value. Guests should be more than satisfied with the facilities, which include a generous stretch of manicured beach, an impressive Roman-themed spa with five hammam pools and 14 restaurants and bars.

+ 164 B3 ✉ Al Sufouh Road
☎ 399 5555;
www.leroyalmeridien-dubai.com

Sheraton Jumeirah Beach Resort and Towers $$–$$$

The Sheraton, refurbished in 2003, remains popular with European holidaymakers and is good value. There are 255 rooms, most with sea views and there are rooms for people with disabilities on every floor.

Families are looked after well, with a childrens' club and playground. The landscaped gardens are a forest of date palms and sun umbrellas. Facilities include a freshwater pool, gym, squash and tennis courts and eight eateries.

+ 164 A3
✉ Al Sufouh Road ☎ 399 5533;
www.sheraton.com

Where to...
Eat and Drink

Prices

Expect to pay for a three-course meal for one, excluding drinks and service

$ under $60Dh $$ 60Dh–100Dh $$$ over 100Dh

Al Hadiqa Tent $–$$

Several of the resorts along this stretch of beach offer Arabic-style tented areas in their grounds. The Sheraton is always popular with its guests in the evening when an à la carte Arabic menu of swarma and meze is served to diners reclining on cushions. They're good fun for visitors of all ages although it's worth noting that it's only the adults who finish their meals with a smoke on a shisha pipe. The beach bar is close to the tented area.

➕ 164 A3 🏖 Sheraton Beach Resort, Al Sufouh Road ☎ 399 5533
🕙 Daily noon–3 am

Al Mahara $$$

The submarine elevator, with its own captain, takes you down to the dining room around a central column aquarium with thick acrylic plastic walls that don't distort the view of the tank's inhabitants. More than 50 tropical species, including colossal groupers and savage-looking eels, are contained in the aquarium. The excellent menu is varied and includes seafood options. The tasting menu is a good option and the wine list is superb. Men must wear a jacket and tie.

➕ 165 E3 🏖 Burj Al Arab ☎ 301 7600 🕙 Daily 12:30–3, 7–midnight

La Baie $$$

La Baie is the Ritz-Carlton's formal dining room, supplying a gourmet experience to guests and gastronomes alike. Chef Damien Chorley sends out modern European dishes with the emphasis on light and healthy courses rather than the cream-laden concoctions you might expect. The restaurant opens out onto the Gulf and dining on the terrace is a memorable experience.

➕ 164 B3 🏖 The Ritz-Carlton, Al Sufouh Road ☎ 399 4000; www.ritzcarlton.com
🕙 Mon–Sat 7–11

Bussola $$$

A new addition to Mina Seyahi, Bussola offers beachfront dining in a beautiful but relaxed environment. At night candles are lit among the palm trees and swinging lounge music is played softly. Bussola is one of the best Italian restaurants at this end of Dubai, with an accomplished repertoire of traditional Italian classics and a choice of 32 varieties of pizza. Bussola is a great start to a night out at the beach.

➕ 164 C3 🏖 Le Meridien Mina Seyahi, Al Sufouh Road ☎ 399 3333; www.minaseyahi.lemeridien.com
🕙 Daily 9 am–midnight

Chandelier $$

On the right as you enter the Marina complex, Chandelier has a large outdoor area with tables and chairs plus a cushioned area for shisha.

Inside the stylish, two-tier restaurant serves an extensive meze menu with tasty treats such as falafel, tabbouleh and fattoush – lettuce, tomato, cucumber, green onions, mint, parsley and radish served with toasted bread. Grilled meats, such as lamb skewers and arayes (baked mince lamb in Arabic bread), are also served.

Note that the restaurant does not have an alcohol licence. The fountains outside attract splashing children and families and there's a pleasantly relaxed atmosphere.

🏠 **164 B2** ⊠ **Dubai Marina**
☎ 366 3606;
www.chandelier-uae.com
🕐 Daily 8.30 am–11.30 pm

Inferno $$

Inferno is certainly in a hot location, with a sunny outdoor terrace overlooking the marina's yachts. If the weather is too hot to sit outside, take a pew at the long tables in the orange-and-red, oriental-themed dining room.

This is a casual place with the grill chefs producing Arabic-flavoured dishes such as grilled fish, steaks, lamb kebabs and classics such as dried lemon-marinaded lamb. There's no alcohol licence but you wash down the spicy meats with something from the juice bar. The venue above is a cigar bar, the Velvet Lounge.

🏠 **164 B2** ⊠ **Dubai Marina**
☎ 368 9193
🕐 Daily 8 am–midnight

Johnny Rockets $$

Turn left as you enter the Marina complex for this 1950s diner, where it is *Happy Days* every day. Johnny Rockets is convincing right down to the red leather banquettes, the soul and doowop classics on rotation, the bow-tied waiters, table-top jukeboxes and formica bar top. Stick to the mouthwatering burgers: the Original Burger is good value, the Smoke House comes with Tillamook Cheddar and smoky sauce. Drinks include root beer and floats. The sunny terrace overlooks yachts in the marina.

🏠 **164 B2** ⊠ **Dubai Marina**
☎ 368 2339; www.johnnyrockets.com
🕐 Sat–Thu noon–midnight, Fri 1–midnight

Ottomans $$–$$$

Have a taste of Turkish delight at this 2nd-floor restaurant in the Grosvenor House tower, serving confidently prepared Turkish and Middle Eastern cuisine. The square dining room is broken up by pillars and is patrolled by a pair of musicians playing traditional Turkish songs. Service is excellent.

🏠 **164 C3** ⊠ **Grosvenor House, Dubai Marina** ☎ 399 8888;
www.grosvenorhouse.lemeridien.com
🕐 Mon–Sat 7:30 pm–midnight

Pierchic $$$

In a city of stunning restaurants, Pierchic makes a bid for the top table with a romantic location at the end of a pier stretching from Al Qasr's private beach into the Arabian Gulf. The Mediterranean cuisine is sublime, as it should be for the price, but the views are even better. The clientele are mostly couples and the overall vibe is stylish but serene. Fish is a speciality.

🏠 **165 D3** ⊠ **Al Qasr, Madinat Jumeirah** ☎ 366 6730;
www.jumeirah.com
🕐 Daily noon–3, 7–11.30

Shoo Fee Ma Fee $$$

Part-lounge bar, part Moroccan restaurant, this sumptuous venue has the best view of the faux-Arab Madinat Jumeirah complex from its terrace.

The Moroccan food can be a little heavy for the after-hours drinking and shmoozing that goes on, so choose a light salad or tapas-style snacks before sinking into the cushions with a shisha (pipe).

🏠 **165 D3** ⊠ **Souk Madinat Jumeirah**
☎ 366 8888; www.jumeirah.com
🕐 Sat–Thu 6–12:30, Fri 4–12:30; drinks until 2 am

Splendido $

With a sun-soaked terrace, views over the Gulf and a menu of simple, classic dishes, Splendido has hit a winning formula. Of course, as a Ritz-Carlton restaurant, it's still a lavish experience, never more so than for Friday brunch (12:30–3:30).

🏠 **164 B3** ⊠ **Ritz-Carlton, Al Sufouh Road** ☎ 399 4000;
www.ritzcarlton.com
🕐 Daily 7–11, 12:30–5, 7–12:30

Where to...
Shop

Gold and Diamond Park

A recent expansion has seen the number of shops grow from 37 to over 60, with a further 154 units dedicated to manufacturing. Although the shops all sell a similar selection of gold jewellery, there's something here for every wallet. Shop around because competition is fierce thanks to low visitor numbers – the park is a little out on a limb until development along Sheikh Zayed Road catches up with it. Free tours of the jewellery-making area take 30 minutes and add an extra dimension to what could otherwise be just another shopping trip (tel: 347 7788).

✚ 165 E1 ⊠ Interchange 4, Sheikh Zayed Road ☎ 347 7574;
www.goldanddiamondpark.com
🕐 Sat–Thu 10–10, Fri 4–10

Ibn Battuta

No mall goes as far as Ibn Battuta in adding an extra layer to the shopping experience. In the case of the single-storey Ibn Battuta this involves organising the mall into six geographical areas corresponding to the travels of 14th-century scholar Ibn Battuta, who travelled from his birthplace in Tangiers across the Eastern hemisphere to China, India, Persia, Egypt, Tunisia and Andalusia.

Each area is colour-coded and themed according to its region, so in the red-tiled China Court you'll find a full-size Chinese Junk and in the purple Andalusia Court a replica of Alhambra's Fountain of the Lions. The tour of the world's greatest civilisations certainly adds interest to a day out shopping and the colour coding, combined with some incredibly elaborate interior design, such as the elegant tiled dome in Persia or the mosaic floors of Egypt, can help you work out where you are.

Thankfully, there are shops as well as the "edutainment". Each region is distinct but beyond the style of décor there is only a loose order to the selection of shops in each. You will find department stores, including the ubiquitous Debenhams, in Persia, alongside heath and beauty shops, children's stores and homeware outlets. In the India Court, designer fashion holds sway, with mainstream outlets such as Topshop alongside trendy brands such as jean's label Evisu. The Tunisia Court, resembling a 14th-century North African marketplace although with slightly better hygiene standards, is home to the Géant supermarket and other food shops.

Convenience and general-purpose stores are in the Andalusia Court for locals who want to drop off their dry cleaning or to do their banking.

In Egypt, family-interest shops dominate, with a Lego store and several clothing outlets for children,

sports shops such as Nike and a Magrudy's for books and music. The final region, China, at the far end of the mall is where you'll find Dubai's first IMAX screen and 21 other cinema screens. There are also seven restaurants in the China Court - the branch of the Lime Tree Café is the best bet for tasty snacks and a good coffee – and a useful Thomas Cook office for changing travellers' cheques. Ibn Battuta may not be the largest mall in Dubai, but it has a good selection of shops and, as malls go, is a rather special place to roam around.

✚ Off map ⊠ Interchange 5 or 6, Sheikh Zayed Road ☎ 362 1900;
www.ibnbattutamall.com 🕐 Sat–Tue 10–10, Wed–Fri 10–midnight. Food court daily 10–midnight

Mall of the Emirates

This super-sized shopping centre dwarfs most others in Dubai. You're not likely to visit every one of the 400 shops in one trip and there are enough entertainment options, including a Magic Planet for children, cinema screens and Ski Dubai (▶119–120), to merit a second or even third visit. There are three levels to the Mall of the Emirates but, unlike Ibn Battuta mall, shops are only loosely grouped together by type, except in the glitzy Via Rodeo section where you'll find Italian and French designer labels. But perhaps the most significant name in the mall is that of Harvey Nichols, the London department store's first Dubai outpost.

Parents with children will be relieved to find one of two superb Magic Planet play areas (see Deira, ▶54); with arcade games, a funfair and exciting activities, the children won't want to leave. Next to Magic Planet is Peekaboo, a childcare centre for younger children. Areas such as The Kitchen and Book Corner aim to keep energy levels steady and all the play areas are soft to prevent bumps and bruises. Note that children under three have to be accompanied by an adult.

Shop-wise, there's something for everyone. Once again, clothes shops figure prominently with sporty, casual, dressy and designer clothes for men and women. You'll find most of the brands in other malls too but there are several shops selling skiing and snowboarding gear, presumably inspired by Ski Dubai.

Food options include Café Ceramique, where children (and adults) can put a design on a piece of plain crockery and have it fired for you to take home: the café is close to the Carrefour supermarket on the first floor.

Parking is available at the Mall of the Emirates, but you're best advised to take a taxi, especially during the sales-period of the Dubai Shopping Festival in January, when bargain-hunting shoppers lay siege to the mall.

🔲 165 D1 ✉ Interchange 4, Sheikh Zayed Road ☎ 409 9000; www.malloftheemirates.com
🕙 Sat–Tue 10–10, Wed–Fri 10–midnight

Where to...
Be Entertained

BARS

Barasti Bar

The Barasti is in the little black book of every fashionable bar-hopper in town. It has stood the test of time and now the outdoor bar and terrace is one of the leading nightspots in Dubai. You can also enjoy a shisha smoke as you watch sunset over the Gulf. The Barasti has the magic mix of being fashionable but unpretentious.

🔲 164 C3 ✉ Le Méridien Mina Seyahi Resort, Al Sufouh Road
☎ 399 3333 🕙 Daily 9 am–2 am

Buddha Bar

A parade of expensive sports cars deposits Dubai's beautiful people at the door of this recent addition to the city's hot spots. The Buddha Bar, fresh from Paris, is a dark, seductive venue furnished with dark, red lanterns and a giant gold Buddha statue. One wall is a 9m (30-foot) high glass panel allowing drinkers and diners to gaze over the Dubai Marina development. Thai eats are served but the cocktail list deserves the closest attention. Later in the evening the music becomes livelier and the focus switches from the restaurant to the bar. Come here for a drink and to see the most exotic interior of Dubai's bar scene.

🔲 164 C3 ✉ Grosvenor House, Dubai Marina ☎ 399 8888;
www.grosvenorhouse.dubai.com
🕙 Mon–Fri noon–2 am, Sat–Sun noon–3 am

Jambase

Jambase is the most consistent live music venue at this end of town. The venue, below Trilogy nightclub, has an in-house band keeping people moving with jazzy music. You can eat here – American classics mainly, such as crawfish – but you're better coming for a drink and a dance before heading upstairs to Trilogy. Note that smart casual dress is expected. Over 21s only.

🕀 165 D3
⊠ The Souk, Madinat Jumeirah
☎ 366 6730;
www.madinatjumeirah.com
🕒 Daily 7 pm–2 am

The Rooftop

Kick back with a cocktail at this chilled out bar on the roof of the One&Only Royal Mirage. Relaxation is the object here, with cushions to laze against, soothing ambient music and views of the Burj Al Arab's technicolour light-show, if you can take your eyes off the stars above.

🕀 164 C3 ⊠ One&Only Royal Mirage Hotel, Al Sufouh Road
☎ 399 9999 🕒 Daily 5–1 am

Skyview Bar

Non-guests have to make a reservation at this cocktail bar 200m (650 feet) above sea level. And the Skyview's entry requirements are the most stringent in the city: no jeans, no trainers, no sandals and shirt with a collar for men. But it's worth the effort for the mesmerising views over the World development in the Gulf and along the coast. Sadly, the décor is as chaotic as elsewhere in the Burj Al Arab.

🕀 165 E3 ⊠ Burj Al Arab ☎ 301 7600 🕒 Daily 11 am–2 am

Trilogy

At weekends Trilogy is, usually, the place to party. With a capacity of 2,000 people and three floors of throbbing dance music from a line-up of resident and guest DJs, including international stars, it's not the place for an intimate evening out; for that head up to The Rooftop, which has awesome views of the Burj Al Arab. Bars and chill-out rooms are spread liberally around but if you prefer, book one of the VIP glass cages to be your personal domain. Trilogy is at the entrance of Madinat Jumeirah.

🕀 165 D3 ⊠ The Souk, Madinat Jumeirah ☎ 366 8888;
www.madinatjumeirah.com
🕒 Mon–Sat 9 pm–3 am

SPAS

Givenchy Spa

This minimalist spa uses Givenchy products in a sedate, slightly formal, environment. They offer a variety of facials, massages and treatments such as wraps and peels. Beyond the spa, the hotel also boasts the best hammam in Dubai.

🕀 164 C3 ⊠ One&Only Royal Mirage Hotel
☎ 399 9999;
www.oneandonlyresorts.com
🕒 Daily women only 9:30–2, mixed 3:30–8

Retreat Health and Spa

Be rejuvenated at this excellent spa in Grosvenor House on the Marina. It has separate areas for men and women and a range of massages, including the Balinese massage.

🕀 164 C3 ⊠ Grosvenor House West Marina Beach hotel, Dubai Marina
☎ 317 6762;
www.starwoodhotels.com
🕒 Daily 6:15 am–9:45 pm

The Ritz-Carlton Spa

The Ritz-Carlton's spa has much to recommend it, with more than 40 different Balinese or European treatments and eight treatment rooms. For the ultimate in pampering take a one-day Signature Package such as the 5-hour Eastern Delight package of a Javanese Lulur full body treatment, a traditional Balinese facial, and Indonesian scalp treatment and a health drink.

🕀 164 B3 ⊠ The Ritz-Carlton Hotel, Al Sufouh Road ☎ 318 6184;
www.ritzcarlton.com
🕒 Daily 6 am–10 pm

CULTURE

Cinestar

This 14-screen cinema is on the first floor of the mall and shows the usual stream of Hollywood blockbusters. Opening hours are the same as the mall (▶ 132) with frequent screenings during the day.

🔢 165 D1 ⊠ Mall of the Emirates
☎ 341 4222;
www.cinestarcinemas.com

Grand Megaplex and IMAX

Dubai's first IMAX screen is at this cinema complex in the China Court of Ibn Battuta mall. Opening hours are the same as the mall with frequent screenings during the day.

🔢 Off map ⊠ Ibn Battuta mall
☎ 366 9898; www.ibnbattutamall.com

Madinat Theatre

There is just one theatre venue for drama, dance and stand-up comedy in Dubai: the 442-seat Madinat Theatre. The theatre has good sight lines and acoustics and comfortable seating. And it has been well-received by Dubai's theatre-starved population.

🔢 165 D3 ⊠ The Souk, Madinat Jumeirah ☎ 366 6888;
www.jumeirah.com
🕙 Times and prices vary

ACTIVITIES

Diving
Pavilion Dive Centre

This PADI-approved dive centre offers Discover Scuba Diving sessions for first-timers and courses and trips for experienced divers. Charters depart Dubai and Khor Fakkan on the east coast of the Emirates near Fujairah. Equipment and transport are included.

🔢 165 E3 ⊠ Jumeirah Beach Hotel
☎ 406 8827;
www.thepaviliondivecentre.com
💲 Expensive

Golf
Arabian Ranches Golf Club

The primarily residential Arabian Ranches development has the first truly desert golf course in Dubai. The design, by Jack Nicklaus's design company, uses the desert to present an unusual challenge: no water features but a lot of sand traps on this par-72 course.

🔢 165 off D1 ⊠ Dubailand
☎ 366 3000;
www.arabianranchesgolfdubai.com
💲 Expensive

The Montgomerie

This Colin Montgomerie-designed course is close to the Emirates Golf Club (▶ 126) and introduces some of the features of a Scottish links course. The third hole not only uses the outline of the United Arab Emirates, but is the largest single golfing green in the world.

🔢 164 B1 ⊠ Interchange 5, Sheikh Zayed Road ☎ 390 5600
💲 Expensive

Parasailing
Sheraton Jumeirah Beach

If you like the idea of being towed by a speedboat while wearing a large parasail, try the experience at the Sheraton hotel on the beach, which has its own speedboat.

🔢 164 A3 ⊠ Al Sufouh Road
☎ 399 5533; www.sheraton.com
💲 Expensive

Sailing
Dusail

Motorboats and a yacht can be hired from this firm based in Dubai Marina. They also offer fishing packages and 2-hour sightseeing cruises, departing from the Marina at the Jumeirah Beach Hotel.

🔢 164 C3 ⊠ Dubai International Marine Club ☎ 396 2353;
www.dusail.com 💲 Prices vary

Skiing and Snowboarding
Ski Dubai

It might be sweltering outside, but inside this indoor ski resort it's snowing (▶ 119–120).

🔢 165 D1 ⊠ Mall of the Emirates
☎ 409 4000; www.skidxb.com
💲 Expensive

Walks & Tours

1 Fujairah 136 – 138
2 Al Ain 139 – 140
3 Al Maha 141 – 142
4 Jumeirah Beaches 143 – 144
5 Hatta 145 –147
6 Bur Dubai 148 – 150
7 Desert Driving 151 – 154

1 Fujairah
Drive

What it lacks in oil, Fujairah makes up for in natural beauty. The only emirate with an Indian Ocean shore line, Fujairah is blessed with beaches, mountains and lots of winding roads to speed you from one to the other. No wonder that it is a favourite retreat of frazzled workers from Dubai.

The road from Dubai to the tiny emirate of Fujairah, population 144,000, is a well-trodden route at the weekend. The appeal for many is as much the swooping roads through the Hajar mountain range as the golden beaches waiting on the other side. The biggest difficulty will be getting out of Dubai. You need to head to Sharjah before turning inland. The flow of traffic will be going the opposite direction in the morning. From the clock tower roundabout in Deira follow Route 74, signposted Al Sharjah, straight through central Sharjah. Then follow signs for Sharjah airport. Go over the first roundabout you

DISTANCE 320km (198 miles) round-trip **TIME** Allow one or two days, staying overnight at a beach resort (Hilton or Le Meridien in Fujairah) ⊞ 170 C1
START/END POINT Clock tower roundabout on Al Maktoum Road ⊞ 170 C1
WHAT TO TAKE Map, additional car insurance if venturing into neighbouring Oman
WHEN TO GO Any day of the week; start early because it is a 3-hour drive each way, with stops.

Fujairah's beaches are a welcome retreat from city life

come to, while following signs for the airport, and take the second exit at the next roundabout, again following signs for the airport.

You're now on the Al Dhaid road, also known as Route 88 but not signposted as such yet. It's a wide, three-lane motorway lined with wrought-iron lamposts and palm trees. On the right is Sharjah University, with majestic fountains in the gardens. Then comes **Sharjah Discovery Centre** (tel: 06 558 6577; Sat–Tue 9–2, Wed 9–2, 3:30–8:30; Thu–Fri 3:30–8:30), a science theme park for children. Keep in the left lane as you pass the green gardens of **Sharjah National Park** (Sat–Thu 4–10, Fri 10–10), a landscaped area of 630,000sq m (688,976sq yards) with ponds and a dry ski slope, on the right. As you leave Sharjah's suburbia, the scenery changes to yellow, scrubby sand dunes.

Left: Quirky sculptures enliven an otherwise ordinary roundabout

Continuing along Route 88 you will pass the **Sharjah Arab Culture Monument** to your right at Interchange 8. The desert surrounding the pinnacle is a protected conservation area and you're advised to have a four-wheel-drive vehicle to explore its shifting sands. Also off Interchange 8 is the **Sharjah Natural History Museum and Desert Park** (tel: 06 531 1411, www.shjmuseum.gov.ae; Mon–Thu, Sat 9–7, Fri 10–8), on the opposite side of the motorway. This is a good place to stretch your legs; children can visit a petting farm. The Wildlife Centre has more than 100 species

from vipers to oryx. A nocturnal house allows visitors to glimpse the night-time activities of species such as the mongoose, honey badger and jackal. Not all the species are indigenous: baboons and hyenas have somehow made their way over from Africa, but despite these anomalies Sharjah's Desert Park is an interesting place to stop for a break.

Return to Route 88 and continue to **Al Dhaid** (now signposted). On entering Al Dhaid, turn left at the first roundabout, driving down the shop-lined main street. Turn right at the next roundabout and go straight over the next, staying on Route 88 and following signs for Masafi. As you enter the foothills of the Hajar mountains, watch out for Friday Market: stalls on both sides of the road selling carpets, fruit, vegetables, plants and, bizarrely, inflatable children's toys.

Stay on this wide, well-made road until it reaches Fujairah, after winding through the barren hills. The scenery is of a bleak, dusty

landscape of hills and valleys – it's not the sort of place you would want to walk through. Fujairah's roads are managed by a series of roundabouts. Indeed, roundabouts are something of a tourist attraction in this quiet town, with quirky sculptures placed in the centre of them. To go straight to the seafront follow signs for the corniche, which will take you straight ahead at most of the roundabouts. The Hilton resort lies at the north end of the corniche and is a good place for refreshments – non-guests can use all the restaurants and, preferably, the beachside café. At weekends the seafront from the Hilton south to Kalba is crowded with beachgoers enjoying the gardens and wide, sandy beach. There are plenty of car parking spaces.

Fujairah is the newest emirate since it was part of Sharjah until 1952. To visit the **Fujairah Museum** (tel: 09 222 9085, Sunday–Friday 8–1, 4–6), a ramshackle building containing exhibitions about Fujairah's history, turn left after you enter Fujairah and follow signposts. There's talk of moving the museum's contents into the fort (visible from the museum) when its restoration is complete; check at the Fujairah Tourist Office (Fujairah Trade Centre, Sheikh Hamad bin Abdullah Road, tel: 09 223 1554).

From Fujairah it is 55km (34 miles) north to Dibba, following Route 99. Stick to Corniche Street (seafront) through the town of **Khor Fakkan**, straight over the roundabouts and past the petrol station styled like a castle. Khor Fakkan is renowned for its scuba diving, with several sites, including some coral reefs offshore. After you exit Khor Fakkan, look for Al Bidiyah mosque on the left, which dates from 1446. You can stop the car beside the

road and look around the exterior of the mosque outside prayer times. Bidiyah village itself dates from around 3,000 BC and is one of the oldest settlements on the Indian Ocean coast. Behind the mosque two watchtowers are a reminder of the invasions that plagued this coast through the centuries.

At the next turning bear right on Route 87 for the pretty town of **Dibba**. There's an incongruous high-rise resort (Le Meridien's Al Aqah Beach Resort) before you enter the town and the hotel is sure to be joined by other developments soon.

From Dibba you can charter a boat to take you to Snoopy Island (the profile of the island looks like the cartoon character in repose) where there is excellent diving and snorkelling. You can book the trip at the Sandy Beach Diving Centre at the Sandy Beach Motel (tel: 09 244 5555, www.sandybm.com).

Dibba was the site of many battles between Islamic forces from Saudi Arabia and Arab tribesmen in the 6th and 7th

centuries; the Islamists won eventually, leaving huge cemeteries at Dibba. After you exit Dibba, turn left onto Route 18 and after 10km (6 miles) take the right exit for Sharjah. You're now back on Route 88 so retrace your steps through Al Dhaid and Sharjah. On passing Sharjah airport and the university remember to turn left at the roundabout at the end of the Route 88 and go ahead at the next roundabout for Dubai. Do not enter Sharjah since the roads are poorly signposted and you will get lost; if you miss the turning, turn around and try again. Note that the traffic is particularly treacherous in Sharjah. Dubai is signposted to the left from outside Sharjah.

The fort in Fujairah's Old City

Where to Stay

Hilton Fujairah

✉ Coffee Pot Roundabout, Al Gurfa Street
☎ 09 222 2411; www.hilton.com

Le Meridien Al Aqah Beach Resort

✉ Near Dibba, Fujairah
☎ 09 244 9000; www.lemeridien.com

2 Al Ain
Drive

The highest mountain in the United Arab Emirates is Jebel Hafeet mountain and you can drive all the way to the top. From here you can look out over Al Ain below and see why the city is known as the "Garden City". Al Ain doesn't just have gardens though; it also has a lot of roundabouts and navigating the city can be confusing.

How you negotiate your way through Dubai's traffic jams is down to where you are starting from. Al Ain is signposted from Sheikh Zayed Road's Interchange 1 but if you're based in Deira the easiest way out of town may be down Garhoud Road, past the airport then right, around the ringroad (Route 611) aiming for Academic City, until you see signs for Al Ain and Hatta. Get on the three-lane Route 66, which is a straight, if undulating, drive of about 100km (62 miles) all the way to Al

DISTANCE 300km (186 miles) round-trip **TIME** One day; try to avoid leaving Dubai at 8–9 am or arriving back at 5–6 pm **START/END POINT** Interchange 1 ⊞ 167 E2
WHAT TO TAKE Map, binoculars **WHEN TO GO** Any day of the week

Al Ain camel market

Ain. Shrubs have been planted alongside the length of the road to stop sand blowing across it – the plants have to be watered three times daily!

To your right, you might spot camel farms among the dunes. Midway between Dubai and Al Ain there's a rest area and several fuel stops. When you're 30km (18.5 miles) from Al Ain you will start to see mountains on your left. Al Ain is known locally as much for its roundabouts as its gardens – the reason will become apparent as soon as you enter town. "Tourists Follow Brown Signs" is the sound advice offered and you should heed it. You can largely ignore the green Arabic signs.

Go straight over the first roundabout. At the second roundabout, **Hili Fun City** is the (first) exit to the right. Take this exit if the family are clamouring to visit a average funfair. Otherwise, take the left (third) for Al Ain's **National Archaeological Park** (daily 4–11, except holidays 10–11, 1Dh) where you'll find exhibits recovered from some of the 5,000-year-old tombs at Hili.

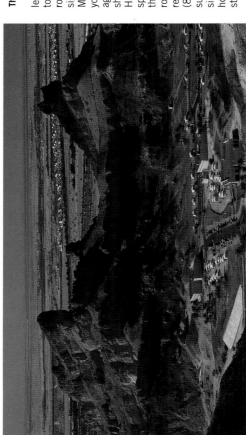

The city of Al Ain began life as an important oasis on the traders' camel trains from Oman. It's still famous for its greenery, the result of underground springs, some of which you can wallow in near Al Ain's top attraction, **Jebel Hafeet,** the highest mountain in the UAE at 1,160m (3,806 feet). A good road takes you to the mountain's summit from where there are great views of the city.

From the National Archaeological Park, go straight over the next two roundabouts and

The view from Jebel Hafeet

left at the third. Now follow signs for the town centre straight over the next seven roundabouts. Here, you should pick up brown signs for Jebel Hafeet and, in green, Mubazzarah. Bear left for Jebel Hafeet, which you will see rising in front of you. Head left again at the roundabout with the mountain sheep sculpture, following signs for Jebel Hafeet and Mubazzarah, a resort with hot springs for visitors on the right-hand side of this road. After the Mubazzarah turning, the road gets very twisty and the speed limit is reduced to 30kph (18mph) for the 13km (8-mile) drive uphill. At the top there are super views over the Emirates from both sides. You can relax over a snack at the Accor hotel at the summit, or watch the sunset and stay the night.

Where to Stop

Grand Hotel Jebel Hafeet
☎ 03 783 8888; www.mercure.com

3 Al Maha
Drive

DISTANCE 70km (43 miles) **TIME** To see the wildlife you will have to stay overnight at Al Maha
START POINT Pick-up at Interchange 1 ⊞ 167 E2
WHAT TO TAKE Everything, including binoculars, is provided **WHEN TO GO** Winter

Wild oryx pay a neighbourly visit to Al Maha

The Dubai Desert Conservation Reserve is one of Dubai's treasures: a 225sq km (87 square miles) wildlife sanctuary in the sand dunes, where rare oryx are reared and indigenous plants and animals thrive. It's a magical place. The catch is that you have to stay at the associated resort, Al Maha, to explore the reserve.

Down a track off the Dubai-Al Ain highway, about 70km (43 miles) from the city, there lies one of Dubai's most remarkable attractions. A vast area of desert has been ring-fenced and stocked with the fauna and flora of the Arabian peninsula. The Al Maha Desert Resort and Spa is at the centre of this nature reserve and it is a place where wild oryx, with their fearsome scimitar-like antlers, roam freely among the 40 tented luxury lodges. Guests can watch gazelles root for vegetation as they sit down to breakfast on the terrace, or take a camel ride to watch the sunset with a glass of champagne.

Accommodation at Al Maha takes the form of luxury tents

Knowledgeable guides helm wildlife drives or teach archery, falconry or horse riding. But Al Maha is no back-to-basics safari experience; every whim of the guests is met by the 160-strong staff. The lodges each have their own plunge pool, plus binoculars and wildlife-spotting books. The tented suites have mahogany beds from Oman and sandstone tiles from Ras Al Khaimah. Somehow the presence of such beautiful wildlife in such close proximity – the oryx really do wander up to the lodges – means that the luxury of the accommodation doesn't register. It's clearly a special resort, but the desert outshines it.

Al Maha, the emirate's largest conservation area, opened in 1998. They had an initial breeding stock of 70 oryx in two varieties: the Arabian and the scimitar. Now there are 360 oryx in the reserve, as well as four types of gazelle, including Thomson's and Reem's. Around 40 varieties of bird visit the reserve and eagle-eyed visitors will spot the tracks of reptiles and rodents. All around the resort is the rippled landscape of Dubai's desert.

Useful Information

Dubai Desert Conservation Reserve
🖥 www.ddcr.org

Al Maha
Guests typically stay two or three nights; you would probably see enough by staying just one night.
☎ 343 9595; www.al-maha.com

4 Jumeirah Beaches

Tour

Golden sand, clear blue sea and reliable, even roasting, sunshine: Dubai's beaches appeal to many visitors.

START/END POINT Jumeirah Beach Corniche, close to Dubai Marine Beach Resort ✚ 168 B5
TIME One day, taking taxis between beaches

All Dubai's beaches, except the public beach at Al Mamzar Beach Park (▶ 46), are on the Jumeirah side of the Creek. The coast stretches from the built-up suburbs behind Jumeirah public beach near Port Rashid all the way past the Burj Al Arab hotel to Jebel Ali port, a distance of some 40km (25 miles). The shore is a mix of free-to-use public access beaches, public beach parks where a nominal entry is charged and private beaches managed by hotels. Hotel beaches are often cleaned and may have facilities such as changing area, sun loungers, refreshments and water sports. Remember that if you are staying at a city centre hotel that has a sister hotel with a beach you may be allowed to use it free of charge; this applies to the Sheraton, Le Meridien, Jumeirah and Hilton hotels

among others. Dubai's shore has no bays so breakwaters are used to partition the beach.

In general, water quality is good, but note that there is an undertow so weak swimmers should stick to the hotel swimming pool. Some beaches may provide a lifeguard and may forbid swimming when there is no lifeguard on duty. The offshore construction work

in the Gulf on the three Palm Islands and the World development is causing problems for some hotel beaches with additional detritus and lower visibility. Hopefully, this will be a temporary problem.

Dubai's authorities are placing increasing restrictions on water sports such as jet skiing and kitesurfing on the public beaches. Kitesurfers are moving further away from the central beaches to practise their sport in less developed areas without breakwaters to hamper them. Jebel Ali beach, which stretches from the Jebel Ali Golf Resort and Spa to the border with Abu Dhabi, is Dubai's most unspoiled beach but the plan to build the Jebel Ali Palm Island at the nearside may change this. Currently this is the favourite destination of kitesurfers and those who want to laze among real sand dunes rather than the landscaped gardens of the hotel beaches.

Tourists enjoying the beach at Jumeirah

HOW TO USE PRIVATE BEACHES

Le Meridien Mina Seyahi Beach Resort and Marina

Beach access at this stylish hotel costs 100Dh (Sunday–Wednesday), 200Dh on Thursday and Saturday (including brunch) and 250Dh on Friday.

📞 399 3333

Sheraton Jumeirah Beach Resort and Towers

Access to the Sheraton's beach is free for guests at the city's other Sheraton hotels, but otherwise adults will have to pay 100Dh and children (6–16 years) 60Dh (Saturday–Wednesday). On Thursdays the price rises to 120Dh for adults, while on Fridays there is a buffet lunch (with beach access) which costs 120Dh for adults and 90Dh for children. Children can use the Pirates Club, which is supervised.

📞 399 5533

Jumeirah Beach Club

Non-members can use the beach here if they book the Beach Club's "One Day of Pampering" package at 499Dh, including lunch and two spa treatments.

📞 310 2759

One&Only Royal Mirage

Outside peak periods, the Royal Mirage's beach is open to non-guests – call in advance. If non-guests are accepted, access to the pool and beach costs 125Dh, but children are not permitted to use the hotel's children's facilities.

📞 399 9999

Habtoor Grand Resort

Access to the Habtoor's beach costs 150Dh for adults and 90Dh for children (under 12), with prices rising to 200Dh and 120Dh respectively on Fridays.

📞 399 5000

The Ritz-Carlton

The most expensive beach belongs to the Ritz-Carlton, with adults charged 200Dh and children 100Dh during the week, and 300Dh and 125Dh on Thursdays. Spaces are limited on Fridays to hotel guests. Water sports are available.

📞 399 4000

Jumeirah Beach Hotel

The price of access to this hotel's beach is 350Dh per person but includes a 100Dh food voucher, subject to availability.

📞 348 0000

Oasis Beach Hotel

The Oasis Beach Hotel's reputation for good value extends to its beach pass for non-guests, costing 85Dh for adults (children under 12 half price). On Fridays visitors can enjoy a barbecue and beach access for 160Dh. Water sports such as waterskiing and windsurfing are available for an extra fee.

📞 399 4444

Hilton Dubai Jumeirah

Adult non-guests pay 100Dh for beach access at the Hilton or 55Dh if they are aged under 12. Fridays cost 130Dh for adults and 55Dh for children. Facilities include the Kidz Paradise Club and a children's play area on the beach. Activities include beach volleyball, waterskiing, windsurfing, sailing, parasailing and fishing.

📞 399 1111

Tips

While the Dubai authorities have no objection to the wearing of bikinis on beaches, topless sunbathing is not permitted. And it is advisable for both men and women to cover up when they leave the beach area. Jumeirah's beach is a mix of public and private sections. You can pay to enter the private beaches or sunbathe for free on the public beaches; be warned, however, that female sunbathers can attract a male audience in the public areas.

5 Hatta

Drive

Hatta is a small mountain town with two important attractions: a fine hotel and a series of rock pools accessible by four-wheel-drive vehicles. If you take only one trip out of Dubai, make it this one.

There's plenty of evidence of the water that rushes off the surrounding Hajar mountains at Hatta: roads are built across wadis (dry river beds), the town's hotel is an oasis of greenery and there are the Hatta rock pools themselves. The deep, dark pools of water among blasted and eroded rock are a 45-minute off-road drive into the mountains and if you go at the weekend you'll be sharing the experience with a lot of weekenders from Dubai. It's easy enough to make the one-hour drive to Hatta, but you'll need detailed directions to the pools; you can pick up a map and

DISTANCE 120km (75 miles) **TIME** Allow one day, or stay overnight at the Hatta Fort Hotel
START/END POINT Interchange 1, Sheikh Zayed Road 🔒 167 E2
WHAT TO TAKE Four-wheel-drive vehicle, water, food, tow rope, shovel, mobile phone
WHEN TO GO Winter, busy at the weekends

Hatta Fort Hotel

kilometre-by-kilometre directions through the mountain tracks from the Hatta Fort Hotel. You need the blue route pack.

To reach Hatta, take **Route 44** out of Dubai. It is signposted from Interchange 1 on Sheikh Zayed Road and passes the Ras Al Khor Wildlife Sanctuary (▶ 71). This road will take you all the way to Hatta and there are filling stations on the way where you can buy food and fuel.

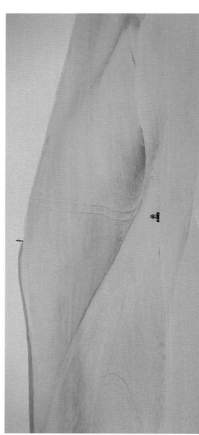

As you leave the environs of Dubai the sand dunes start to take over the landscape. At first they're scrubby, then they become the classic, wind-sculpted dunes of the Emirates' deserts. About **halfway to Hatta**, at the 50km (31-mile) point, a number of quad and motor-bike tour operators have set up shop on both sides of the road. This place gets very busy at weekends with locals from Dubai renting quad bikes. Note that quad bikes are not the safest contraptions and can injure riders if

they are rolled – exercise caution. Dune buggies have roll cages and are a much safer option if you have to unleash the inner rally driver. Owners of four-wheel-drive vehicles also bring them here to drive in the desert. In the distance, to the left, the rust-coloured **Big Red** is the largest, most famous dune in Dubai. It provides an irresistible challenge to off-road drivers. Don't be tempted to venture off-road unless you are with another vehicle and know how to drive safely in the desert.

After a petrol station, there's a row of shops selling pottery and carpets and the foothills of the Hajar mountains are in the distance. As you enter Hatta you'll encounter a round-about: Hatta Fort Hotel is to the left, and Hatta and its attractions are to the right. If you carry straight on you'll enter Oman in 10km (6 miles).

Hatta Fort Hotel is an attractive, small-scale resort set on a verdant hillside. Visitors can eat at the restaurant and purchase detailed maps of the mountain roads in the lobby's gift shop. They can also organise supported

The ultimate off-roading experience – choose from quad bikes, dune buggies and four-wheel-drive vehicles

tours to Hatta rock pools; this may be a good option if you prefer not to hire a car.

As you enter central Hatta you'll spot sign-posts for the Hill Park; this is simply a vantage point. Ignore them and continue uphill through the town until you see the signs for **Hatta Heritage Village** to the left. The road twists and turns until it reaches the village (tel: 852 1374; Sat–Thu 8–8:30, Fri 2:30–8:30; during Ramadan Sat–Thu 9–5, Fri 2–5) to the left. The village was opened in 2001 and aims to show what life was like in the mountains; like the Heritage House in Dubai (▶ 45), it uses tableaux to provide a glimpse into rural life. Defence against raiders and invaders was one preoccu-pation of the villagers and a fort is the centrepiece of the Heritage Village. It was built in 1896 by Sheikh Maktoum bin Hashr Al Maktoum. There are another 30 buildings in the village, including a Sharia mosque, a traditional house and social house, used for weddings and meetings. The village's site dates back 2,000–3,000 years but most buildings are no older than 200 years.

On leaving the village stay on the same road and continue away from Hatta. At the next

junction, a roundabout in front of a mosque, bear left and follow the road round a bend. After 1km (0.5 miles) take the second right, down what looks like a residential road with a series of speed bumps. Follow this straight road for 7km (4 miles) through Qiman village. On the other side of the village take the gravel track to the right. This is the route to **Hatta's rock pools** and it is a 10km (6-mile) off-road drive, along dirt tracks and wadis, to a parking area. Keep right as vehicles may be returning from the pools at speed and there are plenty of blind hill brows and bends. Note that there is no mobile phone reception here so if you crash or break down you will have to help yourself or rely on someone passing. However, with a four-wheel-drive vehicle, it is not a difficult drive.

If you have started early and want to make a day of it, you can continue past the rock pools, after you've had a dip, and drive along a series of wadis (dried-up waterways) and make a circuit looping back to the Hatta Fort Hotel. It's a 121km (75-mile) route and should take 6 hours; follow the detailed directions of the hotel's blue route map. Off-road driving is great fun and extremely popu-lar in Dubai. Most tour operators offer days

Exhibits at the Hatta Heritage Village

trips from Dubai to Hatta or you can rent four-wheel-drive vehicles from most of the major car rental firms in the city (▶ 26).

To return to Hatta Fort Hotel, turn around and go back the way you came.

Where to Stay

Hatta Fort Hotel
☎ 852 3211; www.jebelali-international.com

6 Bur Dubai
Walk

Bur Dubai is one of the oldest districts in Dubai and certainly the most rewarding to explore on foot. The key sights are strung along the Creek, which provides a dynamic backdrop to the walk.

DISTANCE 2km (1.3 miles) approximately **TIME** 30 minutes to 3 hours depending on stops
START POINT Sheikh Saeed Al Maktoum House ✚ 170 B4

1–2

Start from the **Sheikh Saeed Al Maktoum House** at the mouth of the Creek, where the waterway bends inland. From here you can see the Al Ras quarter of Deira across the water and two mosque minarets in Bur Dubai – at prayer time the muezzin's wail carries across the water. Sheikh Saeed Al Maktoum House, where Dubai's former ruler lived from 1912 to 1958, documents Dubai's transition from desert village to trading port, a transition he instigated. The galleries inside use period photographs to tell the story (▶ 61–62). With a bus and coach parking area to the right, you'll face the block-like Ministry of Finance and Industry. Follow the Creek

around to the left, where there are some sunshades. Before you get to the Bur Dubai *abra* stations, from where workers cross the Creek to the Deira side, the path runs past some kebab and shisha stalls. *Abras* carry between 15,000 and 30,000 people across the Creek every day. It's no wonder the *abra* stations can be a mêlée of waiting and disembarking passengers.

2–3

After the busy Bur Dubai *abra* station turn right then left into the covered alleyway of the **Old Souk** where you will pass all kinds of stalls selling clothes, snacks, fabrics, electronics and, at the Golden Arrows stall, novelties such as shark jawbones. Silks and satins come here from the Far East; prices can usually be negotiated.

Traders take a well-earned break

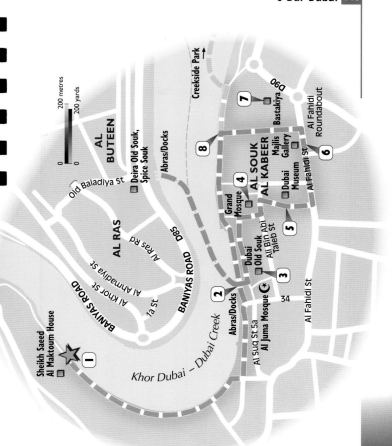

3–4

Continue until you reach the end of the souk and the **Grand Mosque**. This mosque is one of Dubai's largest, with a capacity for 1,200 people. It also boasts the tallest minaret of any mosque in Dubai, at 70m (229 feet) – it is this minaret that you can see from Deira and from the start of the walk.

4–5

Before you pass the mosque, turn right, away from the Creek and uphill. The **Dubai Museum** (➤ 62–63) in the squat Al Fahidi Fort, is ahead. The entrance is on the far side, past a ship used for pearl diving called a *sambuk*. Al Fahidi Fort is one Dubai's oldest buildings, dating from 1799, when it was built as a sea defence from marauding pirates and hostile navies. Renovations began in 1970 to turn it into a museum and a new area has opened under the courtyard, illustrating Dubai's 4,000-year history in a series of interesting themed galleries. A visit is recommended.

5–6

After exiting the museum, turn left along Al Fahidi Street, crossing a small intersection to join a strip of neon-lit shops. At the end of Al Fahidi Street, before the roundabout, you'll arrive at the **Majlis Gallery**, one of Dubai's most highly regarded art galleries. You can stop for refreshments at the excellent Basta Art Café next door, which has a serene interior courtyard.

6–7

After the Majlis Gallery, turn left to head back to the Creek, through the renovated **Bastakiya** quarter (▶ 64–65), a traditional neighbourhood that is now one of Dubai's most important heritage sites.

7–8

Back at the Creek you have two options. You can turn left, walk along the cobbled waterfront and pick up an *abra* to cross the Creek for a shopping trip to the **Spice Souk** (▶ 40) if you're staying in Deira. The journey will cost only 1Dh and is preferable to sitting in traffic. Or, you can turn right and hire a private *abra* from the owners gathered on the steps a few metres along the waterfront. It will cost 50–70Dh to go farther up the Creek

to Creekside Park via a quick stop-off at the Spice Souk. On the way you can tick off the buildings on the other side of the Creek: the Intercontinental is the oldest five-star hotel in the city and lies behind a row of moored dhows almost opposite Bastakiya. The thin, curved building is the National Bank of Dubai and the next triangular building, in blue glass, is the Dubai Chamber of Commerce. The dhow wharfs beyond those towers are where the traders moor their dhows

for the night. You'll pass under Maktoum Bridge before you spot the unmistakeable Dubai Creek Golf and Yacht Club on your left. On the right side of the Creek is Creekside Park where you can have lunch before taking a taxi back to your Bur Dubai or Jumeirah hotel.

Travel along the Creek by foot or take trip on one of the many local *abras*

7 Desert Driving

Tour

DISTANCE Varies
TOUR OPERATORS ➤ 154

As soon as you leave the confines of Dubai city, you will find yourself surrounded by scrubby plains then sculpted desert sand dunes. Some of this land is privately owned, such as Al Maha (➤ 141), other places, such as the sand dune called Big Red on the way to Hatta (➤ 145), are available for all the public. For many people, visitors, expats and locals alike, exploring these dunes is as essential a Dubai experience as flexing the credit card in the shopping malls.

To see this part of the Sahara-Arabian desert first hand you have two options. You can travel with one of the tour operators listed on page 154. Most offer desert safaris in four-wheel-drive vehicles and some, such as Arabian Adventures, can also arrange desert driving lessons so you can learn how to control a vehicle in sand. It's not as easy as it

looks. These tours can range from half-day excursions to overnight desert camping trips. Normally everything, including water and collection from your hotel, is provided and included in the price.

The alternative to joining a tour party is to rent your own four-wheel-drive vehicle. With a vehicle that is hopefully less tempermental than the average camel you will be free to join the locals on the dunes and explore the shifting sands at your leisure. But, as romantic as it sounds, there are some ground rules. If you haven't taken a desert driving course with one of the operators on page 154 and if

Four-wheel-drive safari tours are growing in popularity

this is your first time driving off-road you are better off booking an organised desert safari. The deserts of the United Arab Emirates are harsh environments and no place to get into trouble. The next rule is to always travel with more than one vehicle – you may need to be pulled out of a sand trap by it and it is always safer to have a back-up vehicle in case one breaks down. This may mean that your group will have to hire two cars even if you would all fit into one.

Once you have two vehicles ready to go, remember to pack a tow rope and shovel in case you need to dig your way out of soft sand and enough water for everyone (several litres per person). Taking food and a first-aid kit is also advisable. Experienced desert drivers also pack an extra-large jack (not just to repair punctures with but also to lift the car out of trouble) and a large plank of wood on which to mount the jack so it doesn't sink into the sand. A compressor will also allow you inflate and deflate tyres as required. Finally, be aware that mobile phones will not always have coverage and should not be

relied upon. Always tell someone where you are going and when you expect to return.

How to Drive in the Desert
Having observed the two key rules of desert driving – always travelling in a convoy of two vehicles or more and always taking enough water for everyone – you'll want to turn off the road at the first opportunity. The most obvious place to practise desert driving is on the sand dune known as Big Red, which is about half an hour from Dubai on Route 44 to Hatta. The first thing to do is let your tyre pressure down from about 35psi for driving on the road to about 18psi for driving on sand. Softer tyres won't sink as deeply into the sand and offer more grip. More than anything, desert drivers strive to avoid

Driving on sand is tricky but exhilarating

soft sand. There are some tricks you can use to spot soft sand, but it can take months of practice before you get good at it.

These are the basic tips:

• Dunes with sharp ridges are freshly made and therefore soft.

• The sand in the lee of a dune is known as a pocket and is usually soft so don't drive over a dune's ridge unless you know what is on the other side. Note the wind direction so you can guess the orientation of sandy pockets.

• If the sand's ripples are close together the sand is hard; the farther apart the ripples, the softer the sand.

• Stick to a maximum speed of 30kph (18mph).

• If you start to slide, steer in the direction of the slide otherwise you will pop the tyres off the wheels' rims.

If you do get stuck in sand the second vehicle will have to tow you out, otherwise you will need to use the shovel. If you do get lost you can use the wind or sun to navigate by – but since a GPS unit (global positioning system) is compulsory in off-road vehicles by federal law that usually won't be necessary.

Where to Drive in the Desert

Big Red sand dune on the road to Hatta is the most obvious destination for off-road driving. You can take

your own four-wheel-drive or even hire a dune buggy or quad bike. Note that quad bikes can be dangerous and a vehicle with a roll bar will offer more protection in an accident. The coast road to Ras Al Khaimah also offers numerous off-road opportunites at places such as Wadi Bih. Although well over half the United Arab Emirates is desert, other ecosystems include mountains, salt flats and plains and exploring the Hajar mountains and wadis is highly rewarding. A popular weekend excursion for Dubai dwellers is to drive to the rock pools at Hatta rock pools (▶ 145) – although there's a track, you should take the same precautions as you would in the desert.

The UAE Desert Challenge

This annual desert rally is a major event in the Emirates and takes place over a six-day period each November. The route usually starts in Abu Dhabi and off-road bikers, drivers and truckers rampage east towards Dubai across some spectacular desert scenery. If you're in Dubai at the time it is worth trying to see a stage start or finish. See page 21 for more details.

The Big Red sand dune is the top off-roading destination

TOUR OPERATORS

Alpha Tours
Private tours, wadi bashing, cultural evenings and desert adventures.
☎ 294 9888; www.alphatoursdubai.com

Arabian Adventures
Wide range of tours including city tours, desert safaris, dhow cruises and activities such as sand boarding and desert driving.
☎ 308 4888; www.arabian-adventures.com

Desert Rangers
Desert safaris, fishing, dhow cruises and a wide range of adrenalin activities including sand boarding, rock climbing, desert driving courses and dune buggying.
☎ 340 2408; www.desertrangers.com

Desert Rose Tourism
The usual desert tours and activities plus a personal guided tour of Dubai with your own driver.
☎ 335 0950; www.holidayindubai.com

Gulf Ventures
Can organise one-off experiences and tours, including hot-air ballooning, polo lessons, speedboat rides and camel safaris.
☎ 209 5568; www.gulfventures.org

Lama Desert Tours
Offer a diverse selection of tours including a 4-hour shopping trip, desert driving, trekking, tours to Hatta, Al Ain, Abu Dhabi and the east coast.
☎ 335 7676; www.lamadubai.com

Net Tours
Safaris with camels, falconry and sand skiing or trekking at Hatta. Also offer a shopping tour of Dubai.
☎ 266 6655; www.nettoursdubai.com

Orient Tours
A Sharjah-based operator with an imaginative range of tours including the coastal caravan route to the emirate of Ras Al Khaimah, a tour of the Emirates' mountains and a night camping under the stars in the desert.
☎ 282 8238; www.orienttours.ae

Offroad Adventures
Try wadi bashing, desert driving, overnight camping or a variety of water sports.
☎ 343 2288; www.arabiantours.com

Voyagers Xtreme
Anything from day trips, sky diving and desert driving to their "One Wild Week in the Emirates" adventure.
☎ 345 4504; www.turnertraveldubai.com

Wonder Bus
See Dubai from a semi-amphibious bus that can drive on the roads and motor along the Creek. The 2-hour tour starts from the BurJuman Centre.
☎ 359 5656; www.wonderbusdubai.com

Big Bus Company
Operate eight double-decker buses touring Dubai with informative English commentaries.
☎ 324 4187; www.bigbus.co.uk

Car Hire
Avis: tel 295 7121; www.avisuae.com
Budget: tel 295 6667; www.budget-uae.com
Hertz: tel 224 5222 www.hertz.com
National: tel 335 5447; www.national-me.com
Thrifty: tel 800 4694; www.thriftyuae.com

Practicalities

GETTING ADVANCE INFORMATION

- Official site of the Department of Tourism and Markting: www.dubaitourism.ae

- Local newspaper: www.gulfnews.com

- Dubai airports: www.dubaiairport.com

- Shopping malls: www. dubaishoppingmalls.com

- Police www.dubaipolice.gov.ae

BEFORE YOU GO

WHAT YOU NEED

		UK	Germany	USA	Canada	Australia	Ireland	France	Italy
● Required ○ Suggested ▲ Not required △ Not applicable	Some countries require a passport to remain vaild for a minimum period (usualy at least six months) beyond the date of entry – check before booking								
Passport/National Identity Card		●	●	●	●	●	●	●	●
Visa (regulations can change – check before booking)		▲	▲	▲	▲	▲	▲	▲	▲
Onward or Return Ticket		●	●	●	●	●	●	●	●
Health Inoculations (tetanus and polio)		▲	▲	▲	▲	▲	▲	▲	▲
Health Documentation		▲	▲	▲	▲	▲	▲	▲	▲
Travel Insurance		○	○	○	○	○	○	○	○
Driver's Licence (national)		●	●	●	●	●	●	●	●
Car Insurance Certificate		●	●	●	●	●	●	●	●
Car Registration Document		●	●	●	●	●	●	●	●

WHEN TO GO

Dubai

⬤ High season   ⬤ Low season

JAN	FEB	MAR	APR	MAY	JUN	JUL	AUG	SEP	OCT	NOV	DEC
19°C	19°C	22°C	25°C	27°C	32°C	35°C	35°C	32°C	30°C	25°C	19°C
66°F	66°F	72°F	77°F	81°F	90°F	95°F	95°F	90°F	86°F	77°F	66°F

☀ Sun   🌦 Sun/ Showers

The peak season is from October to May. Within this period December and January are the busiest months of the year, when hotels must be booked in advance.

Dubai has a desert climate. Rainfall rarely exceeds 120mm (under 5 inches) per year. Temperatures range from a low of 15°C (59°F) in winter to a high of 48°C (118°F) in the summer. Humidity is also extremely high in the summer, exceeding 90 per cent. January, the most temperate month, has an average daily temperature of 19°C (66 °F). In winter, temperatures will fall farther in the mountains and at night when a pullover or jacket may be required. Sunshine and blue skies are to be expected all year round.

In the UK
125 Pall Mall, London
SW1Y 5EA; tel 020 7839
0580

☎ 06 4889 9253

In North America
25 West 45th Street,
Suite 405, New York, NY
10036

☎ 212 575 2262

In Australia and New Zealand:
75 Miller Street, Sydney,
NSW 2060

☎ 61 2 9956 6620

GETTING THERE

Dubai is at the crossroads of Europe and Asia, flying time from London is 7–8 hours, the flight from New York is 13 hours.
Dubai International Aiport (➤ 26) welcomes more than 80 airlines from all over the world thanks to an open-skies policy.

TOURIST INFORMATION

*The Dubai Department of Tourism and Commerce Marketing
(www.dubaitourism.ae) has several overseas offices:
UK and Ireland: 125 Pall Mall, London SW1Y 5EA; tel 020 7839 0580
US and Canada: 25 West 45th Street, Suite 405, New York, NY 10036;
tel 212 575 2262
Australia and New Zealand: 75 Miller Street, Sydney, NSW 2060; tel 61 2 9956 6620
France: 15 bis, rue de Marignan, 75008 Paris; tel 33 144 958 500
Gemany: Bockenheimer Landstrasse 23, D60325 Frankfurt; tel 49 69 71 000 20
India: A/121 Mittal Court, Nariman Point, Mumbai 400 021; tel 22 400 27114
Italy: Via Pietrasanta 14, 20141 Milan; tel 39 25740 3036
Japan: 21 Building 21 Aizumi-cho 23, Shinjuku-ku, Tokyo 160-0005;
tel 81 35367 5450
Russia: 10 Letnikovskaya Street, Moscow 115114; tel 7095 980 0717
Saudi Arabia: Saudi Business Centre, 1 Maddina Road, Jeddah; 2652 4283

TIME

Dubai is four hours ahead of GMT. There are no seasonal adjustments to the clock.

CURRENCY AND FOREIGN EXCHANGE

The national **currency** of the United Arab Emirates is the dirham. 100 fils makes one dirham, but fils are rarely used.

Dirham notes come in denominations of 5Dh, 10Dh, 20Dh, 50Dh, 100Dh, 200Dh, 500Dh and 1,000Dh. 1Dh coins are also used.

Credit cards are widely accepted and ATMs will dispense cash to foreign card holders. Most banks will change money without any problem.

Travellers' cheques can be cashed at currency exchanges, some banks and hotels. Check the rates carefully: hotels and the airport exchanges offer less generous rates than exchanges such as Thomas Cook. US dollars and pounds sterling are the most common travellers' cheques' currencies. You will need your passport to change them.

TIME DIFFERENCES

GMT	Dubai	New York	Germany	Italy	Sydney
12 noon	4pm	7am	1pm	1pm	10pm

WHEN YOU ARE THERE

CLOTHING SIZES

UK	Rest of Europe	USA	
36	46	36	
38	48	38	
40	50	40	
42	52	42	Suits
44	54	44	
46	56	46	
7	41	8	
7.5	42	8.5	
8.5	43	9.5	
9.5	44	10.5	Shoes
10.5	45	11.5	
11	46	12	
14.5	37	14.5	
15	38	15	
15.5	39/40	15.5	
16	41	16	Shirts
16.5	42	16.5	
17	43	17	
8	34	6	
10	36	8	
12	38	10	
14	40	12	Dresses
16	42	14	
18	44	16	
4.5	38	6	
5	38	6.5	
5.5	39	7	
6	39	7.5	Shoes
6.5	40	8	
7	41	8.5	

NATIONAL HOLIDAYS

1 Jan	New Year's Day
2 Dec	UAE National Day

The following are all national holidays but dates vary according to the Islamic lunar calender:
• Eid Al Adha
• Islamic New Year
• Prophet Mohammed's Birthday
• Accession of Sheikh Zayed
• Lailat Al Mi'Raj
• Eid Al Fitr

During Ramadan, a three-week fast usually in autumn, businesses reduce their opening hours.

OPENING HOURS

○ Shops   ● Post Offices
● Offices   ● Pharmacies
● Souks   ● Banks

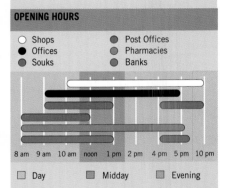

8 am 9 am 10 am noon 1 pm 2 pm 4 pm 5 pm 10 pm

☐ Day   ☐ Midday   ☐ Evening

Friday is the holy day in the Muslim world so the weekend in Dubai is generally Thursday and Friday, although some businesses close Friday and Saturday. Most shops and other services are closed for at least part of Friday. The opening hours of shopping malls are typically Saturday to Thursday 10–10 and 4–10 on Friday; independent shops 8–1, 4–10 (although hours vary considerably).

The opening hours of banks are typically Saturday to Wednesday 8–1, Thursday 8–12. All are closed on Friday. Post offices are open Friday to Wednesday 8 to midnight; Thursdays 8 to 10pm. Some pharmacies are open 24 hours.

EMERGENCY

POLICE 999

FIRE 997

AMBULANCE 998 or 999

PERSONAL SAFETY

- Dubai is one of the safest cities in the world but take the same precautions you would anywhere else: lock valuables in your hotel room's safe, and make copies of important documents and store them separately.
- The biggest threat to your safety is travelling by road – see the driving section ►28.

Tourist police assistance:
☎ 800 4438 (toll free)

TELEPHONES

Public phones are widespread and although some take coins, most only accept cards. These can be bought at shops and supermarkets.

International Dialling Codes
Dial 00 followed by
UK:	44
USA /Canada:	1
France:	33
Australia:	61
Germany:	49

To use your mobile phone in Dubai check whether your service and phone permit international roaming. Coverage in Dubai is generally very good.

High-speed internet facilities are widely available in Dubai's hotels, many offer a wireless service. You may have to pay.

POST

Post within the UAE usually takes 2–3 days, but to Europe, the US and Australia it can take up to 10 days. Buy stamps from post offices and some shops. Hotels will post mail for guests. All incoming mail goes to a post office box and has to be collected.

ELECTRICITY

The electricity supply in Dubai is 220/240 volts at 50 cycles. US-made appli-

ances may need a transformer. UK appliances will work without one. Sockets accept three, square-pronged plugs.

TIPS/GRATUITIES

Many restaurants now add a service charge to your bill, so check before leaving a tip.

In general it is usual to add 10 per cent if you are happy with the service you have received. However, tips are not always expected.

CONSULATES AND EMBASSIES

UK
☎ 309 4444

Germany
☎ 397 2333

France
☎ 332 9040

Australia
☎ 321 2444

USA
☎ 311 6000

HEALTH

Insurance It is essential to take out full health insurance when visiting Dubai. Medical standards in the UAE are high, but the cost of treatment is expensive.

Doctors State healthcare is generally very good. Emergency treatment is provided free of charge, but if you want to see a doctor for a non-emergency consultation you will have to pay 100Dh. Many hotels will also have their own on-site doctor.
Dental Services Good dentists are also widely available. Ask your hotel to direct you to the nearest one.

Weather The most important preventative action is drink a lot of water (several litres daily) to reduce the risk of dehydration in the heat. Covering up with a sun hat is also a good way to minimise the risk of sunstroke.

Drugs There are pharmacies throughout Dubai, providing many medicines without a prescription. There are no specific diseases to prevent against. Malarial mosquitoes are present outside cities but few people take malarial prophylactics.

Safe Water Tap water is safe to drink. Bottled water is widely available. Local brands are less expensive to buy.

LOCAL CUSTOMS

Dubai is a Muslim country meaning that alcohol and pork are banned to Muslims and most Muslim women will wear a headscarf. However, non-Muslims are free to drink alcohol in the city's hotels and some restaurants serve clearly labelled pork dishes. Women are under no pressure to cover their heads, unless visiting the Jumeirah Mosque, but both sexes are expected to cover up when they leave the beach.

There are several Christian churches in Dubai and one Hindu temple.

TRAVELLING WITH A DISABILITY

Facilities for visitors with a disability are improving. There is a desk in the aiport departure hall where transport around the airport can be organised. Some new hotels and newly built facilities, such as Zabeel Park, offer excellent access for people with a disability, including wheelchair ramps and parking places close to the entrance. For more information contact the Dubai Centre for Special Needs (tel 344 0966; admission@dcsneeds.ae).

CHILDREN

Children are at the centre of the Emirati family and are welcomed almost everywhere. Only occasionally age limits are imposed.

TOILETS

The best facilities are in hotels, bars and restaurants but Dubai has few public toilets.

CUSTOMS

You are allowed to import no more than 2,000 cigarettes, 400 cigars, 2kg of tobacco, 2 litres of wine or spirits.

The official language in Dubai is Arabic, but English is widely spoken. People are always happy, and proud, to practise their foreign languages, but even if you only speak a few words in Arabic you will generally meet with an enthusiastic response. The following is a phonetic transliteration from the Arabic script. Words or letters in brackets indicate the different form that is required when addressing, or speaking as, a woman.

GREETINGS AND COMMON WORDS

Yes **Naam**
No **Laa**
Please **Min fadlak (min fadlik)**
Thank you **Shukran**
You're welcome **Afwan**
Hello *to Muslims* **As-salamu alaykum**
Response **Wa-alaykum as-salam**
Hello *to Copts* **As-salamu lakum**
Welcome **Ahlan wa-sahlan**
Response **Ahlan bika (ahlan biki)**
Goodbye **Ma-asalama**
Good morning **Sabaah al-khayr**
Response **Sabaah an-nuur**
Good evening **Masaa al-khayr**
Response **Masaa an-nuur**
How are you? **Kayfa haalak (kayfa haalik)**
Fine, thank you **Bikhayr, shukran**
God Willing **In shaa al-laah**
No problem **Laa toojad mushkilah**
Sorry **Aasif (aasifa)**
Excuse me **An idhnak (an idhnik)**
My name is...**Ismii ...**
Do you speak English? **Hal tatakallam al-inglizyah? (hal tatakallamin al-inglizyah?)**
I don't understand **Laa afhaml**
I understand **Afhaml**
I don't speak Arabic **Arabiclaa atakallam al-arabiyyah**

EMERGENCY

Help! **Tarri!**
Thief! **An-najdah!**
Police **Liss!**
Fire **A-shurttah**
Hospital **Mustashfaa**
Go away **Ab-eed (ab-eedy)**
Leave me alone! **Atrukni wahdi! (atrukeeni wahdi!)**
Where is the toilet? **Ayna dawrat al-meeyah?**
I'm sick **Ana mareedd (ana mareed-dah)**
We want a doctor **Noureed ttabeeb**

SHOPPING

Shopping **A-tassaouuq**
Shop **Dukkan**
I would like... **Oreed...**
I'm just looking **Atafarraj faqatt**
How much...? **Bi-kam...?**
That's my last offer **Hadha akher kalam**
That's too expensive **Hadha ghaali jedanl**
I'll take this one **Sa-aakhuz hadha**
Good / bad **Jayed/ Sayi**
Cheap **Rakheess**
Big / small **Kabeer/ Sagheer**
Open / closed **Maftooh/ Moughlaq**

NUMBERS

0	**Sifr**	15	**Khamsata-ashar**
1	**Wahid**		
2	**Ithnain**	16	**Sittata-ashar**
3	**Thalathah**	17	**Sabaata-ashar**
4	**Arbaah**	18	**Thamaniata-ashar**
5	**Khamsah**		
6	**Sittah**	19	**Tisaata-ashar**
7	**Sabaah**	20	**Ishriin**
8	**Thamanyah**	21	**Wahid wa ishriin**
9	**Tisaah**		
10	**Asharah**	30	**Thalathiin**
11	**Ihda-ashar**	40	**Arbaaiin**
12	**Ithna-ashar**	50	**Khamsiin**
13	**Thalathata-ashar**	60	**Sittiin**
14	**Arbaata-ashar**	100	**Miiyah**
		1000	**Alf**

DAYS

Today	**Al-yawm**
Tomorrow	**Al-ghad**
Yesterday	**Ams**
Tonight	**Al-lailah**
Morning	**As-subh**
Evening	**Al-masaa**
Later	**Fema baad**
Monday	**Yawm alithnayn**
Tuesday	**Yawm althulaathaa**
Wednesday	**Yawm alarbiaa**
Thursday	**Yawm alkhamiis**
Friday	**Yawm aljumaah**
Saturday	**Yawm alsabt**
Sunday	**Yawm al-ahad**

DIRECTIONS AND TRAVELLING

I'm lost **Ana taaih (ana taaiha)**
Where is...? **Ayna...?**
Airport **Mattar**
Boat **Markib**
Bus station **Mahattat al-baass**
Church **Kanisah**
Embassy **Sifarah**
Market **Soq**
Mosque **Masjed**
Museum **MatHaf**
Square **Maydaan**
Street **Shaari**
Taxi rank **Mawqif at-taxi**
Train station **Mahatat al-qitar**
Is it near / far? **Hal howa qareeb/ baeed?**
How many kilometres? **Kam kilometre?**
Here / there **Hunna/ hunnak**
Left / right **Yassar/ yameen**
Straight on **Ala tuul**
When does the bus leave / arrive?
  Mataa ughader/ uassal al-qittar?
I want a taxi **Oreed taxi**
Stop here **Qeff hunna**
Return ticket **Tadhkarah zihaab wa rigooa**
Passport **Jawaz as-safar**
Bus **Baass**
Car **Sayarah**
Train **Qittar**

RESTAURANT

Restaurant **Mataaml**
I would like to eat... **Oreed an aakul**
What's this? **Ma Hadha?**
Alcohol / beer **beerah**
Bread **Khoubz**
Coffee / tea **Qahwah/ Shaay**
Meat **Lahm**
Mineral water **Meeyah maadaniah**
Milk **Haleeb**
Salt and pepper **Milh wa filfil**
Wine red / white **Nabeez ahmar/ abyadd**
Breakfast **Ifttar**
Lunch **Ghadaa**
Dinner **Aashaa**
Table **Maaida**
Waiter **Nadil**
Menu **Qaaimat at-ttaam**
Bill **fatourah**
Bon appetit **Bil hanaa wal-shifaa**

MONEY

Money **Niqood**
Where is the bank? **Ayna al-bank?**
Dirham **Dirham**
Half a pound **Nisf Junaih**
Small change **Fakkah**
Post office **Maktab al-bareed**
Mail **Bareed**
Cheque **Sheak**
Travellers' cheque **Sheak siyahi**
Credit card **Bittakat iiteman**

GLOSSARY TO THE TEXT

Abaya black, full-length outer garment for women
Abra water taxi
Balaleet noodles made from eggs, onions, cinnamon, sugar and oil
Barasti palm-frond shelter
Barjeel wind towers for ventilation
Bedouin nomadic tribe
Bin son of
Burj tower
Corniche coastal road
Dishadasha dress-like shirt for men
Dhow cargo ship
Emirate any of the six family-run states, together known as the United Arab Emirates
Fareed meat and vegetable stew served on a layer of very thin slices of bread (regarg)
Haram forbidden (by Islam)
Harees a basic dish of diced meat, cracked wheat and water
Hijab scarf for women
Iwan vaulted space around a court-yard of a mosque
Kuswari spicy mix of pulses, pasta and rice
Lukaimat dough balls
Majlis meeting room
Maristan (Islamic) hospital
Meze small plates of food, appetisers
Midan square
Mina ferry terminal
Minaret tower on a mosque
Mohalla flat bread sweetened with honey and date syrup
Muezzin man who calls muslims to prayer
Ramadan month-long religious fast in autumn
Sikka alleyway
Sharia street
Shawarma meat roasted on a spit
Sheesha water pipe i.e. pipe for smoking (flavoured) tobacco that draws smoke over water to cool it
Souk market
Wadi dried-up river bed

Atlas

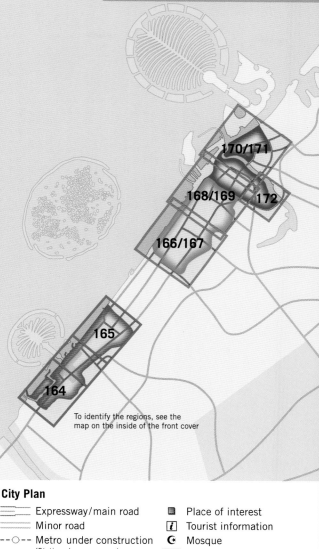

170/171

168/169   172

166/167

165

164

To identify the regions, see the
map on the inside of the front cover

City Plan

≣ Expressway/main road

― Minor road

--○-- Metro under construction
(Stations have proposed names,
locations are approximate)

◼ Place of interest

i Tourist information

☪ Mosque

◼ Important building

◼ Park

164–165
| 0 | 600 metres |
| 0 | 600 yards |

166–172
| 0 | 500 metres |
| 0 | 500 yards |

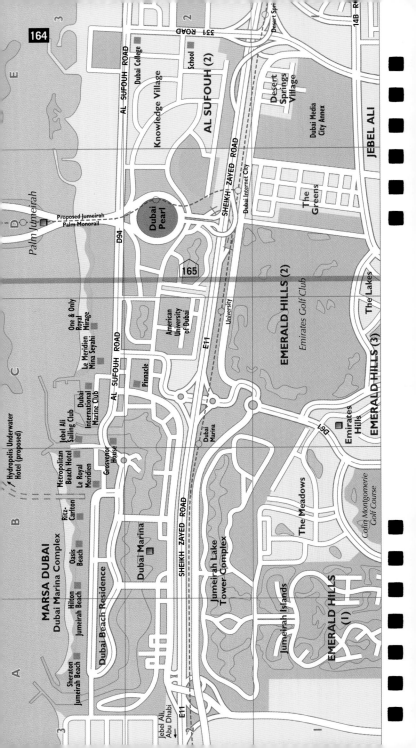

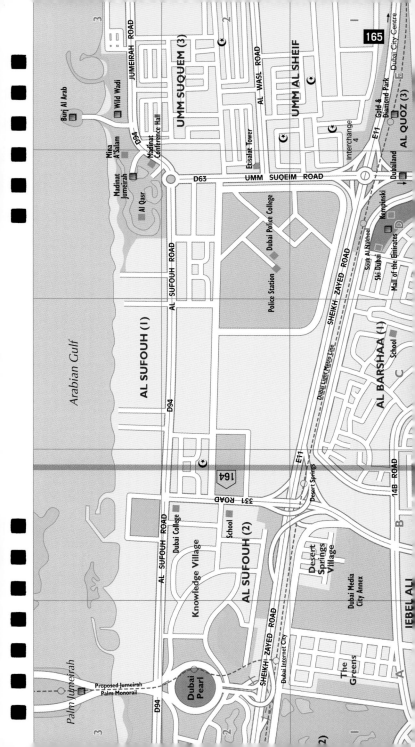

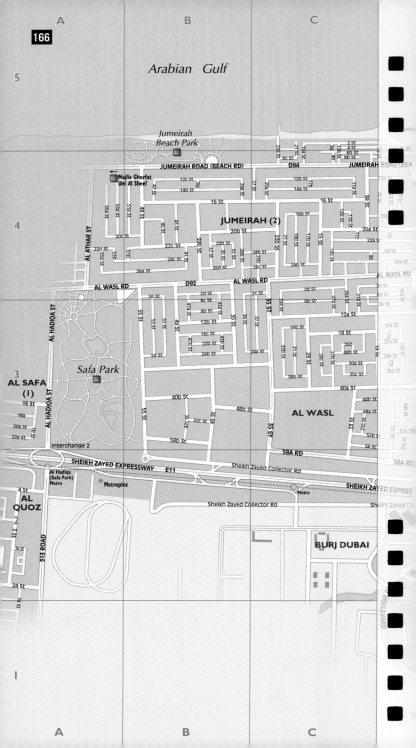

Arabian   Gulf

Jumeirah
Beach Park

JUMEIRAH ROAD (BEACH RD)

Majlis Ghorfat
Um Al Sheef

D94

JUMEIRAH ROAD (BEA

12c St
14b St

12b St

14a St

16 St

JUMEIRAH (2)

20b St

23b St

20a St

22a St

24 St

AL WASL RD

AL WASL RD

D92

AL WASL RD

2d St
6c St
8b St

2c St

2d St

6b St

12a St

12b St

16c St

16b St

18 St

22b St

25b

24b St

24a St

48b St

30a St

36b St

25c St

40a St

40b St

AL WASL

44b St

48a St

40b St

48b St

52b St

52c St
45 St

56 St

58b St

58A RD

58A RD

Interchange 2

SHEIKH ZAYED EXPRESSWAY

E11

Sheikh Zayed Collector Rd

SHEIKH ZAYED EXPRES

Al Hadiqa
(Safa Park)
Metro

Metroplex

Metro

Sheikh Zayed C

Sheikh Zayed Collector Rd

AL SAFA
(1)

16 St

18a

20a St

22a St

4 St

AL
QUOZ

313 ROAD

16 St

24 St

BURJ DUBAI

Safa Park

AL HADIQA ST

AL ATHAR ST

55 St

53 St

51 St

49 St

45 St

43 St

22d St

20c St

26e St

22c St

24c St

39b St

22b St
24d St

31 St
29b St

24b St
26c St

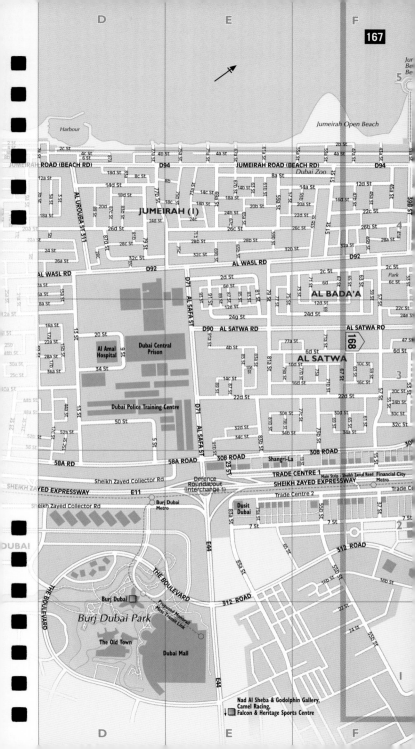

D E F

5

Harbour

Jumeirah Open Beach

Jur
Be
Be

2c St   4c St   D94   4b St   7a St   4a St   6a St   5a St   5a St   4a St   47 St   43a St   39B St
6 St   5a St   54 St   47a St
JUMEIRAH ROAD (BEACH RD)   JUMEIRAH ROAD (BEACH RD)   Dubai Zoo   D94

12a St   18d St   8c St   8b   8a St   12d St   45a St   45a St
14d St   18d St   14c St   65a St   14b St   67a St   14a St   16d St   45 St   22c St
20d St   18d St   7b St   18c St   18a St   20b St   59a St   20a St   22a St   26b St   28a St   41 St
JUMEIRAH (1)   24d St   79 St   75c St   28b St   26c St   28b St   32a St   45b St   D92
26d St   28c St   26c St   71 St   65b St   26c St   51 St   45b St   D92
24 St   32c St   69b St   65c St   32b St
26a St   AL WASL RD   D92   AL WASL RD
2d St   2c St   6d   AL BADA'A
6a St   91 St   126 St   6a St   81 St   7a St   79 St   75 St   12d St   57 St   22c St   24e St
24g St   24d St   57 St
Al Amal   20 St   D90   AL SATWA RD   77a St   AL SATWA RD   47 St
Hospital   Dubai Central   6d St   6d St
Prison   34 St   4b St   6d St   AL SATWA   10c St
83a St   87a St   100 St   7b St   73 St   67 St   53 St   20c St   24b St   30c St
14c St   16d St   73 St   7b St   67 St   16c St
Dubai Police Training Centre   22d St   22d St   57 St   32c St
50 St   32d St   77c St   30e St   30d St   69 St   34a St
34c St   4b St   75c St
58A RD   58A ROAD   308 ROAD   Shangri-La   308 ROAD   30
Sheikh Zayed Collector Rd   Defence   TRADE CENTRE 1   Main Strip - Sheikh Zayed Road   Financial City
SHEIKH ZAYED EXPRESSWAY   Roundabout   SHEIKH ZAYED EXPRESSWAY   Metro
E11   (Interchange 1)   Trade Centre 2   Trade Ce
Sheikh Zayed Collector Rd   Burj Dubai   Dusit   7 St
Metro   Dubai   7 St   312 ROAD
2
THE BOULEVARD   E44
THE BOULEVARD   312 ROAD   16b St
Burj Dubai   Proposed Metrorail   22 St
Burj Dubai Park   Mass Transit Link
The Old Town   24 St
Dubai Mall   1
Nad Al Sheba & Godolphin Gallery,
Camel Racing,
Falcon & Heritage Sports Centre

D E F

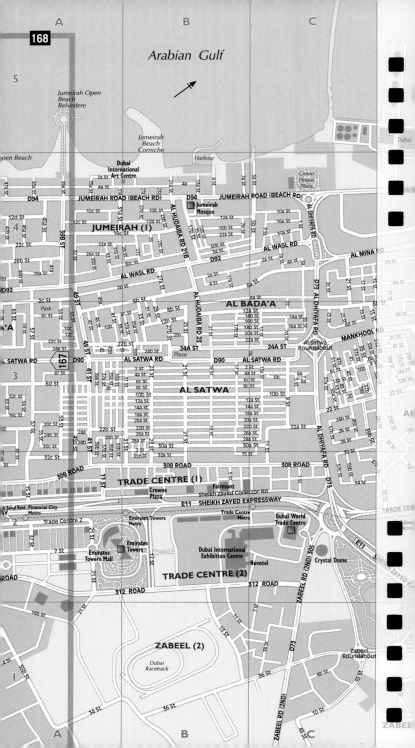

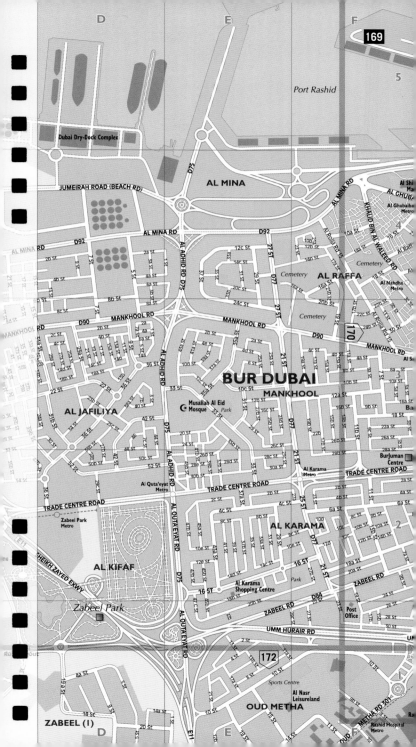

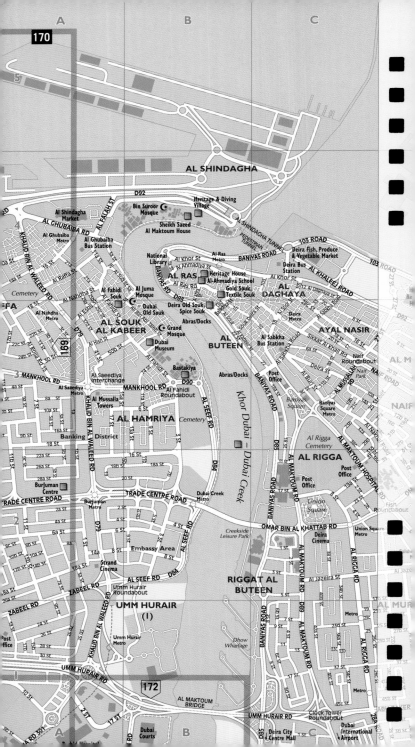

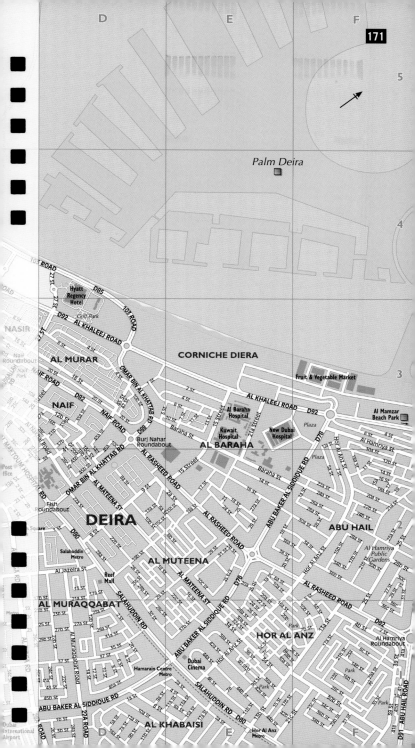

D   E   F

5

Palm Deira

4

10A ROAD
27 ST
25 ST
Hyatt Regency Hotel
D85
D92
Gulf Park
AL KHALEEJ ROAD
103 ROAD
OMAR BIN AL KHATTAB RD

NASIR
16 St
Naif Roundabout
Naif Park
AL MURAR
NAIF ROAD
4 St
20 St
18 St
12b St

CORNICHE DIERA

AL KHALEEJ ROAD   D92

Fruit & Vegetable Market

3

Al Mamzar Beach Park

NAIF
D82
NAIF ROAD
Al Nahda Street
D88
Burj Nahar Roundabout
2 St
Baraha St
15 Street
21a Street
Al Baraha Hospital
Kuwait Hospital
New Dubai Hospital
AL BARAHA
Plaza
Al Hamriya St
10A ST
Al Hamriya St
12b St
14 St

Post Office
Al Maktoum Hospital Rd
Fish Roundabout
OMAR BIN AL KHATTAB RD
AL MATEENA ST
AL RASHEED ROAD
9 St
15 Street
Baraha St
14 St
ABU BAKER AL SIDDIQUE RD
Plaza
22a St
28a St
24b St
20a St

DEIRA
D80
Salahuddin Metro
AL MUTEENA
AL MATEENA ST
D78
AL RASHEED ROAD

ABU HAIL
Al Hamriya Public Gardens
28b St

2

Al Jazeira St
Reef Mall
SALAHUDDIN RD
10c St
D78
AL RASHEED ROAD
D82
Al Hamriya Roundabout

AL MURAQQABAT
Al Muraqqabat Road
25 ST
27a St
29b St
37 St
ABU BAKER AL SIDDIQUE RD
SALAHUDDIN RD
Park
HOR AL ANZ
Hor Al Anz St
75 St
4b St
D82

Metro
Hamarain Centre Metro
Dubai Cinema
SALAHUDDIN RD   D91
Park
Al Hamriya Road

ABU BAKER AL SIDDIQUE ROAD
AL KHABAISI
AL MURAQQABAT ROAD

Dubai International Airport

D   E   Hor Al Anz Metro   F

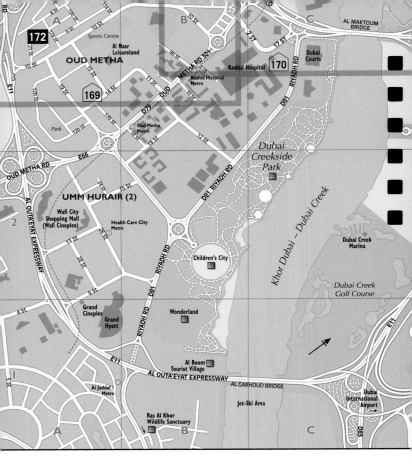

Abu Baker Al Siddique Road 171 E1
Abu Hail Road 171 F1
Al Abra St 170 B4
Al Adhid Road 169 D3
Al Ahmadiya Street 170 B4
Al Athar Street 166 A4
Al Burj Street 170 C3
Al Daghaya Street 170 C2
Al Dhiyafa Road 168 C3
Al Esbij Street 170 A3
Al Fahidi Roundabout 170 B3
Al Fahidi Street 170 A3
Al Falah St 170 A4
Al Ghubaiba Road 170 A4
Al Hadiqa Street 166 A3
Al Hamriya Roundabout 171 F1
Al Hamriya Street 171 F3
Al Hisn Street 170 A3
Al Hudaiba Road 168 B4
Ali Bin Abi Taleb Street 170 B3
Al Jazeira Street 170 C2
Al Khaleej Road 171 D3
Al Khor Street 170 C2
Al Maktoum Hospital Rd 170 C3

Al Maktoum Road 170 C2
Al Mateena Street 171 D2
Al Mina Road 169 D4
Al Muraqqabat Road 171 D1
Al Mussallah Road 170 C3
Al Nahdha Street 170 A4
Al Nakhal Road 170 C3
Al Quta'eyat Expressway 172 A2
Al Quta'eyat Road 169 E2
Al Raffa Street 170 A4
Al Rasheed Road 171 E2
Al Ras Road 170 B4
Al Rigga Road 170 C1
Al Rolla Road 169 F4
Al Sabkha Road 170 C3
Al Saeediya Interchange 170 A3
Al Safa Street 167 E3
Al Satwa Road 168 B3
Al Satwa Roundabout 168 C3
Al Seef Road 170 B2
Al Soor Street 170 C3
Al Souk Al Kabeer St 170 B3
Al Sufouh Road 164 E2
Al Suq Street 170 A4
Al Urouba Street 167 D4
Al Wasl Road 165 E2
Al Wasl Road 167 E4

Baniyas Road 170 C3
Baraha Street 171 E3
Beach Road (Jumeirah Road) 168 A4
Burj Nahar Roundabout 171 D3
Clock Tower Roundabout 170 C1
Defence Roundabout (Interchange 1) 167 E2
Deira Street 170 C3
Fish Roundabout 171 D2
Hor Al Anz St 171 F2
Interchange 1 (Defence Roundabout) 167 E2
Interchange 2 166 A3
Interchange 4 165 D1
Jumeirah Road 165 E3
Jumeirah Road (Beach Rd) 168 A4
Khalid Bin Al Waleed Rd 170 A3
Mankhool Road 169 E3
Naif Road 171 D3
Naif Roundabout 170 C3
Old Baladiya Street 170 B3
Omar Bin Al Khattab Road 171 D2
Oud Metha Road 169 F1

Riyadh Road 172 B2
Salahuddin Road 171 D2
Sheikh Zayed Collector Road 167 D2
Sheikh Zayed Collector Road 167 D2
Sheikh Zayed Collector Road 168 B2
Sheikh Zayed Expressway 167 E2
Sheikh Zayed Road 164 D2
Sikkat Al Khail Road 170 C3
Souk Deira Street 170 B3
The Boulevard 167 D2
Trade Centre 1 167 E2
Trade Centre 2 167 E2
Trade Centre Road 169 E2
Umm Hurair Road 170 A2
Umm Hurair Roundabout 170 A2
Umm Suqeim Road 165 D2
Zabeel Road 169 F2
Zabeel Road (2nd) 168 C1
Zabeel Roundabout 168 C1

abras (water taxis) 27, 44, 148, 150
Abu Dhabi 7, 8, 9
accommodation 29
    Bur Dubai 72–73
    Deira 47–48
    East Jumeirah 98–99
    West Jumeirah 127–128
admission charges 26
airport 26, 157
Al-Ahmadiya School 46
Al Ain 139–140
alcohol 30, 32, 160
apartments 29
architecture 12–15
art galleries 78, 104, 150

banks 160
bars and clubs 32, 52–53, 77, 103–104, 132–133
Bastakiya 14, 64–65
beach parks 46, 97
beaches 143–144
Big Red 146, 152, 153
Al Boom Tourist Village 71, 78
Bur Dubai 55–78
    accommodation 72–73
    Al Boom Tourist Village 71, 78
    Al Fahidi Fort 62, 149
    Bastakiya 14, 64–65
    BurJuman Centre 66–67, 75
    Children's City 69–70
    Creekside Park 68
    Dubai Museum 62–63
    eating out 73–75
    entertainment 77–78
    Grand Mosque 149
    Heritage and Diving Village 69
    map 56–57
    one-day itinerary 58–59
    Ras Al Khor Wildlife Sanctuary 71
    Sheikh Saeed Al Maktoum House 14, 60–61, 148
    shopping 75–76
    walk 148–150
    Wonderland 70–71
Burj Al Arab 112–113
Burj Dubai 12, 13, 16, 96–97
BurJuman Centre 66–67, 75
buses 26, 27, 154

cable cars 68
Calligraphy House 65
camel farms/camel racing 18, 94, 95, 139
car rental 26, 28, 154
children 160
Children's City 69–70
cinemas 32, 53, 78, 104, 134
climate and seasons 156
clothing sizes 158
consulates and embassies 160
credit cards 31, 157
Creekside Park 68
cruises 44, 71
currency exchange 31, 157
customs regulations 26, 160

Deira 33–54
accommodation 47–48
Al Mamzar Beach Park 46
Al-Ahmadiya School 46
Dubai Creek 42–44
eating out 49–50
entertainment 52–54
Heritage House 14, 45
map 34–35
one-day itinerary 36–37
Palm Deira 38
shopping 51–52
souks 39–41, 52
dental services 160
desert driving 19, 151–154
Dibba 138, 139
disabilities, visitors with 26, 162
diving 19, 134, 138
doctors 160
dress code 30
drinking water 30, 160
driving 28, 156
Dubai Creek 42–44
Dubai Desert Conservation Reserve 141
Dubai Marina 109, 121–122
Dubai Museum 62–63
Dubai World Trade Centre 86
Dubailand 12, 106, 109, 123–124
dune safaris 19, 152, 154

eating out 30
    Bur Dubai 73–75

Deira 49–50
East Jumeirah 99–101
West Jumeirah 129–130
East Jumeirah 79–104
accommodation 98–99
Burj Dubai 12, 13, 16, 96–97
camel farms/camel racing 95
Dubai World Trade Centre 86
eating out 99–101
Emirates Towers 87
entertainment 103–104
Falcon and Heritage Sports Centre 95–96
Godolphin Gallery 93, 94
Jumeirah Beach Park 97
Jumeirah Mosque 84–85
Majlis Ghorfat Um Al Sheef 14, 90–91
map 80–81
Nad Al Sheba 92–94, 95
one-day itinerary 82–83
Safa Park 97
shopping 102
Zabeel Park 88–89
economy 16
electricity 159
emergency telephone numbers 159
Emirates Hills 126
Emirates Towers 12, 87
entertainment 32, 132–134
    Bur Dubai 77–78
    Deira 52–54
    East Jumeirah 103–104
    West Jumeirah 132–134
events and festivals 20–21

Al Fahidi Fort 62, 149
Falcon and Heritage Sports Centre 95–96
food and drink 30
    alcohol 30, 32, 160
    Arabic cuisine 17
    drinking water 30, 160
    Emirati cuisine 17
Fujairah 9, 136–138
Fujairah Museum 137

gambling 32, 93
go-karting 124
Godolphin Gallery 93, 94
Godolphin stable 10–11, 92
    stable tour 93–94
gold 23, 31, 39–40, 125

Gold and Diamond Park
125, 131
golf 18, 20, 54, 126, 134
Grand Mosque 149

haggling 31, 41
Hatta Heritage Village 14,
147
Hatta 145–147
Hatta rock pools 147
health 156, 160
helicopter tours 53
Heritage and Diving
Village 69
Heritage House 14, 45
horse racing 10–11, 18, 21,
92–94
horse riding 19
hot-air ballooning 53–54
hotels see accommodation
Hydropolis 12, 121

insurance 28, 156, 160

Jebel Hafeet 140
Jumeirah Beach Park 97
Jumeirah beaches 143-144
Jumeirah Mosque 84–85

Karama 56–57, 75
Khor Fakkan 138
kitesurfing 104, 143

language 32, 161–162
local customs 160

Madinat Jumeirah
107–108, 114–115
Al Maha 141–142
Majlis Ghorfat Um Al
Sheef 14, 90–91
Maktoum dynasty 6–8
malaria 160
Mall of the Emirates
108–109, 118–120,
131–132
malls see shopping
Al Mamzar Beach Park 46
medical treatment 160
Metro 27
money 157
motorsports 18, 54,
124
Mubazzarah 140
music venues 32
Nad Al Sheba 10, 92–94,
95
National Archaeological
Park 139–140

national holidays 158
newspapers 32

oil reserves 7, 42, 61
opening hours 31, 158

paintballing 78
Palm Deira 38
Palm Islands 12, 24, 38,
125
Palm Jumeirah 125
parasailing 134
passports and visas 156
pearl diving 6, 42, 63, 69
pharmacies 162
places of worship 160
police 159
population 16
postal services 159

quad biking 153

Ramadan 21, 30, 158
Ras Al Khor Wildlife
Sanctuary 71
restaurants see eating out

Safa Park 97
safety, personal 159
sailing 20, 54, 78, 104, 134
sand boarding 19
Sharjah Discovery Centre
137
Sharjah National Park 136
Sharjah Natural History
Museum and Desert
Park 137
Sheikh Mohammaed
Centre for Cultural
Understanding 17, 65
Sheikh Saeed Al Maktoum
House 14, 60–61, 148
shopping 20, 21, 22–23,
31, 66–67, 118–119, 158
Bur Dubai 75–76
Deira 51–52
East Jumeirah 102
West Jumeirah 131–132
Ski Dubai 108–109,
119–120, 134
souks 22–23, 31, 39–41,
52
spas 53, 77, 104, 133
sports and activities 18–19
sun safety 160

taxis 26, 27
telephones 159
tennis 18, 20, 53

theatres 119, 134
theme parks 54, 69–70, 97,
116–117, 123–124, 137
time differences 157, 158
tipping 29, 30, 159
toilets 160
tour operators 154
tourist information 157
traveller's cheques 157

United Arab Emirates
(UAE) 6, 8, 9

walking in Dubai 28
walks and tours
Al Ain 136–138
Al Maha 139–140
Bur Dubai 148–150
Desert Driving 151–154
Fujairah 136–138
Hatta 145–147
Jumeirah beaches
143–144
water sports 18, 78
West Jumeirah 105–134
accommodation
127–128
Burj Al Arab 112–113
Dubai Marina 109,
121–122
Dubailand 106, 109,
123–124
eating out 129–130
Emirates Hills 126
entertainment 132–134
Gold and Diamond Park
125, 131
Madinat Jumeirah
107–108, 114–115
Mall of the Emirates
108–109, 118–120,
131–132
map 106–107
one-day itinerary
110–111
Palm Jumeirah 125
shopping 131–132
Wild Wadi 106,
116–117
Wild Wadi 106, 116–117
wildlife 19, 71, 138,
141–142
Wonderland 70–71

youth hostel 29, 47

Zabeel Park 88–89
Zen garden 87

Picture Credits

SPIRAL GUIDE

Questionnaire

Dear Traveller
Your comments, opinions and recommendations are very important to us.
So please help us to improve our travel guides by taking a few minutes to complete this simple questionnaire.

You do not need a stamp (unless posted outside the UK). If you do not want to remove this page from your guide, then photocopy it or write your answers on a plain sheet of paper.

***Send to:* The Editor, Spiral Guides, AA World Travel Guides, FREEPOST SCE 4598, Basingstoke RG21 4GY.**

About this guide...

Which title did you buy? ______

Where did you buy it? ______

When? mm/ y y

Why did you choose an AA Spiral Guide?

______

Did this guide meet your expectations?
Please give your reasons.

Exceeded ☐ **Met all** ☐ **Met most** ☐

Fell below ☐

______

Were there any aspects of this guide that you particularly liked or thought could have been done better.

______

About you...

Name (Mr/Mrs/Ms) ______

Address ______

Postcode ______

Daytime tel nos ______

Please *only* give us your email address and mobile phone number if you wish to hear from us about other products and services from the AA and partners by email or text or mms.

Which age group are you in?

Under 25 ☐ **25–34** ☐ **35–44** ☐ **45–54** ☐

55–64 ☐ **65+** ☐

Are you an AA member? Yes ☐ **No** ☐

About your trip...

When did you book? mm/ y y

When did you travel? mm/ y y

How long did you stay? ______

Was it for business or leisure? ______

Did you buy any other travel guides for your trip?

☐ **Yes** ☐ **No**

If yes, which ones? ______

The information we hold about you will be used to provide the products and services requested and for identification, account administration, analysis, and fraud/loss prevention purposes. More details about how that information is used is in our privacy statement, which you'll find under the heading "Personal Information" in our terms and conditions and on our website: www.theAA.com. Copies are also available from us by post, by contacting the Data Protection Manager at AA, Fanum House, Basing View, Basingstoke, RG21 4EA.

We may want to contact you about other products and services provided by us, or our partners (by mail, telephone) but please tick the box if you DO NOT wish to hear about such products and services from us by mail or telephone. ☐